EASTERN ENGLAND
WALES
CAMBRIDGE
IPSWICH
WORCESTER
HEREFORD
GLOUCESTER
OXFORD
COUNTRY OF THE THAMES
LONDON
MARGATE
BRISTOL
BATH
READING
MAIDSTONE
DOVER
BRISTOL CHANNEL
GUILDFORD
FOREST COUNTRY
CHALK COUNTRY
SOMERSET
WINCHESTER
RYE
TAUNTON
SOUTHAMPTON
LEWES
DEVON
EXETER
ISLE OF WIGHT
BODMIN
PLYMOUTH
CORNWALL
ENGLISH CHANNEL
N
W
E
S
S. HORNE SHEPHERD.

ENGLAND AND THE ENGLISH

Other Works by Charles Duff

In this Series:

IRELAND AND THE IRISH

General:

A HANDBOOK ON HANGING
THIS HUMAN NATURE
THE TRUTH ABOUT COLUMBUS
NO ANGEL'S WING (Autobiography)

Plays:

IRISH IDYLL
MIND PRODUCTS LIMITED
OILFIELD (with Leo Lania)

(Frontispiece) Buckland in the Moor, Devonshire

Photo: Central Office of Information

ENGLAND AND THE ENGLISH

Charles Duff

LONDON * NEW YORK
T. V. BOARDMAN & COMPANY LIMITED
14 Cockspur Street, London, S.W.1

First published 1954

PRINTED AND BOUND IN ENGLAND BY
HAZELL WATSON AND VINEY LTD
AYLESBURY AND LONDON

CONTENTS

PART II

SEEING ENGLAND

APPENDICES

ILLUSTRATIONS

MAPS

PREFACE

THE general plan of this book follows that of *Ireland and the Irish*. But, as the subject-matter of *England and the English* is infinitely more complex as well as much greater in scope, the treatment here is necessarily different from that in the book on Ireland.

Part I of the present work makes no pretence to be a general 'History of England'. It is a fresh presentation (with a personal interpretation) of certain phases and aspects of English history, including some—that of the Celts, their origin and importance, for example—which are too often either almost ignored or inadequately dealt with in conventional expositions. To the selected historical material presented here I have added items of what I regard as important relevant anthropology, archæology, prehistory and physical geography, with a brief note on climate. It is all intended for general readers. The whole of Part I has this main purpose: it is an attempt to provide in broad strokes a picture of the general background to England and the English of to-day.

In Part II the reader is taken round England and shown a number of selected places, and, wherever it seems necessary, given indications of where he or she will find the more detailed information required by the studious traveller or holiday-maker. Part II is intended to exemplify from the contemporary scene what has arisen from the vast background of Part I. The routes, centres and places selected for this purpose are a personal choice. The maps, photographs and end-papers should help the reader to appreciate more vividly many things which could not be dealt with otherwise in the text.

It is hoped that what is offered will have an appeal for those in the homeland who care so much for their country and countrymen that they may wish to contemplate them through the eyes of a friendly observer. The book should be welcome to readers generally in the English-speaking world who may not have easy access to, or time or inclination to tackle, more advanced or more exhaustive treatises relating to the subjects dealt with here. For those non-English people and others who may be unacquainted at first-hand with the islanders at home, this picture may open the way to a better understanding; and at a time when an understanding of the English, their country and way of life was never more necessary.

Objectivity is attempted in this book, which means that some things in it may be found controversial. If I have been prompted by anything, it is the feeling, after more than forty years' residence among the English, that those who believe that 'England is finished' have not the faintest understanding of these people. I have a quiet conviction that England and the English are still capable of providing many surprises; and that a people with their record and their curious nature do not easily go under. If something of this feeling can be conveyed by what I have written, the book will have achieved its purpose.

In the Bibliography at the end will be found the sources of quotations and the authorities on whom I have relied for facts. Apart from these, I have consulted many standard works, including *The Oxford History of England* and *The Cambridge Modern History*. I wish to thank The British Travel and Holidays Association for information and help, and for photographs marked BTHA. I must record that a reviewer of my book *Ireland and the Irish* quite wrongly assumed that, because official bodies helped me with photos and information, I must therefore be some sort of official propagandist. It is not so. In both books the presentation and interpretation are my own. Acknowledgments are due to Mr. J. C. Berrangé for the photograph of Netley Castle, Hampshire; to Sport and General for The Enfield Chase Hunt Meet and the Test Match at Lord's Cricket Ground; to Fox Photos for Coronation Day; to the Central Office of Information (COI) for Buckland in the Moor; and to S. de Horne Shepherd for the Maps, the design for the dust-jacket, and for the end-papers. I am deeply grateful to those friends and critics who read the typescript and gave me the benefit of their findings; and finally to several good friends (they wish to remain anonymous) who read the proofs.

London, 1954

C. D.

PART I

BACKGROUND

England is only a small part of the outcome of English history. Its greater issues lie not within the narrow limits of the mother island but in the destinies of nations yet to be. The struggles of her patriots, the wisdom of her statesmen, the steady love of liberty and law in her people at large were shaping in the past of our little island the future of mankind.

From JOHN RICHARD GREEN'S *Short History of the English People.*

PHYSICAL MAP
SHADED AREAS INDICATE MOUNTAINS
BORDERS INDICATED
0 10 20 30 40
statute miles
SCOTLAND
CHEVIOT HILLS
NEWCASTLE
R. North Tyne
R. South Tyne
SOLWAY FIRTH
R. Derwent
PENNINE CHAIN
LAKE DISTRICT
R. Tees
MIDDLESBOROUGH
NORTH YORK MOORS
NORTH SEA
ISLE OF MAN
VALE OF YORK
FLAMBOROUGH HEAD
MORECAMBE BAY
YORK WOLDS
BLACKPOOL
R. Ribble
LEEDS
R. Ouse
HULL
WESTERN PLAIN
SPURN HEAD
GRIMSBY
R. HUMBER
MANCHESTER
LINCOLN WOLDS
ANGLESEY
R. MERSEY
R. DEE
LIVERPOOL
R. Mersey
SHEFFIELD
CHESTER
LINCOLN
R. Trent
EASTERN PLAIN
STOKE ON TRENT
NOTTINGHAM
THE WASH
R. Welland
FENS
MIDLAND PLAIN
NORWICH
R. Yare
LEICESTER
CARDIGAN BAY
BIRMINGHAM
COVENTRY
R. Waveney
R. Severn
R. Ouse
WALES
CAMBRIAN MOUNTAINS
R. Avon
CAMBRIDGE
IPSWICH
ORFORD NESS
R. Wye
COTSWOLD HILLS
R. Stour
HARWICH
THE NAZE
OXFORD
CHILTERN HILLS
MARLBOROUGH DOWNS
LONDON
MOUTH OF THAMES
R. Thames
BRISTOL
READING
R. Kennet
NORTH FORELAND
BRISTOL CHANNEL
NORTH DOWNS
MENDIP HILLS
SALISBURY PLAIN
DOVER
FOLKESTONE
EXMOOR FOREST
THE WEALD
LAND POINT
R. Stour
R. Exe
SOUTH DOWNS
SOUTHAMPTON
DUNGE NESS
BUDE BAY
STRAIT OF DOVER
DORSET HEIGHTS
R. Tamar
EXETER
SELSEY BILL
BEACHY HEAD
PORTSMOUTH
DARTMOOR
LYME BAY
ST. ALBAN'S POINT
ISLE OF WIGHT
PORTLAND BILL
PLYMOUTH
START POINT
ENGLISH CHANNEL
ARD POINT

CHAPTER I

THE EARLIEST RECORDS: UNTIL ABOUT 2000 B.C.

1

When Britain was not an Island

THERE was a time long ago when the area we now call Britain was not yet an island but formed a section of the western part of a continental mainland that stretched across the upper hemisphere from the Atlantic to the Pacific. In that remote period the little area which was to become Britain was of no more importance than any other on this earth; and, in the things which interest us, it was not very dissimilar from almost any area we might choose at random in the northern temperate zone. It is necessary to bear this in mind for several reasons. It means, for example, that 'Britain' shared the mainland's flora and fauna; and that the men who might wander into the area and settle there were just like the other primitive men elsewhere on the mainland. Men? Our knowledge of those early pioneers and adventurers is far less than of the flora and fauna; and still less of the flora and fauna than of the rocks. For these provide a lasting record, with fossils and other almost permanent evidence which can be examined at leisure and, with patient application guided by the methods of modern science, made to yield their story: the starting-point of prehistory.

The relevant time-scale is so vast, the period in which the 'British' area of the world was first inhabited by human beings is so very far away from us, and life in general was so different from anything with which the modern world has direct contact, that it is all but beyond our comprehension. Almost every inference drawn from whatever evidence is found relating to that period carries an implied qualification to the effect that, so far as we can judge, the conclusions reached, the 'facts' established, are 'as near as we can get' to truth. That is the most that can be expected. We know from experience

A Thatcher at Work at Long Compton, Warwickshire
BTHA

The Feathers Hotel, Ludlow, Shropshire
BTHA

in the law courts that one flaw or gap in circumstantial evidence can shatter its total import. In a work such as this, the reader expects simplification, and it is only fair to point out that in attempting to simplify there is much which has to be compressed or omitted. But if it is unnecessary here to encroach deeply into prehistory, which is still a field for a few experts, one must take a sweeping look at it—for even this helps us to understand much that is relevant to the story of England.

In the remote period mentioned, the North Sea, the English Channel and the Irish Sea were the beds of rivers on the mainland. In the British area there was in general a similarity about human existence and men's way of life with that of men elsewhere which, considering the very varied differences which we see to-day, at first strikes us as curious. The sameness explains itself if we remember that, in those early days of man, conditions in our hemisphere were everywhere similar. Man had everywhere to face the same problems with the same sort of individual equipment, and in environments in which the principal difference was one of climate.

In the present state of knowledge there would seem to be little purpose in attempting to think of dates for all this. We soon find ourselves involved in astronomical chronology that is guesswork. Yet we are so accustomed to thinking in terms of dates (which provide a useful time-perspective) that it may simplify things to start somewhere. So, for the purpose of considering the British area, let us take the year 100,000 B.C. and start from that point. It is an arbitrarily chosen date in the Palæolithic or Old Stone Age, so named because throughout its incalculable duration, man's principal instruments were made of chipped stone. In regard to this, Stuart Piggott [1] expands: "The term Palæolithic is used to define a large group of humanly made tools and weapons, and in some instances structures such as houses or graves, which may or may not be associated with actual fossil human bones, but all of which occur in natural geological deposits belonging to the Pleistocene phase, an epoch having a duration which is estimated as beginning about six hundred thousand years ago and ending perhaps ten or fifteen thousand years ago." In our arbitrary year 100,000 B.C., Palæolithic man had already settled in the

'British area' of the great mainland. He came there from the north, east and south; he could hardly have come from the west, which was ocean and probably beyond his powers of navigation. Besides, he was a landlubber.

We shall have a glimpse of Palæolithic man later, and meantime record that in the Old Stone Age the upper or northern mainland of the earth was suffering (and was duly to benefit) from quite fantastic movements and activities on the part of Nature. They have not yet been satisfactorily explained.

They began with persistent waves of cold weather which in the fuller phase extended over a vast area in the northern hemisphere—above a line drawn round the west and south of Ireland and across the south of England, then across the Continent and almost straight on to the Black Sea and Urals. Next, whole fields of glaciers advanced over the land at a snail's pace. The fields and rivers of ice came down to the rough line just drawn, and stopped there. They moved from north to south at speeds varying from a few inches to not more than 100 feet a day, crushing all soft obstacles, going round or over hard rocky mountains, submerging most of the land down to the line. But here and there they left little pockets, sheltered spots in which hardy Palæolithic men somehow managed to survive, more often than not as cave-dwellers, and with a way of life rather like that of our Eskimos. Then, after thousands of years and as capriciously as its southward movement had begun, the ice began to melt. It gradually disappeared from the European mainland, to remain permanently in its proper polar region more or less as we now know it. There were recurrences of these astounding phenomena: ice came and went, making at least four Ice Ages relieved by interglacial periods in which the land was cleared of glaciers and life became almost as it had been before the first coming of the ice. The end of the fourth or last Ice Age is variously dated as from 10,000 to 50,000 years ago.

It does not require any great effort of the imagination to see with the mind's eye what must have been the general effects on the landscape of those vast submergences under ice; and then of the large-scale meltings into water which, in immense quantities and often in torrents, ran in all directions to find its levels, forming rivers great and small which duly wound their ways into the ocean. Soil would be washed away from one place to be dispersed over another and settle there. Trees and plants that survived in unaffected pockets would again flourish and bloom as the climate slowly changed from frigid to temperate, in some places even warm. And, as the new and well-conditioned land became tolerable, even inviting, the more adventurous or restless of those men, who for thousands of years had lived on the more comfortable side of the 'ice curtain', would begin to explore and wander farther and farther into that *terra incognita*, the new unknown world, which the vagaries of climate had liberated from ice and now exposed to the life-giving sun, its soil recast, resettled and enriched.

In this terrific panorama of cataclysmic Nature, the British area was the most westerly rugged aspect and faced the ocean. Even during the Ice Ages some Palæolithic men remained there to fight the elements, adapting themselves in sheltered pockets to the appallingly severe conditions of their environment: and surviving—somehow. They survived until they were joined by other 'softer' and probably more advanced Palæolithic men from the gentler south. With the end of the ice, the whole mainland could settle down. But it was not until some 10,000 years ago that the area in which we are most interested began to settle into its present shape. The washing-away of land was in some places on such a scale that what had been river-beds before the Ice Ages had now become sea. In this way the British area was cut off from the mainland by what we call the North Sea and the Channel; a little later and similarly, the Irish Sea completed the process of making Britain an island. These new seaways were then narrower than they are now, but quite definitely they were *sea*-channels. So that, considering the enormous time-scale with which we have been dealing, it was in a comparatively recent period that this western area finally changed from being part of the mainland of 'Europe' to remain permanently as the group which we recognize as the 'British Isles'.

The year in which that part of the mainland comprising our England, Wales and Scotland was changed by the prodigious humour of cataclysmic Nature into a tight little island, separated by a most useful sea-dyke from Continental Europe, has not been precisely established. That does not matter. We can be content with the approximate estimate: 6000–8000 B.C., or at most about ten thousand years ago. In thinking of this approximation, we must never allow ourselves to forget that for tens of thousands of years men had been living on the piece of land which had now become an island. Even allowing for the modicum of guesswork which is a privilege accorded to the prehistorian, we can at least be quite sure of that fact. There is even justification for the assertion that in all probability Britain was inhabited at as early a date as all but a very few other places on the earth. We are certainly dealing with a very old country, and one in regard to which hardly a day passes but the geologists and archæologists discover fresh evidence disclosing new and often astonishing facts relating to its great antiquity.

The physical event of becoming an island in just that geographical position is a fact which dominates English history down to this day. It must affect the future, whatever this may be. What was to become an 'island homeland' had been placed in a miraculously favourable position, as subsequent history was to demonstrate again and again, even as recently as 1939. For the moment it made little difference to the inhabitants of the island. Yet it meant that whatever infiltrations or waves of people came there, bringing new ideas from the mainland, could go no farther—except to Ireland. It was the fringe of the Old World.

After the end of the last Ice Age the island's surface steadily improved: from uninspiring scrub and tundra Britain gradually changed into a pleasant, fertile land with everything for human life and the increasing needs of progressive man. It was as yet sparsely inhabited by wandering bands of hunters and food-gatherers in scattered groups: families, tribes and clans, all of them probably a little suspicious of one another. There were many swamps, but the surface became covered with forests, and there were many animals and birds, including waterfowl, with fishes in the rivers and surrounding sea; and an abundance of shellfish along the coasts. More rain came with more regular south-west winds, but the climate was otherwise not very different from that of to-day. This draws the physical boundaries of the small piece of territory with which we are concerned. We have to consider man in this setting.

2

Early Inhabitants

The year 100,000 B.C., chosen as a starting-point in time for considering the area we call Britain, may not be far removed from the epoch which has left us the earliest important remains of man in this country. For many years Piltdown man held the field as our most ancient Briton, but in 1935 his priority in this respect was shaken by the discovery of Swanscombe man. While digging (1911–1913) in a gravel-pit on Piltdown Common, near Fletchling, Sussex, Charles Dawson came upon what he recognized as fragments of a very early human skull. Experts then agreed that these cranial fragments must represent a man of the Old Stone Age, but later scrutinies proved that Piltdown man—'Dawson's Dawn Man'—although accorded third place of honour in the list of fossil men—he ranks after Java man and Peking man, and comes before Heidelberg man, Neanderthal man and well before Cro-Magnon man—is not completely convincing as evidence. The fragments found include not only pieces of the upper part of a skull that is certainly human, but also a lower jaw and a canine tooth like those of a great ape. Furthermore, there could be no certainty about the geological date of the deposit in which the remains were found. Thus, with the geological time-reference useless, and the apish jaw-bone possibly unrelated to the cranial fragments, only the cranial fragments by themselves could be considered as valid evidence. (In 1953 some experts asserted that the jaw-bone was a hoax, but, even assuming that it was, the fact would not impair the value of the cranial evidence, imperfect as that must be without the geological site-reference.) Sir Arthur Keith speculated that Piltdown man, like Java and Peking man, branched off from the main human stem; and that in Piltdown man we have the remains of a specimen of 'Dawn Man', the early ancestor of modern races of mankind. As an offshoot from the human stem, this 'Dawn Man' must have proved a failure; after a long period of survival, he became extinct. No need to go further into details here; sufficient has been said to indicate that, whatever his defects, Piltdown man must be very old—he probably dates back to little less than 100,000 years. The point which anthropologists have not overlooked is that he must represent a type which may have existed in considerable numbers; and so further searches are deemed necessary. One can imagine their joy when, in 1935, in the Barnfield Pit at Swanscombe in Kent, cranial fragments with recognizable hand-axes were found, all in deposits of known geological age. Now at last the experts could say with certainty that this latest and much more satisfactory discovery provided a skull which differed hardly at all from that of modern man! The discovery was one of first-rate importance, for it provided evidence that this first authentic and most ancient Briton may represent a human ancestry dating as far back as the Pliocene period of geological time; that is, possibly even before the Ice Ages.

From other evidence found at Piltdown and elsewhere, we can form some picture of the primitive hunting and food-gathering existence of those first known Britons who lived in that dim, remote age of about 100,000 years ago. Men were hunters who provided meats; women and children were gatherers of vegetation, which made the salads and desserts. They lived in groups based on the family, and they were mobile, wandering about from one good place for food in search of the next. Around them were animals which have long disappeared from our landscape: the great mammoth, the hairy rhinoceros, the hippopotamus, the reindeer, the musk-ox, the sabre-tooth tiger. Hunting those monsters with very primitive traps and weapons was dangerous sport. Men had to be strong, active, alert and possessed of a good knowledge of how to find their subsistence; and the women must know their essential botany. Only the fittest and most intelligent survived. There was an incalculable period of this primitive existence, with a very small mobile population of those aboriginal Britons, before we come to the infiltrations, influxes and invasions from north, east and south, which ended by establishing on this farthermost edge of the world a population worthy of the name.

Between the years 2500 and about 2000 B.C. (or possibly a little later), there was an infiltration amounting in its final phase almost to an invasion of Britain by considerable numbers of a most interesting people who, for want of a better name, English archæologists have called 'Beaker Folk' because of a distinctive type of pottery always associated with them. The influx of Beaker Folk was not, I think, accompanied by great violence, for they do not appear to have been primarily warlike; or perhaps it was that the aborigines kept well away from them. Piggott says, "The characteristics of the Battle-axe folk seem to have permeated the racially mixed Beaker invasion of Britain"—which explains some of the weapons found among their remains, and the speculations to the effect that they were warlike. Much is known of Beaker culture; otherwise our knowledge of the Beaker Folk is slight and alters as scholarship advances. Evidence of the existence of Beaker Folk has been found in many parts of Europe: in Sicily, Sardinia, Italy and elsewhere, but most impressively in the Iberian Peninsula. The origins of these remarkable people, their high standard of culture and their quite astonishing voyagings is a fascinating but still rather mysterious story. About all we can yet be really certain of are the places in which they settled, the general nature of their culture and technical details of their arts and crafts. One school of thought regards them as the tail-end of an obscure civilization which produced the megalithic monuments that are scattered over Europe. The wide diffusion of their particular kinds of beaker indicates a cultural unity. In the search for their origins, the Spanish archæologist and prehistorian Bosch Gimpera has assembled and ordered important evidence,[2] and, although many points still remain to be cleared up and many gaps to be filled, his findings point to Spain as the country of their first appearance. Some highly reputable scholars believe that the Beaker Folk who went to Britain were the original stock of the Goidels, the group of Celtic peoples speaking Goidelic, which was to become the Gaelic of Ireland, Scotland and the Isle of Man, as distinct from the Brythonic, which was to become the language in general use in pre-Roman Britain and which still actively survives in Welsh. Useful ethnic evidence is lacking, but such as exists indicates considerable resemblances between Beaker Folk and the other Celts who, in view of the many existing misconceptions and misreadings of the facts, it cannot be too strongly asserted were not just one distinct race but *several ethnic groups* of peoples who formed themselves into loosely knit communities, societies and even primitive federations on the basis of a common way of life. On this general basis they found themselves more or less in agreement (though it did not always prevent them from quarrelling and fighting with one another!). So that there is no need to be surprised if we should find indications of the Germanic, the Alpine, the Iberian and Celto-Iberian ethnic groups among anthropological evidence left by Beaker Folk in Britain or elsewhere. If a speculative simplification is permissible on existing evidence, it is that the Beaker Folk were a section or offshoot from the Celtic agglomerations which stretched from the east to the west of Europe, from the Danube to the Iberian Peninsula, embracing northern Italy, a considerable part of Germany and France, reaching the western European seaboard and eventually Britain and Ireland. Beaker Folk migrated from Spain to Brittany and the Channel Islands, and it is within the bounds of possibility that the first wave of Beaker settlers in Britain came from there.

The first considerable Beaker immigration took place almost at the end of the Neolithic or New Stone Age and the beginning of the Bronze Age. The date is estimated as *c.* 1800 B.C. And those people left a cultural stamp on Britain which continued to influence craftsmen and others down to the coming of the Romans and even afterwards. They compel respect, those people, for they represent a cultural and ethnic enlivenment which in time affected a great part of Britain. Macalister [3] writes: "The newcomers established themselves firmly over what are now the southern and eastern littoral counties, from Hampshire to Kent, and thence northward as far as Elgin. Inland from the coast their relics are less thickly concentrated; but, even there, they are sufficiently extensive to testify to the secure hold which the intruders acquired and maintained, in a situation which automatically gave them *control of all overseas trade*." The italics are mine.

Control of all overseas trade! This is important, for it means that they must have maintained constant contact with the Continent from which they had come, and so we may allow for traffickings to and fro with visits from continental relatives and friends, of whom many would return home to tell of the pleasant island that was capable of providing a new and more interesting life, if not a very much better one. The Beaker Folk have been singled out for mention here not merely because of their cultural influence, though that was no doubt very important. They are mentioned because they represent the first considerable invasion of England from the continental mainland. They were the pioneers, the forerunners of a great movement of people which was to change a sparsely populated country into one with a population which covered most parts of it. And that movement was to be succeeded by another invasion, which was to be succeeded by another, which was to be succeeded by another. . . . But we must not go too fast.

Britain had become very attractive to continental peoples, a fact which was to colour the island history.

3

The Nature of the Country: Climate

The main physical features of England to-day are more or less the same as they then were. There has been little change in the climate. Now we have a complex civilization and a vastly increased population. But there are certain factors which have remained constant since the time of the Beaker Folk, and of these the most interesting for our purpose may conveniently be stated at this point.

In the forefront of important facts relating to England was —and still is—its geographical position. We are not far from the warm Gulf Stream and, until the discovery of America, England was on the fringe of the world that mattered, "the end of all things, the road to nowhere—and everywhere". This well-favoured country is situated on a ledge in the ocean which is just covered with water, the significance of which may be better appreciated when we say that if the land beneath the surrounding ocean were raised *only 600 feet,* England would again be a part of the continental mainland. The extreme importance of this is that the ebb and flow of tides are exactly of the right measure to keep river mouths free from silt and the whole of the coast good for navigation. And that coast is indented by Nature to provide generously for good harbours and havens for shipping of every kind. The estuaries of the big rivers can be entered from the open sea, some of the rivers are navigable for distances well inland—as in the great ports of Liverpool, Bristol, Southampton, London and Newcastle. Rivers (and to-day canals) enable goods to be easily and cheaply transported from ports to the interior.

The physical map shows us a mountainous north with the great chain of the Pennines running from the Scottish border to the Midlands. We see that in the whole country there are only three groups of high land: the Pennine region, the Lake District and the peninsula of Devon and Cornwall. The rest of England may be summarily described as plain, of which considerable areas are undulating and only a few parts are really flat, the most notable of these being in the Midlands, with the fenland of Lincoln, Cambridge and Norfolk. There is an abundance of small rivers, few districts being without one or more, and the great navigable rivers are connected by barge-canals, even across the Pennine Chain. Beneath the surface there is much wealth in the form of minerals: coal, iron ore, clay and shale, sandstone, limestone, igneous rocks, salt, tin ore; and the discovery of others has not ceased. But coal surpasses all other minerals in its abundance. It is still one of England's standing sources of wealth, and was the backbone of the Industrial Revolution in the 19th century. Coal represents six-sevenths of England's total annual output of mineral wealth.

The Beaker Folk found a green country, which was then well covered with forests. Most of those forests have disappeared, and green areas of a natural pastoral trend have taken their place. In our own time the great natural beauty of most of England is too often smeared and in parts obliterated by appallingly ugly patches of industrial 'black country' that are still further disfigured by masses of the disgraceful little houses erected in the last hundred years by landlords whose idea of beauty centred in cash, and who therefore attached more importance to their own profits than to hygienic amenities or the comfort of their tenants. Sometimes these horrid dwellings have been replaced by their modern counterparts, which are not only much better in appearance but are now often owned by those who live in them. This is the modern tendency. It is encouraged by every government and by the people themselves, for it may be news to many who do not know the ordinary English working man to learn that in his heart this seemingly inartistic fellow is by no means unappreciative of beauty. When given a chance, he will have as attractive a little home as that of his continental opposite number.

The most striking features of the surface of England are the wide diversity of scenery, with striking contrasts existing from one county to the next, often from one village to the next. It is a country so full of surprises in this sense that, with its incalculable climate, it must in the course of ages have affected English character in at least two important respects; producing that quality of never seeming surprised or mentally disturbed which foreigners call 'English phlegm'; and an innate sense of poetry which is rarely disclosed, and then only to intimates. Furthermore, the mere fact of being an island with such extensive and magnificent lowland areas—the mountains are decorations and have their own values—greatly assists in making homogeneous and stable government a less difficult problem than it is in most other countries. One more glance at the physical map and we see that there are three lowland areas: the western, which extends from the north of Lancashire in a line running southwards between the Pennine Chain and the Welsh mountains below Bristol and into Somerset; the southern, which touches the western in Dorset and extends right along the south of England; and that great eastern and south-eastern lowland area which some writers have called the 'essential England', a term which is unfair to other parts of the country which seem to most of us to be equally 'essential'. No doubt the reason for calling it the 'essential England' is because it contains London, the great metropolitan area now comprising no less than one-fifth of the population of the country: 8,364,000 inhabitants of the

41,147,938. England radiates from London, which is not only its capital city but the capital of the British Commonwealth of Nations. London was once regarded as the 'capital of the world'. A modesty which increases with the passage of time no longer allows any but a few of the diminishing old brigade of Imperialists to speak of our admittedly fine city as the capital of the universe.

In its wonderful position, which was once at the end of the world and now lies between the two greatest powers on earth —a position of boundless possibilities—Britain has for ages been the last refuge in Europe for people of the European Continent whom circumstances or inclination drove from their own countries. There was a time, and not very long ago, when England was completely self-supporting. It could again be so; that is another story. However we regard this little island, whether from its geographical position or because of its natural beauty and excellent resources, it is a favoured spot on this troubled earth. Some readers may immediately say: "But what about the horrible climate?"

The English climate is a standing joke. One is never quite certain how the weather will behave: in one day we may have samples of spring, summer, autumn and winter! Yet in spite of everything, it is on the whole a good and equable climate, if the health and strength of the inhabitants are anything to go by. The prevailing winds are westerly, which means that Britain is warm but never tropically hot in summer; and the heat is never enervating. The winter cold is bracing and does not kill. A feature of the English climate which is too often overlooked by its detractors is that energy can be saved in all seasons of the year. The weather does not stop people from working. Those westerly winds bring useful rain, which is rarely too fierce to cause serious damage. The soil benefits from this rain, and great droughts are unknown. One might add that Britain does not suffer from earthquakes—slight tremors have been known but are rare—or from typhoons, which often play havoc in more highly advertised climates. As for earth tremors, there is a record of an apprentice having been killed by falling masonry in one that was felt in London in 1580; and that is the only fatality known to be attributable to such a cause. To sum up, the frequent changes in the weather are a constant stimulus for man. No person need ever hesitate about coming to England for fear of the climate. Seasoned travellers have been known to find its vagaries a great relief and stimulus after a period in one of those delightful places in which there is no rain for months on end and the sky is blue for the greater part of the year.

The prospective visitor may wish for some practical guidance:

The mean annual temperature of the whole of England (and Wales) is 50° F., diminishing regularly from south-west to north-east, the west coast being warmer than the more bracing east. The coldest month of the year is January, when the mean temperature falls to 40° F. The hottest month is July, when the mean temperature is 61·5° F., with London reaching a mean of 64° F. and that of the south coast 62° F. Those who like to tap the barometer may be interested to know that the average barometric pressure over England is 29·94 inches, but this knowledge is of little value except to weather experts. It is more useful for the prospective visitor to know that the wettest month is October, the wettest parts of England are the Lake District, the Cornwall-Devon peninsula and the southern part of the Pennine region. The least rainy part of England is the eastern lowland area, with the Wash and mouth of the Thames areas having a scantier rainfall than elsewhere. Those famous London fogs will be dealt with later.

What I have thus briefly stated is entirely empirical and should be regarded as a very rough indication of our almost incalculable climate. It must be confessed that such a thing as a safe, reliable and general guide to the English climate is still a meteorological dream. For all that, what I have said may be of some help to the weather-conscious visitor in choosing the most favourable period and area for a visit and in avoiding what he may regard as the least attractive. For weather forecasts English people glance at their daily newspaper, or listen to broadcasts which are given several times daily by the British Broadcasting Corporation; and hope for the best!

The excuse for interrupting the main narrative with this factual dissertation about the physical nature of England

and its much-maligned climate is that everybody who has lived in this country from the period of the Beaker Folk until our own time has been affected by these unchanging main features. The only certainty about the English climate is its short-term incalculability. Could it be the climate that is responsible for what foreigners regard as the incalculable nature of the English?

4

Aspects of Prehistoric England: Perspectives

It requires some effort for us to project our minds backwards into that period of time before men chronicled what was happening in the world around them. When we read the word 'prehistory', our minds are inclined to become blurred. If prehistory is not entirely a blank to us, we fail to think of it as representing human life with busy communities, activities, culture, of the evolution of a pattern in man's existence, not to mention progress. All these things existed in prehistoric England.

The only aspects of that prehistoric England which need concern us here are those represented by survivals and remains which can be *seen*. And even of these we can choose only a few as standing and striking examples of man's efforts in that remote past, adding some indications and speculations as to their significance. In England there are many historic monuments in stone which date from a remote antiquity. We find them in the form of isolated monoliths and dolmens, and in groups, circles and alignments. The stone monuments represent but a small section of the remains, which include various kinds of graves, long and round barrows, cemeteries, megalithic chamber tombs, forts, dwellings, sacred sites, settlements and so forth. England's prehistoric antiquities are mostly to be found south of a line drawn from Worcester to Ipswich; and north of a line drawn from Blackpool to Hull. Avebury seems to be the centre of a circle with a radius of about fifty miles within which lies the majority of the remains, including those of most importance.

Until about a century ago all but a few of these treasures

were neglected and some suffered great damage, but to-day every single one of them that is considered to be of interest is officially cared for and protected; and if new ones are found, they are immediately taken under the official wing of the National Trust. The amount of detailed information relating to them which has been collected and classified is immense. The old stone monuments especially continue to attract as much popular and scientific attention as ever in their long past. Yet, much as we know about the stone monuments, there is one thing which cannot yet be done: read behind them and state what was their significance. In most cases there is failure to agree upon even the period of erection. Curiously enough, English scholars have found out more about the significance and meaning of Egyptian, Greek and Roman monuments in stone than they have about their own, which are hardly less interesting. What it amounts to is this: England is dotted with standing mysteries. There they are, free for all of us to contemplate. "Let it be confessed," writes Grahame Clark,[4] "that scientific archæology has brought us little nearer to understanding them."

The most famous group of 'sacred' stones in England is Stonehenge,[5] though it is neither so grand, so awe-inspiring nor so complex as that of Avebury. Stonehenge has certain features that are unique, especially when we bear in mind that the tools used in its construction were simple quartz hammers and wooden mallets. There are, for example, the huge trilithons with their well-formed mechanical joints to hold the cross-pieces immovable on the great uprights. This in itself represents a very skilled piece of work. The engineering feat of getting those massive parts into position indicates not only considerable technical knowledge but great resources in man-power which must have had an impelling motive behind them, for there were no slaves in that England. Then there is the mysterious horse-shoe arrangement of the inner circle of stones. Yet another puzzle is provided by the different kinds of rock used in the monument, most of which is local sarsen. But for some reason one ring of the horse-shoe is composed of blue stones, which we know for a certainty must have come from the Prescelly Mountain in Pembrokeshire, some 300 miles away! Finally, the south-west pair of uprights is exceptionally large: the weight of each part above ground is estimated at 45 tons.

How was it achieved? What was it for? Here are the remains of what one can only think of as a temple, a central or principal temple of some cult which must have lasted for ages. Such a vast piece of work, involving a great feat of transport by sea and land, indicates a tremendous impelling power which we can only think of as religious—and with a wise old priesthood behind it like that of ancient Egypt. Interesting as these inferences are, it is only when we think of the social and political implications behind Stonehenge that we can begin to realize that the people who erected this great monument must have been far more advanced than we have hitherto been inclined to believe. There is evidence that Salisbury Plain was, in pre-Christian times and going back for perhaps more than 2,000 years, a sort of metropolitan or central area on which all routes converged: a very busy area to which traders and others went regularly for purposes of barter or fun and games—so why not for a religious purpose also? A considerable organized commerce may be inferred, and in that area a considerable permanent as well as fluctuating population.

Stonehenge was associated with the Druids and Druidism by the pioneering 18th-century archæologist Stukeley. Because of the arrangement of the stones in which the line of an axis points to the north of east—that is, where the sun rises at the summer solstice—there could be little doubt that if (as most experts now agree) Stonehenge was a temple, it was a Temple of the Sun for *sun-worshippers* (possibly Celto-Iberians). That was the argument. And here the trouble begins, for, in addition to some forty minor deities, the Druids worshipped the moon and stars! Yet the Druids cannot be ruled out entirely, for there are excellent reasons for believing that there was a final phase in which priests of Druidism made use of the old temple, just as priests of the early Christian Church made use of old pagan shrines (and often even built their own churches on the ruins) long after the pagan cults had disappeared. Stonehenge could be very much older than the period of the Druids, and the year 1880 B.C. or thereabouts which is usually assigned to it. The Druids were Celtic priests and, although it is not impossible that some of them may have arrived in England before the first real invasion of Celts began —you will read of this in the next chapter—they could hardly have arrived in sufficient numbers to 'take over' Stonehenge and make it a centre of Druidical worship. We must speculate again. Stonehenge still holds its secrets.

Avebury, near Marlborough in Wiltshire, though not nearly so well known as Stonehenge, is by general agreement more impressive, and almost equally mystifying. The monumental part in stone is believed to have been built about 1900–1800 B.C.; that is, in the early stage of the Beaker settlement in Wessex, though the original wooden version of the sanctuary cannot be dated and may be anything up to 2,000 years older. Avebury is mentioned here as a further illustration of a far more complex prehistoric England than most people believe to have been possible. In the Stonehenge and Avebury areas there is an abundance of archæological and other evidence to show that the civilization so represented was not only fairly advanced but that it had far-reaching tentacles. Stone axes from Brittany found in Wiltshire barrows admit of explanation. But how can one explain the Egyptian faience beads that have been found in those barrows, which date from about 1500 B.C.? We are forced to conclude that, in the two millennia before the coming of the Romans, England cannot have been too isolated from the rest of the world and, going one step farther, take it for granted that a knowledge of this attractive and comparatively peaceful country had been carried by travellers to many parts of the Continent.

An attempt may now be usefully made to draw up some simple perspectives:

The Palæolithic Age has been mentioned a little earlier, and we need not concern ourselves farther about that appallingly long period of time, except to remember that it came to an end about 10,000 B.C. Some archæologists write of a Mesolithic or 'Middle Stone Age', a difficult period to define because now the remains of man and the evidence of his activities are mixed with those of the Old Stone Age which went before, and the Neolithic or New Stone Age which came after. The Middle Stone Age may date from about 10,000 B.C. to about 3000 B.C., but its most important phase comes well be-

BTHA

Stonehenge, Wiltshire

Its mysteries still unsolved, dates back 4,000 years or more

BTHA

Langan Quoit, Cornwall

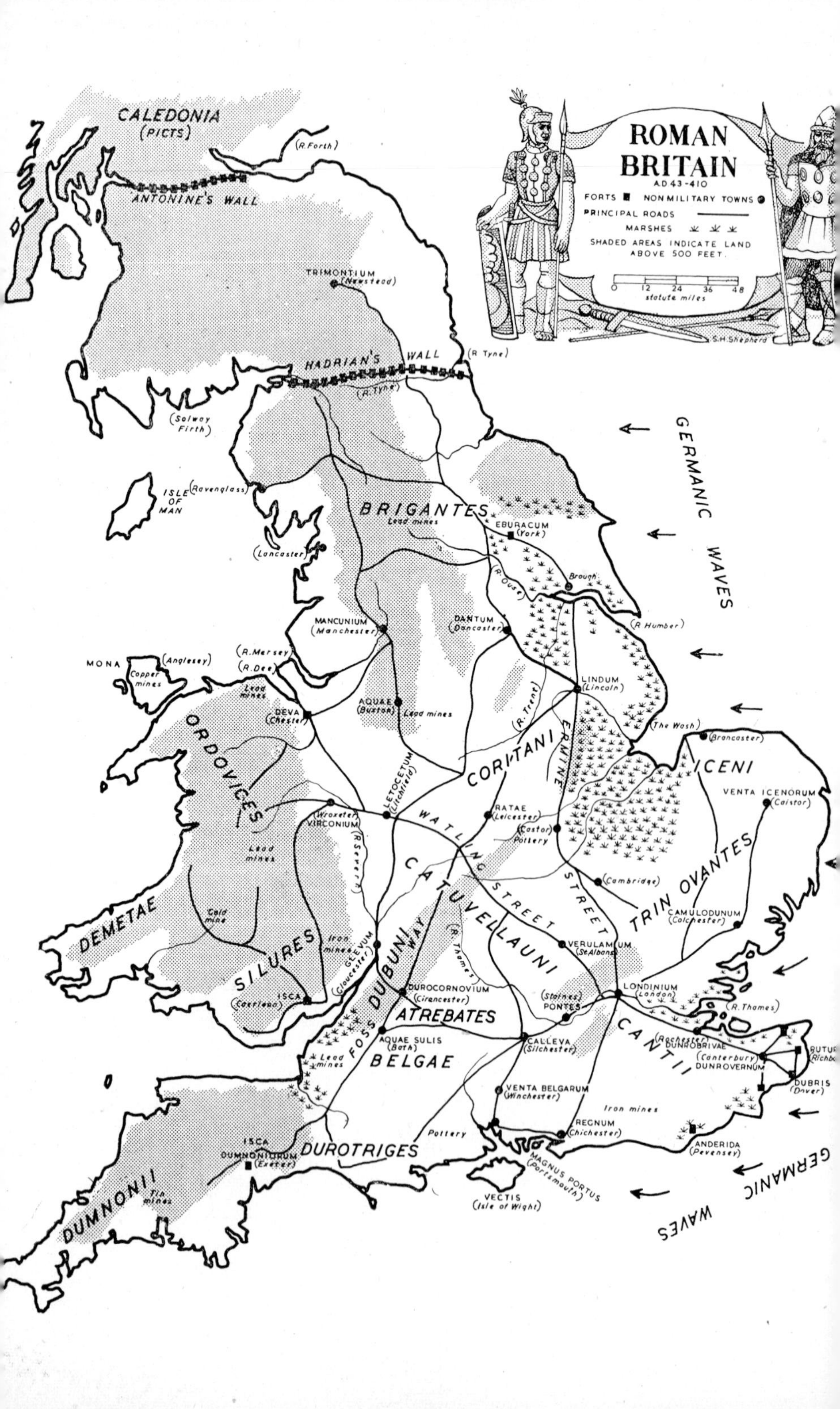
ROMAN BRITAIN
A.D. 43-410
FORTS
NONMILITARY TOWNS
PRINCIPAL ROADS
MARSHES
SHADED AREAS INDICATE LAND ABOVE 500 FEET.
0 12 24 36 48
statute miles
S.H. Shepherd
CALEDONIA (PICTS)
(R. Forth)
ANTONINE'S WALL
TRIMONTIUM (Newstead)
HADRIAN'S WALL
(R. Tyne)
(Solway Firth)
ISLE OF MAN
(Ravenglass)
BRIGANTES
Lead mines
EBURACUM (York)
(Lancaster)
Brough
(R. Ouse)
(R. Humber)
MANCUNIUM (Manchester)
DANTUM (Doncaster)
GERMANIC WAVES
MONA (Anglesey)
Copper mines
(R. Mersey)
(R. Dee)
Lead mines
DEVA (Chester)
AQUAE (Buxton)
LINDUM (Lincoln)
(R. Trent)
(The Wash)
(Brancaster)
ORDOVICES
LETOCETUM (Lichfield)
CORITANI
ERMINE STREET
ICENI
VENTA ICENORUM (Caistor)
(Wroxeter) VIRCONIUM
WATLING STREET
RATAE (Leicester)
(Castor) Pottery
(R. Severn)
Lead mines
CATUVELLAUNI
(Cambridge)
TRINOVANTES
DEMETAE
Gold mine
SILURES
Iron mines
GLEVUM (Gloucester)
DUBUNI
FOSS WAY
(R. Thames)
VERULAMIUM (St. Albans)
CAMULODUNUM (Colchester)
ISCA (Caerleon)
DUROCORNOVIUM (Cirencester)
ATREBATES
(Staines) PONTES
LONDINIUM (London)
(R. Thames)
CANTII
AQUAE SULIS (Bath)
CALLEVA (Silchester)
(Rochester) DUROBRIVAE
(Canterbury) DUROVERNUM
Lead mines
BELGAE
VENTA BELGARUM (Winchester)
DUBRIS (Dover)
Iron mines
Pottery
REGNUM (Chichester)
ANDERIDA (Pevensey)
ISCA DUMNONIORUM (Exeter)
DUROTRIGES
MAGNUS PORTUS (Portsmouth)
VECTIS (Isle of Wight)
DUMNONII
Tin mines

tween the two and is very much shorter. It was an important period for England, which had settled down into its geographical status as an island. It was now that England began to develop island characteristics. The climate changed from dry as on the continental mainland to the moist which we have to-day, because of the rain brought by the prevalent south-westerly winds. This greatly improved the grasslands and possible pastures, and was the beginning of that 'green and pleasant land' of which the poet has written. Next came the Neolithic or New Stone Age, a comparatively short but highly important period because of the infiltrations at times amounting to immigrations of more advanced peoples from the mainland. The period is roughly dated from about 3000 B.C. to later than 2000 B.C., and we know from the remains which have been found that the immigrants steadily transformed and greatly improved the existing way of life and culture. We can regard the New Stone Age as revolutionary in this sense—it is the period of the earthen long barrows, of the introduction of hoe agriculture and stock-raising, of megalithic tombs and of flint-mining. Most striking of all is the interesting and artistic pottery the new peoples introduced; in essentials it is of a kind that is to be found common to the whole of Europe west of the Rhine and the greater part of the north African littoral. There are some wonderful cultural remains of the period, notably those found at Windmill Hill in Wiltshire and in the Peterborough megaliths. Many new inventions suddenly appeared, a recognizably urban life began, trading developed, useful properties of metals were constantly being discovered and, perhaps most important of all for the simple well-being of the inhabitants, agriculture improved enormously with the new implements that were evolved or invented.

The Neolithic period of England's prehistory is not only one of very great general importance. It is extremely interesting in quite another sense. Here is the first example of what was to happen again in the island history on no less than four more occasions: with the coming of the Celts, the Romans, the Anglo-Saxons and the Normans. What happened on each occasion was that an old and slow-tempo way of life was so stimulated by the impact of a new one that the result was something different from both, and in many ways better or at least healthier than both. The inhabitants of England in that New Stone Age showed an upsurge of such a nature and in so many directions that it is not possible for us to find anything comparable in the island history until we come to the reigns of the great Queens: Elizabeth I and Victoria.

The New Stone Age prepared the way for the Bronze Age, which is usually dated from about 2000 to 800 B.C. This was a period in which the advances already made were not only consolidated but new ideas were applied to new purposes. Men discovered how to make and work bronze. Now came the invasion of those enlightened Beaker Folk, the rise of an 'Urn Folk'—so called because of the cineraries they made for funerary use—all of which enlivened a receptive cultural atmosphere. We cannot be sure that this was the most important period of Stonehenge's history or whether it was now and not earlier that Salisbury Plain had become a kind of capital centre to which most ways led: but we may be certain that it was a very busy period.

We are nearing the end of these simple but necessary perspectives of England's prehistory; necessary because we are still in their direct line. The Bronze Age, for example, runs into the Iron Age, which followed it (in about 700 B.C.) and came gradually. Bronze and iron were used side by side, each for some special purpose as they are to-day, with bronze at first dominating but steadily being replaced by the far more useful, more plentiful and more immediately available iron in which England is rich. We are still in the Iron Age, and shall remain in it until the metallurgists find a better metal for our modern purposes than iron, which will probably go the way of bronze. In the thousand years before the coming of the Romans, England had become a very livable country with an impressive list of attractions. Is it any wonder that this favoured and 'progressive' island off the mainland should attract the attention and envy of mainland people who may not have been finding life easy or who may have wished for adventure and change? History works out its own inevitabilities.

The great movement which took place in the period before the better-known landmark in history, the Roman invasion, requires special treatment, and is usually neglected or ignored.

The coming of the Celts to England was a highly important invasion and settlement, which has hitherto received summary treatment in most history books. Because it happened *before* the Roman invasion, it has too often been dismissed in brief accounts, which tend to place it almost in the realm of myth and legend or, in general, to treat it as of only minor significance.

CHAPTER II

CELTIC AND ROMAN INVASIONS: FROM *C.* 2000 B.C. TO A.D. 429

I

Westward Movement of Continental Celts

THE Celtic occupation of Britain was achieved over a long period which must have begun with minor infiltrations well before 2000 B.C. The infiltrations were followed by several great waves with intermittent smaller ones, but the last movement of Celts to Britain ended about the time of Julius Cæsar's landing in 55 B.C. The Romans found a *completely Celtic country,* except perhaps for a few pockets of aborigines, of whom we know little or nothing.

The reader will wish to know who were the Celts. Where did they come from and why, where did they land, what sort of people they were, what was their way of life and what, if any, was their importance? To answer these questions adequately would require several volumes written by specialists. The best that can be done here is to record the main facts as collected and sifted by reputable authorities, with emphasis on certain aspects of those Celtic movements which ended by providing a hitherto sparsely inhabited Britain with its first homogeneous population. The Celts have been a highly important factor in the general history of European civilization. Their importance as invaders and populators of Britain is certainly far greater than that of the Romans; and is at least equal to that of the Anglo-Saxons and Normans, to whom much more attention is usually accorded. Without the Celtic basis and background, neither England nor the English would be what they are to-day.

We must look for the world in which Celtic societies first came into being in the area between the North Sea and Switzerland and between the Rivers Meuse and Oder, with the valley of the Elbe and the Danubian Plain as the most likely areas from which originated the earliest westward movements of Celts. The first Celtic societies were formed in the Neolithic Age. But the first Celts had appeared long before that, and they must have come to the Elbe and Danube areas, in communities already formed, from far-distant places in the north, north-east and east of Europe, including perhaps southern Russia and possibly even Asia Minor. In order to grasp the significance of the sectional picture of the Celts which relates mainly to Britain, we must accustom ourselves to thinking of agglomerations of peoples with a similar way of life stretching right across Europe from the Atlantic coast to the Black Sea and embracing Spain and northern Italy. They were never at any time politically important peoples; they never even formed a State, and still less an 'Empire' as some writers have asserted. Nevertheless, they were by mere weight of numbers the dominant people—more accurately peoples—over the greater part of Europe until the rise of the Roman Empire.

The Celts were not a 'race'; they never consisted of a single ethnic group. The word Celt is merely the name given to a people or group of peoples, and—this is the important point —the group was always an aggregate of different types. Anthropologists who classify man in accordance with his bone-structure, height, skin, coloration, the shape of his skull and the lines of his features, have conveniently divided the various races of Europe into three basic groups or families. They are the Nordic (better expressed as Teutonic or Germanic), the Mediterranean and the Alpine. They are easily recognizable. Germanic man is usually tall and physically strong with biggish bone-structure; he has fair hair and blue eyes; and he is dolichocephalic—long-headed. He is usually a downland man; he prefers plains to upland regions. Originally the Germanics came to Germany and other European countries via the region of mountain ranges between Europe and Asia, from the steppes of north and north-east Europe; but the date of this is still a matter for conjecture. Mediterranean man is dark, with an oval face and ofter a rather aquiline or 'Roman' nose. He also is long-headed, and of middle height (5 feet 6 inches). He is usually a man of coastal regions. Alpine man differs from the two types mentioned in being brachycephalic—round-headed. He is thick-set and muscularly strong. His coloration varies so much that one school of thought insists that there are two main types, not one: the first, fair or red-headed with blue eyes; the second, dark-haired with dark or brown eyes. The Alpines have often been regarded as the 'original' Celts, but this is speculation, though it accounts for the fact that Alpine man has been called Celtic man.

If this racial question is still plagued with doubts and heated controversy, there need be none on one count: the Celts were a *mixture* of Germanics, Mediterraneans and Alpines; sometimes with one or the other group dominant or, more often, just a straightforward mixture with characteristics of all three groups. There is almost infinite variety among them. But there is also something which most of us have noticed: the almost unmistakable 'air' which characterizes the Celt, man or woman. The mistake often made is to identify the Celts too strongly with any one of their three main elements. They were not an aboriginal people; they absorbed many alien elements, thus adding to their puzzling variety.

There are some very obvious reasons why a vigorous, restless and adventurous people should leave their own fairly thickly populated and troubled areas to find a better place for a habitat. As we have seen, the pleasant land of Britain was already known on the Continent from tales carried there by travellers. We need hardly go farther than one simple outstanding fact which dominates all others: throughout a long period of history, corresponding to that with which we are here concerned, the Celts were being driven westwards by the steady pressure of other peoples who arrived on their territories or were growing up behind them. Henri Hubert,[6] one of the greatest and certainly the most cautious and reliable of writers on the Celts, says: "This general movement of expansion and contraction taking the Celts to the west and confining them there may be called the law of Celticism. It must be studied as a capital fact in European History."

We can accept that law as finally convincing. What may be of more immediate interest are the routes taken and the approximate dates of the various Celtic infiltrations and invasions of Britain. The earliest infiltrations probably took place as far back as the third millennium B.C., and can be regarded as of little significance apart from the making of contacts with the islanders. Then (*c.* 2000 B.C.) came the considerable invasions of Beaker Folk, who comprised at least two groups, making them partly Celto-Iberians and partly Germano-Alpines.

The Germano-Alpines landed on the east coast of Britain, mostly in Yorkshire and around the Firth of Forth; the Celto-Iberians landed in the south, coming from northern France and the Channel Islands, as already stated. These important invasions took place during the 200 years between 2000 and 1800 B.C. Much evidence has been found in round barrows to show that Beaker invaders settled in dense groups here and there on Salisbury Plain, which, as we know, was a kind of metropolitan or central area in prehistoric Britain. The importance of this evidence is that it indicates that in all probability Salisbury Plain was *already* an area of this nature at the time of the Beaker invasion, which represents the first considerable wave of Celts to come to these shores.

We have now reached the end of the Neolithic and the beginning of the Bronze Age. Some continental authorities speculate convincingly that the Beaker Folk were a section of that branch of the Celtic peoples known as Goidels, who were the ancestors of the group of Celts who went to Ireland, settled there and have left the Gaelic branch of the Celtic languages. The other early branch, as we saw, is that of the Brythons, which includes the Gaulish Britons; and they have left the Welsh language and its sister tongue, Breton. These two Celtic languages survive actively to this day. The distinction between the two is an important part of the evidence showing a deep division between the two peoples who from very early days spoke the two principal Celtic languages. The division was to lead to a separation of Goidels from Brythons which, although it was one of the most important events in early Celtic history, need concern us here merely to record the distinction between Welsh and Irish Gaels, adding that the Brythons were kinsmen of the Britons.

After the first invasion of Britain by Goidels (whom English-speaking anthropologists call Beaker Folk), there were three more considerable Celtic colonizations: by the Picts, whose pure Celticism is disputed by some authorities; by the Britons who, if not always 'pure' Brythons, were closely akin to them; and by the Belgæ, who were perhaps Germanic Celts. Between the big colonizations there must have been a constant trickle of Celts from the mainland to Britain, and a small traffic in the other direction. There is something mysterious and unfathomable about the Picts, some of whom were mixed with the Goidels who went to Ireland; the 'Irish' Picts (*Cruithne*) have left remains in Antrim and Tyrone. If the Picts really were Celts, they were possibly Germanics. In the great western movements of the Celts, they followed in the wake of the Goidels about the middle of the Bronze Age; that is, about 1250 B.C., but they probably came to Britain after that. They landed in the east and north-east. From theirs to the next considerable invasion we find a long gap in which no doubt there were continued general infiltrations as before. The new big body of colonists arrived between 550 and 500 B.L. They were Britons—Gauls, that is—and they came from the south, their first landings being in Hampshire. The Britons were the most numerous of all the Celtic groups to land in Britain. Their first wave seems to have spread over England and Wales very quickly. Their remains have been found in most parts of the country, but the oldest and largest group of barrows or grave-mounds of the invasion period is near Hull in Yorkshire; the remains of a two-wheeled chariot similar to those found in Champagne have been found in a Briton tomb. There is no doubt that the Gaulish Britons first introduced the two-wheeled war-chariots, which were later to cause so much trouble to the Romans.

We must note at this point that the various influxes of Celts were not driven out or hardly even disturbed in their settlements by the succeeding waves. Those who settled remained. The final considerable invasion of Celts was by the Belgæ who, like the Britons, advanced as far as they could into the country around the north of Southampton from their eastern and south-eastern landing-places. They did not arrive in masses comparable to those which made the Briton invasion so important. The Belgæ arrived in bands representing already formed small communities and societies, leaving behind them on the Continent the main body of their people. They provided a comparatively small contribution to the already variegated racial make-up of the island. Their invasion took place in two waves, and steady minor infiltrations between about 75 B.C. and the period of Julius Cæsar's landing.

These various groups of Celts penetrated to every hole and corner of Britain in the course of 2,000 years, and they must have absorbed the small aboriginal population. The Britons or Gaulish Celts were far the most numerous, and in the end the dominant group. Britain had now become, to all intents and purposes, a *British* island. And there is reason to believe that the Britons were the liveliest of all the Celts; those with most imagination and verve! They never formed a central state, but continued to live in communities or societies in a sort of loose federation which did not rule out episodes of internecine warfare.

Thus the Celts populated Britain with the mixture of ethnic groups which formed the dominant people in continental Europe at the period when they had achieved their peak point in culture and civilization. This fact, too often overlooked or ignored, is of outstanding demographic and historical importance.

2

The Celts in Britain

There is an authentic story of an ancient Greek named Pytheas of Marseilles, who lived in the 4th century B.C. and made a considerable sea voyage in the course of which he visited our island. He wrote an account of his travels which is unfortunately lost, but Strabo and other respectable writers have quoted from it, and we are reliably informed that Pytheas wrote of "the Pretannic Isles". Whence did he get the name? We do not have to look far: there is an old Welsh word *Priten* or *Pretan*, the same word philologically as the Gaelic *Cruithne*, which the Irish Celts used to describe the Picts, the *Picti* or 'painted men' of Latin writers. From the 4th century at the latest the name *Pretani* was used as a collective word for the inhabitants of the island. Julius Cæsar used the Latinized form Britannia for what ought to have been Pretania from the Celtic root. And so we have the origin —rightly Celtic—of the name Britain. We could reasonably go back much farther than the 4th century, for *Pretan* or *Priten* does not seem to be far removed from Brython, the name given to the very old branch of Celts of which there had been infiltrations long before the 4th century. Not only is Britain an old country, even the name in use to this day is old.

As we have seen, there were four great Celtic colonizations of Britain: by the Goidels, the Picts, the Brythons and finally by the Belgæ. These peoples differed from one another in language and ethnic group, though not greatly in their general way of life. The Goidels were true Celts; they wore the kilt, which they handed on to the Irish, and they to the Scots. The first Brythons had settled in Wales; their kinsmen, the 'Britons', went to most parts of the country. There is still mystery about the Picts, whom some authorities do not regard as Celts, though their arguments seem to be losing ground. There was a strong touch of the Germanic about the Picts, as there was about the Belgæ. It may be that they came via Northern Spain, where they were known as Pictones.

The Britons arrived as early as 550 B.C. The evidence indicates that they were, even at the beginning of their colonization, sufficiently numerous to spread their craftsmanship and their tastes all over the country, and very quickly. The Romans found about twenty British tribes, each a composite formation which may have been organized in Britain or may have come from the Continent in the original tribal formations. Three British tribes—the Brigantes, who lived in northern England; the Parisii and Cassi, of our present Yorkshire and Nottinghamshire—each left a part of the tribe behind them on the Continent. The Brigantes originated from Upper Bavaria and Switzerland; they were a numerous and stiff-necked fighting tribe with many characteristics not unlike those of the modern Yorkshiremen. The Parisii were a tribe which came from the area in which modern Paris is situated; and the Cassi, who settled in our Yorkshire, were more stolid Germanic Celts of a group which probably came from Hessen. This is a perfect example of the close relationship between the Celts of Britain and those of the Continent. It would no doubt be possible to produce a map of that Celtic Britain on which would be shown the exact relationship of each of the twenty tribes with their continental blood brethren. It would help us to an understanding of pre-Roman Britain. The Belgæ were a minor group which never at any time could be compared in numbers with the Goidels; or with the Britons who, because of their numbers and the number of their tribes, became the dominant group. The Belgæ were the only Celts in Britain to use a coinage.

Our present England is dotted with names which are clearly almost pure Celtic with other linguistic elements such as Latin, Anglo-Saxon or Norman grafted on to them. River names such as the Ouse, Esk, Axe, Avon, Thames, Eden, Dee, Trent, Yare, Colne, Tamar and Severn are all Celtic. *Pen* or *Kin,* meaning 'mountain' or 'headland', will be found in Pennine, Penzance and Kintyre. Durham is the old Celtic *dur* (water) and the later Germanic *ham,* and means 'the home on the water'. Oxford means the ford on the running water, from the Celtic word *uisce* (pron. iske) and the Saxon 'ford'. Here are some other names of ultimate Celtic origin, with their Latin endings: Lincoln (*Lindum*); Manchester (*Mancunium* —from *Manchguid*); Gloucester (*Glevum*); Cirencester (*Corinium*); Colchester (*Camulodunum*), Brandcaster (*Branodunum*).

And of Celtic origin also are: London, Dover, Lymne, Isle of Wight, Dorchester, Exeter and Thanet, to mention only a few place-names in common use.

It is still possible, even after more than 2,000 years, to trace some of the old Celtic beaten tracks or unpaved roads, especially in those parts of the country in which the soil is chalky.[7] Such roads were used in the busy commerce between other parts of the country and the great Celtic metropolitan area of Salisbury Plain, with its spiritual centres at Avebury and Stonehenge. As large areas of Celtic Britain were either swamp or forest lowland, which made them difficult for those primitive road-makers, the limestone ridges with their short grass and firm surface well above forests and swampland were chosen. Five of these ridge-routes converge on the low plateau of Salisbury Plain. The Icknield Way, from the Fens along the western slope of the Chilterns, and the Old Road which goes along the North Downs to Canterbury, are in a fair state of preservation, though unfortunately parts of these historic roads have been irredeemably lost. To the old Celtic roads attaches an interesting sociological importance: they were the first national enterprise in Britain! Although the Romans left excellent roads behind them, they were not the first road-makers in Britain. That honour goes to the Celts, who in this only showed co-ordinated effort. It was the pagan Celts who built the original roads from Stonehenge to Farnham—the Harrow (or Hoar, meaning ancient) Way. And from Farnham to the place that was to become Canterbury, and called the Pilgrims' Way. It was first trodden by pagans.

It was not in these or in any other material things that the Celts made their great contribution in Britain or elsewhere. For the most illuminating accounts of this we have to rely on the works of continental writers, and especially on Hubert, to whom I am indebted for much of what has gone before and of what follows. In the 3,000 years before the Christian era, the Celts "enter the history of the world". Let us not forget that there never was a Celtic 'nation' any more than there was a Greek, and that we must always regard the Celts as a group or groups of societies. But for their fundamental weakness they might have dominated the world. That great weakness was a lack of political power-sense, an inability to co-ordinate effort, to organize themselves on a big scale. Their strength lay otherwise: in the arts, in music, literature, as educators, preachers, orators, singers and propagandists. These are certainly not the human activities on which great States are founded or empires built. The Romans, in contrast, knew what was required for this purpose: power and self-discipline. The Celts disliked both. As they were sensitive, receptive and creatively intelligent, it may well have been merely an innate dislike of the authoritarianism which usually accompanies or grows out of power. The reader must decide for himself whether such a dislike indicates weakness or wisdom. To this day the Celts who survive on the western fringe of Europe are not exactly worshippers of authority! While the Romans were in Britain they "kept the Britons in order". When the Romans left, 'order', in the Roman sense of the word, went with them. The Celts love general ideas, dislike discipline and attach paramount importance to the value of the individual and the development of personality. To the Romans the individual mattered less than the State, than what they regarded as the public good, which meant the creation and conservation of unity for political power-purposes. Celtic unity, where it is found, has always been in the domain of bards and poets rather than of statesmen, and is intuitional rather than reasonable. Possibly their Druidic religion was their only real uniting factor; a specifically spiritual religion which lacked both threats and bribes, and had nothing in it of the totalitarian, all-absorbing power-factor. Druid priests were men of wisdom and knowledge, guides to morality, teachers of young and old, the tradition-bearers of the people. Their thoughts were chiefly directed towards immediate Nature; they believed in a mystical conception of the immortality of the soul. It may be recalled that the Achæans, the 'founders' of ancient Greece, were in all probability a branch of the Celts originating from the Danube area; and that we find in Greek civilization of the age of Pericles the characteristic marks of Celtic influence carried to their highest degree in the arts, in culture, philosophy, city societies loosely held together, and in everything that we esteem highly, including the great human freedoms. The Celts transformed the stiff synthetic Latin language into the more flexible analytical French, and into sonorous Spanish and fluid Portuguese—great languages for great talkers. They were the educators, the progressives, the principal elemental motive and dynamic force behind almost every forward step in Europe.

The Celts have always been great talkers with a talent for eloquence and poetry, pleasing inclinations for the romantic, the marvellous, the embroidered and the adventurous; and a very decided gift of humorous observation, to which they add their Celtic wit. They have always been fine warriors, more notable for spontaneity than cool organization, but quite capable of becoming brilliant tacticians and strategists. The Celt when cornered, or with his back to the wall, can be an extremely 'awkward customer'; in general, he is one of the least aggressive of Europeans. He can usually be led, though rarely driven; but to be satisfactorily led he must first be convinced or he may prove wayward. When we consider the sum of the characteristics already outlined, it is not difficult to appreciate why the few political creations of the Celts were among the great failures in ancient European history. They have everywhere been unable to create States which lasted, and that is why they now survive as small communities and in so few places. As individuals and groups they are to be found all over the world, more of them in the United States than in their European homelands—and nearly always unmistakably Celts. Millions of them. Including those people with 'a drop of Celtic blood', the number is incalculable. Their cultural heritage is another thing. Yet of all the features and characteristics which we usually associate with the Celts, there is one which, although not easy to define, throughout the ages proved to be the most valuable and important of them all. It is that they can act as a kind of psycho-biological leaven for others with less brilliant, less imaginative capabilities, but endowed with greater stolidity, greater stability and greater staying powers. This is a congenial role for the Celt. It was the role that was so beautifully played by the 'ancient Britons' when the island was later invaded by the Germanic Saxons, Jutes and Angles after nearly 400 years of Roman occupation, of which the general impact had little or no general or deep effect on the nature of the Britons, who regarded the Romans as intruders to be respected but not necessarily loved.

It was the Celtic leaven, acting on the stolid Germanic nature of those invaders, which was to change Celt and Teuton so profoundly that they became—almost but not quite—the English we know to-day. With the Celts was settled the background of the ultimate demographic pattern which was to emerge.

3

Roman Invasions and Occupation

The picture of those 'ancient Britons' which has been presented to generations of school-children throughout the English-speaking world is, on the whole, rather an unpleasant one. My own youthful impression was that, if they were not exactly a low type of human being, those Celtic Britons were certainly more than half savage, primitive, skin-clad barbarians of an extremely quarrelsome nature who were perpetually fighting among themselves. The fact that they "painted their bodies with woad"—which few did—was never by any chance overlooked; their Druid priests were a bloodthirsty lot with an unappeasable appetite for human sacrifices. And so forth. We do not have to look far to find the origins and reasons for this libellous picture: it came from the Roman conquerors, and was perpetuated by those of our historians and educationists whose classical education and worship of "the glory that was Rome" excluded any knowledge of the great world of the Celts and especially of Celtic culture. We know quite well that in some respects this culture was higher than the Roman; that those Britons wore woollen and linen clothing long before the Romans came; that it is about as truthful to say that they painted their bodies with woad as to say sweepingly of modern Englishwomen that they paint their faces with all the colours of the rainbow. But if the Romans left an unfavourable picture of the Britons, they had good reasons for doing so: the Britons led them a dance, and were never of much use to the conquerors.

Rome, the greatest military and law-imposing power in the world, failed in three and a half centuries to do much more in Britain than to occupy the lowland regions, build a network of military roads, establish forts and armed camps some of which were to become city sites, and keep only the lowland population in order. It was not merely an unprofitable occupation—it was costly. The Romans had the intelligence to choose strong British centres for their armed camps, and they built their great roads to connect the armed camps so that, in the event of an uprising of Britons in any one place, they could rush troops there from several directions. The occupation, which lasted from A.D. 43 to 410, was never at any time entirely an easy one. In the end, the conquerors withdrew from Britain because they needed their forces to meet troubles at home. By all accounts they were glad to see the last of that troublesome island, with its "objectionable climate, its frequent rains and mists", a people which "submitted cheerfully to the levy, the tribute and other imperial charges *providing there was no abuse*. That they bitterly resent: for, if brought to heel in obedience, they would not have slavery"—an illuminating comment by Tacitus. Britons never would be slaves!

Before the conquest and occupation in A.D. 43 under the

Emperor Claudius, there were two preliminary exploratory expeditions under Julius Cæsar: in 55 and 54 B.C. The Romans came to Britain from Gaul, and it was Julius's conquest of Gaul which brought the Briton tribes of the south—the Trinobantes, the Cantii, the Regni, Belgæ and Durotriges—within the Latin orbit. These British tribes were more or less the same people who in northern Gaul had become subjects of Rome; many of these were enjoying Roman citizenship. From Julius Cæsar's time onwards, under the promptings of the Roman leaders, the Gauls gladly lent themselves in Britain to what in our own age became known as 'fifth column work': peaceful penetrations, espionage, the winning over of potential 'Quislings' and so forth—the pattern is familiar to everyone who has read of the two 20th-century German attempts, especially the second one by Hitler, to dominate Europe. Hence, the conquest of Britain was to the Romans under Claudius a military operation which could not have succeeded but for the successful preparatory work done by Julius.

The real reasons why Julius decided to invade Britain are not too clear. There is the general one. He no doubt wished to take into the arms of acquisitive Rome that interesting and possibly rich island on the fringe of the known world. The particular motives are less obvious. There is at least one important political and military reason: Britons from the island were constantly crossing the Channel to fight beside their Gaulish kinsmen against the Roman legions; and in Gaul itself the 'Resistance Movement' against the Roman conquerors was finding in Britain a safe haven for its refugee leaders. Britain was just across the Channel, a background and source of man-power for the Gauls. All this 'had to be stopped', and, indeed, the only way to put an end to it would be to conquer the Britons and leave an army of occupation to maintain Roman law and order in the potentially dangerous island. Gaul was such an important territory for the Romans and the Gaulish Celts so liable to rise against their conquerors, that he must take the risks involved in an expedition to Britain.[7]

In 55 B.C. Julius sent a subordinate to explore the south coast of Britain in the part nearest to the mainland: the

Roman Wall, Northumberland
BTHA

Roman Wall—Housesteads
The stone posts that supported the floors of the old Roman dwellings which were centrally heated by steam
BTHA

Dover area. Meanwhile he himself assembled at Boulogne transports with infantry, archers, slingers and cavalry. The subordinate returned to report that near Deal there was a suitable landing-place. Travellers crossing the Channel warned the Britons in the danger area of these preparations; meanwhile the Roman leader received from their chiefs some promises of submission and undertakings for good behaviour. But no sooner had the Roman armada sailed than the men of Kent decided to resist the invasion. That first expedition, which took place in 55 B.C., failed in its purpose of establishing a foothold from which essential reconnaissances could be made. Next year Julius Cæsar himself tried, this time on a more ambitious scale which was more successful. The exact landing-place is uncertain, but it was not far from Sandwich. He won several good battles and crossed the Thames, penetrating into the territory of the formidable Catuvellauni. The ordered line of the Roman legions, their discipline, military skill and stolid tenacity, proved irresistible to the Celtic warriors, who nevertheless, by a succession of brilliant and spontaneous sallies in their scythed chariots, so greatly harried the Roman forces that in the end the invasion had to be abandoned; not so much because it had failed utterly as because it could not be continued to a useful stage of success. A rising of sympathetic Britons in Gaul finally drew Julius Cæsar and his forces back to that country. Not until A.D. 43 were the Romans, under the Emperor Claudius, in a position to organize an invasion which succeeded, but many years passed before Roman rule was established on the island. Only the lowland Britons ever came under Roman rule; the peoples of the mountainous country to the west (the Welsh) and north (the Picts; and the Scots, who were Irish Celts) were always causing trouble. It was to deal with this trouble, as well as to provide good general lines of communication in the lowland area, that the Romans made their great roads; and built Hadrian's Wall to protect their area of occupation from the Picts and Scots, who were always, it seems, ready for forays against the Roman soldiery and the more detested Latinized Britons.

The conquest was achieved by the methods of Roman military science which had hitherto been effective wherever the

Roman Baths, Bath, Somerset
Some of the most perfect Roman remains in England
BTHA

Romans went. Guerilla warfare was avoided as far as possible, the enemy was enticed into the set piece of Roman tactics: a soldiers' battle, a straightforward clash with the solid legions. When they won the battle—as they nearly always did—the Romans built a fortified camp (*castrum*), in which a permanent garrison was left to keep order. These camps often grew into towns. In many parts of the country the Briton chiefs were won over without a fight and there was an 'arranged' peace. In others there was native resistance which was sometimes fierce and heroic, and in which the Briton leaders, aware that they would certainly be beaten in a soldiers' battle, took every care to avoid the clash and used spontaneous guerilla tactics, which on innumerable occasions reduced the Romans to the verge of despair. Caractacus, son of the great Briton king Cunobelinus (to be known in Shakespeare as Cymbeline), was such a leader; the history of his brilliant campaigns against the invaders makes as thrilling a story as can be found in the national history.

The Romans were not gentle conquerors; even when there was little or no resistance, they were often guilty of bloodthirsty massacres. While dealing with the Welsh problem in A.D. 61, the Roman governor, C. Suetonius Paulinus, a fine soldier, fought his way northwards and reached the strip of mainland facing Anglesea, which he had determined to conquer. A small force of Welsh warriors put up a gallant fight in a hopeless struggle to prevent the Romans from landing on the island, an important Druidical centre. Lined up behind the resisters were women in ceremonial dress holding burning torches and encouraging their men. In the background were the island Druids standing by their sacred fires and holding up their hands in a chanted prayer to the gods for help. This strange sight at first scared the Roman attackers, but they soon recovered their heads and forthwith set upon their opponents, indiscriminately massacred them all and threw the bodies into the sacred fires. The day's bloody work was hardly completed when news came to Paulinus of a great British rebellion which had broken out in his rear.

This was the famous rising of the Iceni (of modern Norfolk), who had been abominably treated by the Romans. With other tribes, including the Trinobantes, they rose at the call peoples—the Siluris of the south, specialists in hill-forts; the Ordovices of the north, good all-round fighters—was simply shut off by the establishment of military centres at Chester, Wroxeter and Gloucester, with fortifications in between. One road ran northwards into Scotland (*Caledonia*) from Hadrian's Wall to Inveresk; a very heavily fortified road this had to be, because of those fierce painted men, the Picts. Another road ran from Ribchester to Skipton and Tadcaster to join the Great North Road at York. Hadrian's Wall built (A.D. 122–126) along the Tyne—from Wallsend, near Newcastle, across the country past Carlisle to Bowness-on-Solway—to join the road from Lancaster, and intended as a last line of defence against marauding Picts and Scots, was an impressive creation of which much still remains.[10] It was eighty miles long; four days' heavy march. The wall is divided into sections by forts, mile-castles and turrets. Parts of it can no longer be seen, for the stones have been found useful for church and farm building; and parts were pulled down by General Wade, who made a road there to help in his military campaign against Bonnie Prince Charlie in the rebellion of 1745. A volume would be required to do justice to this great Roman survival (to which further reference will be made in Part II). The most important of the remaining roads were: the Foss Way, which ran from Lincoln to Exeter; Watling Street (*strata*, a paved route), which ran from London to Chester; Ermine Street, from Lincoln to London, with a connecting road running on to Exeter; and finally there was the very important road—the military lifeline—from the Channel ports to London.

Trade and commerce used these roads when they were not serving a military purpose. There were many others besides those mentioned: roads connecting great native centres inland; roads converging from the west on Canterbury and Winchester. When we take into account the population of Roman Britain, this great network is standing evidence of the elaborate precautions which the Romans deemed to be necessary in order to hold down the Britons. The overriding purpose was military in two senses: the internal one, to keep order; and the equally important one of connecting the mainland of Gaul—where the Romans had great garrisons—with such important centres in Britain as London, Colchester (the Roman capital), Chester and Gloucester. The roads were always straight. If the terrain prevented this, they were built in zigzags to make defence easier. They went over hills, into valleys and cut through swamps—nearly always preserving their straight line. Whoever studies them cannot but feel admiration at the thoroughness with which the roads and their bridges were built, not to mention the military vision in their lay-out and choice of routes. It was a great national enterprise and, with the city sites, the best thing the Romans left in Britain. Incidentally, the old Celtic site of London (Celtic *lunn* or *linn*, a pool; *dun*, a fort: 'the fort by the pool') became the Roman Londinium, a central mart and trading-settlement where goods from the continental empire were handled. It was under the Romans that this geographically ideal centre began to acquire the importance which later made it the greatest commercial port in the world.

We are able now to look back on those invasions—Celtic and Roman—with objective complacency, not forgetting that the first brought incalculable demographic benefits to the country, and the second left behind it many substantial material improvements. Both those invasions, and the later invasions of Anglo-Saxons and Normans, demonstrated a fact which has become for the modern Englishman a commonplace: that an undefended Britain invites invasion. Precisely because of its wonderful geographical position, it is vulnerable from all points of the compass. One is not surprised to read that the Germanic invaders, who were seafarers, easily found their way across the North Sea. Yet, in spite of their maritime inexperience, the prehistoric Celtic navigators also were able to find the best sea-routes from the Continent to Britain; and each wave of later invaders chose the most suitable route for the immediate purpose.

The main body of Beaker Folk (Goidels) chose the highly important routes from the continental littoral, which runs from our present Belgium along the Netherland coast up to some point in Denmark; the same routes as those that were to be taken later by barbaric Anglo-Saxons, and after them by the piratical Vikings of Dano-Norse stock. In the Early Iron Age the Channel routes—from Ostend along to Calais and

Dieppe—had brought to England considerable groups of peaceful Celts representing the remarkable later La Tène and Hallstatt civilizations. From the time of Julius Cæsar's first landing in 43 B.C. until the end of the Roman occupation, these were not only the most important routes for the Romans but the only ones in general use. They fell into disuse during the Anglo-Saxon invasions and settlement of Britain, but with the Norman invasion they resumed their earlier activity and importance, which has continued with a few minor interruptions until now. Following the French coast from Dieppe to Cherbourg, we find other well-established routes which have been used from the Bronze Age onwards, beginning over three thousand years ago and bringing early La Tène culture to the Wessex uplands. The most important of these routes were from Normandy to Hampshire and Dorset. Finally, there was the Atlantic route which extended from Spain to Brittany and thence to south-west Britain, where it divides into two routes, one of which runs eastward along the south coast of England and the other into the Irish Sea, serving Ireland, Wales, Scotland and north-west England.

Though less important, if regarded from the point of view of the numbers of alien peoples which it brought to England, the Atlantic route has been of great importance from a period so far back that the beginning of it is lost in the mists of time. It was most probably by this route that Britain received the Iberians or Celto-Iberians who first brought the idea behind the megaliths. And Spain, if possibly not the original home of that curious and interesting civilization, was certainly one of its most important areas. Its culture came to Britain by the Atlantic route.

If all these remarkable movements were possible *before* the period of our modern and scientific advances in means of communication, there is no need to emphasize the permanent vulnerability of the island. When the Romans abandoned their occupation, they left behind them a whole lowland region whose population had been softened by Latinization and the protracted peace which the Roman garrisons guaranteed within the interior frontiers drawn by their military leaders. So long as the Latinized Britons paid their taxes and remained peaceful, they were allowed to jog along more or less as they pleased. Outside this Romanized area—in the uplands of England, in the Welsh west, in the Pictish and Scottish north—there were still lively native Celtic tribes and communities which had changed hardly at all since the days before Julius Cæsar's landing. More important still, the troubles which the Romans were having at home were being watched by leaders of great hordes of restless barbarians living on the continental littoral from the north-east frontier of Gaul to Scandinavia. The Salian Franks, the Old Saxons, the Frisians and Jutes, the Angles and the Vikings or Norsemen, all had their eyes on Britain. During the later days of the Roman occupation they even put out feelers in the form of marauding expeditions, which caused the Romans to set up a defence system under *Comes litoris Saxonici,* a 'Count of the Saxon Shore'. When the Roman soldiery went, lowland Britain was left not only militarily helpless but under threats from two quarters: from the uplanders on the island itself, and from the waiting hordes across the North Sea.

CHAPTER III

GERMANIC AND SCANDINAVIAN INVASIONS: A.D. 449 TO 1066

1

The Germanic Waves

THE invasion and settlement of the greater part of the island by Germanic peoples from across the North Sea is an event of cardinal importance in British history. The motive which had prompted recurrent raids along the east coast of Britain even during the Roman occupation was in the first instance a simple one: loot. Those raids became so serious that the Romans built a defence system known as the 'Forts of the Saxon Shore', but when the Romans evacuated Britain, the forts were unmanned and the soft Romanized Britons left quite helpless. Now there was an open invitation to the waiting and ready Germanics. From the outset their leaders envisaged a conquest and permanent settlement. They felt that the island would provide for a good and much easier life than they enjoyed at home: Britain would be less crowded than their own thickly populated areas; after an initial and decisive onslaught by their warriors, they could transport large numbers of emigrants, who would settle permanently in the promised land. Their plan was perhaps not so clearly and consciously conceived as all this. But it worked out on these lines, and proved to be highly successful.

We may usefully glance at those Germanic peoples who were to be so vitally important in the island history. The use of the term 'Germanic' first requires a little explanation. Many writers refer to this settlement as 'Teutonic' or 'Nordic'. I use the term 'Germanic' to cover the Saxons, Angles and Jutes, the principal peoples who conquered and settled Britain in the period from A.D. *c.* 450 to *c.* 850. This use is fully justifiable. The Danish-Norse peoples who came after 850 and, with their raids, also left settlements and had considerable influence, were also a branch of the great Germanic family which is often called 'Teutonic', a rather vague term, or 'Nordic', a misleading and in recent years greatly abused term, for there never was a 'Nordic' race or people who could not be more correctly described by the clearer and more easily recognizable term Germanic. Besides, why should we alter the nomenclature used by the early English chroniclers? Dorothy Whitelock [11] writes: "Englishmen in Anglo-Saxon times were aware of the Germanic origin of their race. . . . What is interesting is that the invaders remained so conscious of their Germanic origin. Bede's older contemporary, St. Aldhelm, uses 'our stock' and 'the Germanic race' as parallel expressions," and St. Boniface, a second-generation Englishman of Saxon origin, wrote of the continental Saxons: "We are of one blood and one bone." The term Germanic seems to be the more correct one, as it is certainly the easier to understand.

Nothing could be farther from the truth than the picture of a well-ordered and systematic invasion of Britain by tribal formations, each of them coming from some definite area on the Continent. If there were any methods about the invasion, they were of the roughest and most casual nature: the assembling and transport of a big enough force to smash all opposition in a first onslaught; then a phase in which a mixture of young warriors and farmers came in great numbers to settle; and a final phase with a steady traffic of settler-emigrants from the mainland. The helplessness of the Britons and the overwhelming man-power of the invaders decided the military problem almost immediately. There was little real resistance. The Germanics simply wrought havoc everywhere to awe the Britons into complete surrender. In places they decimated or annihilated the natives. Everywhere they drove them west.

Three groups of Germanic peoples were mainly involved: the Saxons, the biggest group numerically; next, the Angles; and the Jutes, a much smaller contingent. To these there was added an unknown number of little groups representing less-important tribes, but this part of the story is so obscure and of so little importance that it need only be mentioned. What we have to think of is something like a rush from all sides to join the colours of a few adventurous and ambitious leaders who were forming a great overseas expedition with the primary objects of war and loot. Nothing could please Germanic youth more. The main body, of Anglo-Saxons, consisted for the most part of farmers, but there were among them many North Sea fishermen, trained seafarers, who, when not engaged in fishing, went in for piracy and buccaneering. This applied particularly to the group of Jutes, those men from North Denmark and Frisia who were nearly all full-time deep-sea fishermen or pirates or a mixture of both. Thus there was an invasion by a commingling of Germanic peoples who, for the immediate purpose of the attack on Britain, were warriors. They were fierce, courageous and gregarious peoples who easily achieved a common unity for the common purpose: then the conquest and settlement of a militarily helpless island. Britain not only promised to solve their economic problems but to provide immediate scope for the adventurous. The greater part of the first invading force did not consist of mercenaries as has often been asserted. They were volunteers who were to be paid in kind: loot and land.

It is a great pity that there is no contemporary account of the first phase of the Germanic invasion which, with the settlement that followed, was to play so highly important a part in all subsequent English history and to have far-reaching repercussions on European and world history. Our information about it comes from later written sources, from archæology and from linguistic evidence; new items of information about it are still being found by research workers. But it is possible to sort out the confusions of the invasion into a rough, simplified form; thus:

Germanic Invasions and Settlements; from A.D.C. 450 *to* C. 600

I SAXONS	II ANGLES	III JUTES
From the Elbe and South Weser region	*From north of the Elbe and Schleswig*	*From areas not exactly definable but roughly embracing the Jutish Peninsula, Schleswig and Frisia*

I *Went to*	II *Went to*	III *Went to*
Essex Middlesex Hertford North Thames area Surrey Sussex Wessex	Eastern Britain and covered an area from north of the Thames to the Forth, including all East Anglia but excluding Essex	Kent, first from the east by sea, then from the west by land; also Hampshire, Isle of Wight and the area north and around Southampton

See map facing page 64.

By the time the Germanic peoples were in the stage of settling down, the eastern and southern half of Britain was theirs; the other and western half was occupied by Britons who had withdrawn there. In the north-west the purely Briton area was called Strathclyde ('the Clyde tract'), and this area extended from the River Clyde southwards as far as Warwick, almost to Bedford, joining on the way with the area then known as 'North Wales', which included the whole of the Wales we now know. The southern Briton area was called 'South Wales' and embraced our Devonshire and Cornwall. A narrow stretch of Wessex ran northwards along the east side of the Severn, with a point running slightly into Wales and another stretching north almost to the Mersey, leaving a narrow piece of British territory joining Strathclyde with North Wales. The period taken for the Germanic settlement of the areas here outlined cannot be accurately estimated: it might be anything up to one hundred and fifty years. But the general map of the country is clear enough: distinct areas of Saxons, Angles and Jutes to the east, south and south-east; and native Britons to the west.

The Germanic farmer-fishermen-adventurers had a Runic alphabet derived from Roman characters modified to suit such simple uses as carving a leader's name on a shield or monument, but quite unsuitable for general literary purposes. That is why they left no literary records. They were, in the mass, illiterates—heathenish worshippers of a deity representing magic called Woden, and his mythological son called Thor, a warrior giant of enormous strength—"kind to his friends but implacable to his foes". The duality has its significance: the worship of magic and force. The Germanics had little culture, far less than the Britons' own Celtic culture; still less if we take into account the considerable Romanization which had taken place, thus giving the Latin alphabet to many enlightened Britons who, most probably, perished in the invasion onslaught. But the Saxons, Angles and Jutes all had a sense of *power*; and it would seem of the *Führer*-principle, of following a leader. This they canalized into a monarchical and crude aristocratic system, which in England was to evolve into the personal relationship of the warrior to his chief: the basis of the later aristocracy and feudalism. At home on the Continent the system remained rigid and narrow, but after the free-for-all invasion and settlement of Britain, it evolved here on reasonably liberal lines, especially after the first busy period of murder and rapine which, with the lands won, must have satiated the various lusts, including that for power. This was perhaps the first sign of something politically new and important to come from the Germanic invasion, a new evolutionary process which was to continue throughout the centuries with excellent results.

The first wave of the first of the Germanic peoples to land consisted of Jutes, led by the chieftain Hengest, assisted by his less-important colleague Horsa. The story goes that under a pact with the British chief (or 'king') Vortigern, they were called in to defend the latter against the wild Picts of the north. However that may be, Hengest and his Jutes never went north, but to Kent in the extreme south-east, where they landed on a date given by English authorities as between A.D. 450 and 455. The Jutes settled in Kent; Hengest and Horsa were given the Isle of Thanet. Soon a quarrel arose between them and the Britons, on which excuse the invaders proceeded to take and occupy what became their Kingdom of Kent. The Anglo-Saxon *Chronicle* records that in the year A.D. 455, at a place called Agæles, a battle was fought by Hengest and Horsa against the Britons under Vortigern in which Horsa was killed. From then onwards Hengest reigned in Kent. Three more battles are recorded in the *Chronicle* to have taken place in that area; the issues are unstated, but the ultimate outcome is in no doubt. The Britons were driven out of Kent, which became a Jutish kingdom with a long list of Kentish kings from the line of Hengest, who died in A.D. 488 leaving his son Æsc to reign until A.D. 512.

The pattern and conquest of Kent, and the establishment there of a 'kingdom' with an hereditary line of kings, more or less represents what took place elsewhere in the areas occupied by the Germanic invaders. There were seven such kingdoms: Northumbria, East Anglia, Essex, Kent, Sussex, Wessex and, in the centre, Mercia. The whole of this 'Heptarchy' area acquired the Old English name of *Engla Land*, the 'Land of the Angles' who, at least in regard to the name, stole the Saxon thunder—how and why nobody seems to know! England it remained. The name was used to include the farther territories which the invaders gradually took from the Britons, until within a hundred years or so it was used for the whole of the England we know. 'West Wales' was to disappear into Cornwall and Devonshire; Strathclyde into Lancashire and Cumberland. Caledonia, or 'Scotland', and 'North Wales' (the Wales of modern geography) remained as separate Celtic areas.

By A.D. 700 England was well established on the map of the world, and has remained there ever since, as, demographically, the most important part of the whole island.

Into this period come King Arthur (A.D. *c.* 500) and the Knights of the Round Table, whose extraordinary adventures in literary form are known as the 'Arthurian Legend' or 'Arthurian Cycle' which, considered generally, lives up to the description given later by the wise old Norman poet Wace: "Not all a lie, nor all truth, nor all fable, nor all known, so much have the storytellers told and the fablers fabled in order to embellish their tales, that they have made them all seem fable."

Arthurian wonder-tales come into the great Welsh classic, *The Mabinogion*,[12] and also into that monument of noble English prose written by Sir Thomas Malory (*fl.* 1470) called *Le Morte d'Arthur*. There has been and still exists a tendency on the part of scholars to regard the tales as all sheer invention, but this indicates some failure to grasp the gnomic nature of the language of Celtic legends in general, and in particular those which bear upon the man Arthur and the stories associated with his name. The Celts' inclination is to embellish, embroider and 'gild the lily' whenever events or personages are to their liking and 'make a good story'. But this inclination does not prove that the original basis of the story is untrue. On the contrary, it can provide reason for a fairly safe hypothesis that beneath the verbal embellishments there is a foundation of reality. So it was with 'King' Arthur and his 'Knights of the Round Table'. Let us look for a moment at what may be accepted as the authentic base. Arthur was a Romanized Briton who lived about A.D. 500. Like Queen Boudicca in regard to the Romans, he was horrified by the Germanic invasion of his country, and wished to see preserved as much as possible of the Britain he had known, now prostrate under the heathen barbarians. He was never a king or prince, still less an emperor (*amheradawr*), the title given to him in the Welsh accounts. It can, nevertheless, be granted that he was a native British chieftain or a descendant of chiefs. His military ability can be explained: under the Romans he held quite an important post as *Comes Britanniæ* ('Count of Britain'), a military official whose commission was of a roving nature, and included the task of defending the island wherever it was attacked. As there were no Roman soldiers to help him, he raised levies of volunteers among the native Britons, and these he inspired to the point of training themselves in accordance with the military science he and many of them had learned from the Romans. His army was small in comparison with the Germanic hordes with which he had to deal. So here we have one more brave but inevitably hopeless effort. The story is that he defeated the enemy in twelve great battles, but the truth seems to be that all were merely successful encounters except one; and in this he gained a considerable and decisive victory over the Saxons in Wiltshire. Taking it all round, he waged successful warfare against the enemies of his country. In the end he was betrayed by some of his own people, probably by kinsmen and his wife. He fell in battle. This is the most that can be claimed as the historical basis for the marvellous stories which the native Britons began to tell about him; stories which the fertile imaginations of the bardic Welsh expanded and embroidered, taking in some of the old Celtic myths and thus providing many parallels with the early Irish heroic cycles, notably the Fenian and especially the Oisin tales. The Irish additions are important. Into the Fenian cycle from which they were taken come stories of the *Tuatha Dé Danaan*, the mythological god-like "people of the goddess of Dana", a deity representing Nature and fertility. "Recent research", says an authority on the subject,[13] "has shown that two notable features of the Arthurian story, the Round Table and the Grail, can most reasonably be accounted for as survivals of Nature worship, and were probably parts of the legend from the first." Further romantic and faery additions grew on to the original story, which continued to flourish and expand and later took in a long series of Charlemagne romances—until we have Malory's masterpiece, about which the illustrious printer-editor William Caxton wrote: "Herein may be seen noble chivalry, courtesy, humanity, friendliness, hardiness, love, friendship, cowardice, murder, hate, virtue and sin. Do after the good and leave the evil and it shall bring you to good fame and renown."

Thus we see in an otherwise dark period of history the beginning and growth of a legend, a very beautiful legend which has been worthily recounted for us by one of the great masters of English prose. Let us not forget the real Arthur, the Briton leader who sacrificed himself in a hopeless idealistic struggle against the invaders of his land.

2

Foundations of English Society

Although we have been dealing with historical facts of great importance, this is not a history of England. The attempt that is being made here is merely to outline in the simplest terms those facts and circumstances which in one way or another have permanently contributed towards the making of the England we know to-day. Of these facts the Germanic invasion and settlement proved to be of the highest importance, for it laid the foundations of English society, by which is meant the base, the understructure of the social way of life,

449-1066
ANGLO-SAXON ENGLAND
ROMAN WALLS
MARSHES
SHADED AREAS INDICATE DANELAW
statute miles
0 12 24 36 48
S. Horne Shepherd
BERNICIA
STRATHCLYDE
(still Welsh)
NORTHUMBRIA
GALLOWAY
(PICTS)
R. Tyne
JARROW
Roman Wall
DURHAM
SCANDINAVIAN INVASIONS
STREANAESHALCH
(later Whitby)
CUMBRIA
(Lake District)
FURNESS
ISLE OF MAN
(Viking base)
DEIRA
YORK
R. Ouse
R. Ribble
R. Humber
Isle of Anglesey
R. Dee
R. Mersey
LINDSEY
LINCOLN
R. Trent
CHESTER
NOTTINGHAM
The Wash
MERCIA
(NORTH FOLK)
EAST ANGLIA
LEICESTER
STAMFORD
R. Welland
LICHFIELD
MIDDLE ANGLIA
WELSH MOUNTAIN REFUGE
MAGE-SAETE
Dyke circa 784
ELY
(SOUTH FOLK)
NORTHAMPTON
R. Severn
BEDFORD
R. Ouse
R. Avon
ESSEX
(EAST SAXONS)
MID SAXONS
LONDON
R. Thames
R. Thames
HWICCE
BATH
WESSEX
(WEST SAXONS)
CANTERBURY
R. Severn
KENT
(JUTES)
WINCHESTER
Forest of Andredesweald
SUMORSAETAN
WILSAETAN
(SOUTH SAXONS)
SUSSEX
JUTES
DORSAETAN
WALES

the very early customs and organization of the nation which we know. There were innumerable later modifications in the superstructure; but the foundations remained firm. The Celto-Anglo-Saxon-Jutish foundation demands attention, if we are to understand what follows.

The principal inclination of the Germanic peoples, after they had finished with the military problem of dealing with the Romanized Britons, was to settle down in rural townships and till the soil on the open-field system of village agriculture, grouping their wooden houses and homesteads around the hall of their leader or 'lord'. The new settlements were not made along the Roman roads, but near rivers, although in the active phase of conquest the invaders had made good use of those roads to get from one place to another. The new society was essentially agricultural, the country became one of farmers in groups each with its lord. Although most of the Roman landmarks and towns were abandoned by the Britons in the helter-skelter of evacuation to places of safety in the west, many of the more important towns, such as London, York, Lincoln, Chester and Canterbury, survived—a very few, including notably London, to grow into greater importance than before. London remained for long a British centre, one almost untouched during the invasion period. In the end the invaders joined and mixed with the Briton-Londoners, and shared in the amenities of that well-placed city. As the seven Germanic 'kingdoms' were set up and their frontiers became more or less established, their 'kings' attacked one another, each one impelled by the greed of power and the desire to increase his territory. The England of the Heptarchy, the Seven Kingdoms, was politically chaotic, and by the 6th century it was racked with several kinds of minor wars. There were little wars between the kings themselves; wars between kings and Britons; and even some wars between Britons and Britons. Behind all this the fundamental evolutions and developments never ceased: England was steadily becoming an agricultural country, quite well organized in small units which often worked collectively for agricultural purposes; and Germanics who had laid down arms began, at first in a few places, later in many, to show a tendency to mix and marry with Britons. This tendency is impossible to measure with any accuracy, but

Bolton Castle, Yorkshire
BTHA

one need hardly doubt its existence. The dominant language was Anglo-Saxon, and the Brythonic Celtic (Welsh) surviving in all-Celtic Wales and in the Devon-Cornwall area, became 'overlaid', swamped, and all but obliterated by Anglo-Saxon in the areas settled by the invaders. But the disappearance of a language in a given area or areas does not necessarily mean the disappearance of the people who spoke it. Biological survival is much stronger than linguistic in circumstances such as those which prevailed in Britain at that period. That Angles, Saxons and Jutes often married Briton wives can be assumed —that happens with conquerors and conquered—but not necessarily that the conquered Britons married womenfolk from the invaders' camp, though no doubt there were instances. Roman-British civilization was smashed in the internecine wars of the new settlers and in the wars between Celts and invaders. The biological process would go on, and possibly even gather force, as it did here: until, after a couple of hundred years, when the Britons in the areas settled by the Germanics were speaking Anglo-Saxon, had adapted themselves to the new conditions and were marrying and mixing freely with Angles, Saxons and Jutes without the slightest inhibitions. If this tendency cannot be measured, the inference of its existence is a safe one. It would not quickly show itself. But it certainly showed itself many years later in the new type of 'Englishman' who came into existence: a very different person from the rather dull type of farming Anglo-Saxon, and a less emotional, more level-headed person than the pure Celt. While these biological and economic changes were going on, an impetus was given to the advance of Christianity by an event which must be regarded as of great spiritual, political and cultural importance—the landing of a Roman abbot named Augustine with a party of monks on a mission to evangelize the heathen English. Augustine landed in A.D. 597 in the Isle of Thanet—"on the very spot where Hengest had landed more than a century before".

We must look back in order to understand the importance of the impact of this band of evangelists on the newly settled population of England. From the 2nd century A.D. until well into the 3rd, Christianity had been a sort of underground movement among Romans and Britons; a fairly successful one, for reasons not difficult to appreciate. Both the Romans and Celtic Britons were pagans. Their paganism had this much in common: it was easy-going, and there was no missionary zeal or even proselytizing among the approvers of Jupiter and the other Roman gods and the followers of the forty or more Celtic deities and their local cults. Romans and Britons tolerated each other's cults so much that they began to mix and blend ideas, to combine and work out a kind of common spiritual denominator for joint worship. This Romano-Celtic collaboration functioned well, but—as might be expected—the Celts gained dominance in it. When the underground Christian movement appeared, it was not unwelcome; and gradually it found adherents, especially among the Celts. Those Celts—great preachers and teachers—on the whole proved to be far more enthusiastic about Christianity than the Romans, and so this new and attractive religion spread far and wide over Britain. It was a purely Christianizing movement, without central organization or an established 'headquarters' church. The Germanic invasion isolated these Christians from Rome. And so, when Augustine arrived, he found in the island not only the great new population of absolutely heathen Angles, Saxons and Jutes, but a Celtic or Romanized Celtic population whose religions were either full Celtic paganism, a paganism of Romano-Celtic blend, or the unorganized, widely scattered little communities of primitive Christians. This is a highly simplified picture of a situation which presented many problems and complexities to the missionaries. It was Pope Gregory I who sent Augustine on the important mission of bringing into the Church and under centralized Rome the various religious groups, pagan, Christian and heathen, of which the mass of the population consisted. The beginning of the story is delightful. Years earlier, when Gregory was a young deacon at Rome, he had noted some beautiful fair-haired youths in the slave-market. He asked the traders whence they had come and what they were. "They are Angles," he was told. "Not Angles but angels," he commented. Later, as Pope, he had to deal with the involved religious problem of their country.

Augustine was fortunate to have landed in Kent, for the Jutish King Æthelberht was kind to him and gave the group every facility for their mission: a dwelling-place in Canterbury, full freedom to preach. Augustine was an energetic, forthright missionary, well grounded in the ideas of St. Paul, and with a clear conception not only of the spiritual but of the political element of his mission. And so it came about that Canterbury, already the earliest royal city in Germanic *Engla land,* now became the main centre of Latin influence. The Latin language, which had all but disappeared except among a few Christian missionaries, once again became in England the language for worship, for correspondence, for literature. The burning, almost fanatical zeal of imported Irish missionaries provided the necessary drive in Christianizing and civilizing the Germanic elements in the population. The Irish were well helped by the Britons. The whole island, well into Scotland and Wales, was permeated with ardent teachers. The movement, furthermore, served to bring Britons and Germanics closer together than ever; the new religion with its fresh humanism tended to wipe out any surviving 'racial' barriers. And so, by the end of the 7th century, we have again a different stratification of England; this time of an England with the Latin language and therefore access to the heritage of Rome. This meant not only Roman Christianity. A knowledge of Roman law and letters had come, which meant that the mixed and chaotic English laws could be sorted out, codified and reduced to permanent and convenient dimensions. From then onwards there is written record in prose. From then we have Bæda's famous history in Latin, known to us as Bede's *Ecclesiastical History of the English Nation,* finished in A.D. 731, and containing an account of not only ecclesiastical matters but of the most important social and political events in English history until that date. What is for us almost a blank period ended. Augustine had brought back a light that had vanished except in a few places. The English now adapted the Latin alphabet to their Anglo-Saxon language, and began to take into their language useful words from Latin. Thus, in still another England—the England of letters—there was a new impetus. We are now dealing with a country which, by the 9th century, had settled down, socially and economically, on Anglo-Saxon-Christian principles. And the English had available the cultural knowledge of the

Romans and their civilization. To sum up, the population east of Wales was mainly Germanic, but with Celtic pockets surviving here and there, strongly in Northumbria and other hilly places.

3

The Scandinavian Invasions

Life in England of the Heptarchy—the Seven Kingdoms of the Angles, Saxons and Jutes—was beginning in many parts of the country to take on a discernibly new and interesting pattern in the first part of the 9th century, notwithstanding the incessant quarrelling and minor warfare between the kings of Northumbria, Mercia and Wessex. The period from A.D. 800 to 850 was a progressive and hopeful one. The majority of the Anglo-Saxons gave the towns a wide berth and settled in the countryside, in village communities, as farmers of the good lands; many worked at clearing the woodlands of trees. The process of clearing away the forests which then existed almost everywhere was well and vigorously undertaken by those energetic farmer-lumbermen; they had laid aside their weapons for so long that now they hardly knew how to use them. The pattern that was taking shape was somewhat as follows. The Celts kept to the hills, where they lived mostly in hamlets. The greater part of the countryside was dotted with Anglo-Saxon village communities. In the towns and cities there was a mixed population of Romanized Britons, continental traders and of the more sophisticated Germanics. But country village life dominated, and this was based on a free and freeholding peasantry with serfdom, and subject only to the king their lord. In the towns the new civilizing influences were at work. The natural wealth of England meant that in spite of wars, fluxes, economic growing-pains and the lack of major political objectives, life was becoming better and better. Time was all that was required for the heptarchical kaleidoscope to settle into a clearly definable pattern. And then came a great upheaval.

In north-western Europe the kingdoms of the group of Germanic peoples called Swedes, Norse and Danes had by this time achieved a settled order under a succession of strong leaders who were kings. Their kingly rule was established on the old Germanic principle of leadership, in which society in general was held together by the bond between the ordinary man and his 'lord', a very powerful bond existing traditionally and demanding a life or death loyalty. But there were so many men in those countries who refused to accept the leadership of the kings and the bond which went with it, that a considerable population of vigorous, restless seamen-warrior-farmers found themselves cut off and felt that they must look for a new and different way of life for themselves. From a period of time beyond the memory of man those Scandinavian peoples had been amphibious. Between good and favourable periods working on the land or as fishermen-pirates or coastal traders, and bad periods due to a failure of the harvest or a lack of scope for piracy or trade around the shores of the North Sea or the Baltic, they would turn their eyes towards the sea and dream of what it could bring them. And now there was England—a great and attractive country at no distance that mattered for such skilled warrior-navigators. And so the leaders of the outlawed Swedes, Norwegians and Danes began to get together, first with a view to collaborating in raids on England; later with more ambitious ideas of conquest, exploitation or even settlement. This collective effort of piratical Scandinavian outlaws was accompanied by that dynamic upsurge which produced the Viking movement. It was one of the most remarkable in history, and in some ways one of the most puzzling; for we are not even sure whether to take the word Viking as meaning simply 'warrior' or 'creek man'. The Vikings were to go to many places and achieve great things. They went to northern France in A.D. 911, forced King Charles the Simple to accept them, settled in the part now called Normandy after them, and worked miracles there. They were to go as far afield as Greenland and Constantinople. They went inland across Russia to the Dnieper and down that river to the Black Sea. They went to Ireland and established at river mouths bases from which they ravaged the monasteries and wrought general havoc until finally defeated in battle (1014) and driven out. In England their problem was different from any they had to deal with elsewhere. For England was now largely populated by peoples of their own Germanic race.

And so, after some preliminary and almost unopposed plundering expeditions along the coast, they invaded England in great numbers. Their invasions (A.D. 865–878) were not in essentials very dissimilar from those of the Angles, Saxons and Jutes; but the Vikings concentrated on achievement by the inland waterways. The open long-ships of the Vikings, with their single sail and oars, could not only sail the stormy open seas and attack where they pleased on coasts, they could go into creeks and be rowed up the rivers well into the interior. Those Scandinavian invasions of mixed Swedes, Danes and Norwegians—often collectively called Norsemen or Northmen—proved successful. The English were taken unawares, for most of them had long abandoned their arms and warlike habits. England of the Anglo-Saxons was now to have the same sort of horrific experience as Celtic Britain had with the earlier Germanic invaders. But the Viking pirates gave shorter shrift and less quarter than their predecessors. They looted and plundered in all directions. They seized York and made it the centre of a kingdom, north of which they exacted only tribute. They won right and left, and could settle where they pleased. The English peasants, with nothing but shield and spear, could not face the invaders with any hope of success; for those invaders, with their fleets of hundreds of long-boats, were highly skilled wielders of the battle-axe, great bowmen and trained to fight in a disciplined, co-ordinated manner. They never went far from their boats, which always provided them with a safe way of retreat when pressed. They won their campaign, and seemed to be in a position to hold down the greater part of England when among the English a great leader appeared: Ælfred, King of Wessex, and known to history as Alfred the Great. He not only cleared the Danes from his own kingdom, but undertook a systematic reduction of the 'Danelaw', the part of England under Danish domination which comprised East Anglia, Lincolnshire, Leicestershire, Nottinghamshire with parts of the adjacent counties. In the Danelaw, English and Danes often merged, and the two peoples got on well together. From then onwards for years England was a war-racked country. Battles with the Scandinavians were fought up and down the country. Alfred did not see the end, for he died in A.D. 901, one of the greatest of English kings; great not only in war but as a far-sighted, humane, cultured and highly esteemed leader of his people. He was the first of the Heptarchy kings to realize that what this disunited England needed more than anything else was *unity* and an end of internal strife of all kinds. This lesson was driven home to him by the Scandinavian invasion; but he did not live to see it take practical shape. Unity was in the end achieved, though in a way which he might not have liked. While the struggle went on between the English and the invaders, at home in Scandinavia the Danish King Swegen, a man of vision and ambitious ideas, aimed at the creation of a great Scandinavian Empire with England as its most important or central territory. Death interrupted his plans, but they were vigorously taken up by his son Cnut, 'Canute the Dane' of our national history. Cnut formed an expedition and sailed for England, where the news of his arrival off the coast, and the prospect of a seemingly hopeless new war, brought together the leaders of the three great kingdoms of Northumbria, Mercia and Wessex—the greater part of Anglo-Saxon England, that is—in an act of compromise which acknowledged Cnut as their lord. A final attempt to prevent Danish domination was made by Eadmond 'Ironside', son of ex-King Æthelred ('the Unready'); but after a few months of struggle it failed, with a decisive victory for the Danes at Assandun, now Ashingdon, Essex.

Cnut brought peace to England; but that peace did not last for long. In his time began another kind of struggle between king and people, one which was to continue for centuries. By his good sense Cnut might have solved that problem, but the lawlessness and bloodshed under his successor Hardicanute not only lost all the goodwill Cnut had won: it lost England for the Danes, and brought about an English restoration in 1042 in the person of Edward, son of Æthelred, who had long been in exile in Normandy. This Edward, the last king of old English stock, was a man whose gentle attitude and piety gained for him the name of 'the Confessor'. With him we begin to see the roots of the monarchy of to-day. He was succeeded in 1066 by Harold, who was to be the last of the Saxon kings of England.

4

The Pattern in Formation

For some time before the reign of King Alfred the Great of Wessex, the idea of unity had been in the air. The kingdoms —other than Northumbria—at times tried to work on the old Germanic leadership principle, modified into 'overlordship' (possibly by the influence of contemporary ideas of feudalism evolving on the Continent), and even so far back as the 9th century there was an overlord 'Ruler of Britain' to whom other kings paid tribute and whose leadership was accepted in war. The Anglo-Saxons were certainly groping their way slowly, very slowly, towards a solution of that major problem for an island: unity. It can hardly be claimed that they succeeded very well. For a brief moment Cnut almost succeeded; and then, after the Anglo-Saxon Restoration in the person of Edward the Confessor, the English Wise Men of the Witan Council tried again. Although they made some progress, their success was again only partial; and it was never well consolidated. The supreme 'leadership' problem was to be solved later in a way which none of those kings could have foreseen. For all that, the English monarchy of to-day is connected by thin threads with the line of Anglo-Saxon kings beginning with Ecgberht (A.D. 802–833). The line runs from him through Æthelred II and Edmund Ironside, one of whose daughters, Margaret, married Malcolm III, King of Scots. And their daughter Matilda married Henry I of England (1100–1135), a son of William the Conqueror, the Norman leader who came to England in 1066 to set a new pattern of life. William I himself married a Matilda, the daughter of King Beaudouin (Baldwin) V of Flanders, and this Matilda traced her descent in the female line from Alfred the Great: a son of William and this Matilda became Henry I of England. The line of connexion is there, in so far as royalty is concerned. But something more important remains of that pre-Norman Celto-Germanic country—not yet a nation—which existed before the important year 1066 that we are now approaching. There was the population, and the general way of life which that population was still engaged in working out.

Celtic society had ceased to exist except among the Picts and Scots north of the Clyde, in the considerable area called Strathclyde which ran downwards from the Clyde to Kendal extending half-way across northern England; and in Wales and in the Devon-Cornwall peninsula. Even north of the Clyde it had faded except on the western fringe of Scotland, as Caledonia was then called after the Irish *Scotti*. As we have seen, the Anglo-Saxon invaders left the upland regions of England to the Celts; and there, and in a few other places, they continued to exist. They had not an easy life, being constantly harassed and often chased from pillar to post. When the Scandinavians came, they found the Celts friendly. Many Celts joined them, to have new amenities and a prosperity they had not known since the departure of the Romans. This explains why it is that in the 'Danelaw' area we find more evidence of a surviving Celtic influence and temperament than in the rest of England, apart from a few small pockets here and there. But if we leave out this unmeasurable and perhaps problematical biological factor, the Celtic 'influence' had all but vanished into the racial melting-pot. It still remains strong only in those 'fringe' areas or in the pockets.

The Anglo-Saxons established England's agriculture on a sound basis—the open-field system—and when we consider that until comparatively recent times the whole country lived on that agriculture, this was a most important achievement. It was fundamental. Farmers owned and worked their land as freemen, and now there emerged three 'classes' of freemen: the thane (or *thegn*), at first a direct military retainer of the king well below an earl, later an important landowner (a primitive 'squire', forerunner of the Lord of the Manor) who held land direct from the king or from an overlord by military service. Thanes not only farmed land of their own, they granted freeholds to lower-ranked freemen (churls) in return for military and other services and kind. From the military services so rendered, they made up their quota to the king. Below these churls was a still lower 'class' of serfs in two categories: bondmen, slave-labourers who could be disposed of; and bondmen also little better than slaves, who 'went with the land' and could be disposed of only with the land. The Scandinavian wars wrought havoc with this system, to which the Anglo-Saxons had been accustomed even before they came to England. Those wars caused a considerable loss of freedom to all three classes of freemen, to earls, thanes and churls; and even to the serfs. From then not only did the division of classes become stricter and stiffer; but those in the higher rank imposed obligations on those who came next, and each rank adding some of their own, the obligations were always passed on to the next. The people in the lowest category were thus overwhelmed with obligations and tied hand and foot by restrictions. It was this unhappy state of affairs which started a movement among the oppressed landworkers which was to continue in one form or another for centuries, and to evolve in many directions. And yet, although the wars with the Danes started these troubles among the English, in the Danelaw itself the landworkers' freedoms survived much longer. But we must never allow ourselves to forget that it was the Anglo-Saxons who started and developed in England the agricultural village community as a self-contained economic and social unit. This was to be the backbone of the country for centuries, and it has left distinct traces which survive down to our own time.

From that long period of Germanic settlement, beginning soon after the Roman evacuation of Britain and ripening into the rough civilization of pre-Norman days, we have several of the 'classes' which survive into our own times. There was an upper stratum of society, an aristocracy with the king at the top; and then below the earls came the thanes, local overlords. Below the thanes were the two classes of tenants: the free; and the unfree, the serfs. The countryside overshadowed the towns and cities. This pattern was to continue, but with many modifications. Politics, as we understand the word, did not exist. The Church, with headquarters at Canterbury, helped by its teachings to keep society together—and the serf in his proper place, though not without regard for the poor man's rights, the disregard of which good Archbishop Wulfstan considered an abuse which brought the wrath of God on the heads of his countrymen. Many of the serfs were Britons, so much so that the word Briton was at one time used to mean 'slave'. This was one of the reasons which prompted so many of the Britons to enlist in the ranks of the Scandinavian invaders, and thereby to lose their slave-status; for hatred of slavery and love of freedom was in their Celtic bones.

Anglo-Saxon law was customary and uncodified; much of it was passed on orally. Much of it was still in the primitive stage, and although masses of Anglo-Saxon legal records have survived, they are of interest only to scholars, often for linguistic rather than legalistic reasons. Yet in some respects they provide us with valuable indications of the way people *thought* in pre-Norman England, for law is nearly always a compromise between what rulers and ruled consider necessary for the good ordering of society. At least two aspects of Anglo-Saxon law now strike us forcibly as very strange: the oath system by which the right or wrong of a case was decided; and the system of compensation in money or kind by which crimes and torts were settled. Dorothy Whitelock [11] tells how it worked, and I follow her. By the oath system a plaintiff swore his case and called in support vindicators ('compurgators'), who testified on oath to the justice of his claim. Then the defendant swore his case, and called his compurgators. Are we not familiar with the method? But now comes a nice subtlety. The value of the total of cogency on each side was calculated mathematically on the basis of the status and property of the compurgators on each side! Thus, a man's oath could be described as one of 'so many hides of land'—the 'hide' was originally an area considered sufficient to support a peasant household, and varied from about 40 to about 90 acres—and compurgators' oaths were valued on a scale depending on their status. Thus, a 'king's companion' who was a communicant could swear for sixty hides; a churl for five. The oath's value was sometimes expressed in terms of money: 'an oath of a pound in value'. A churl's oath was valued at five shillings. Normally the 'size' of the oath required was related to the amount of fine involved if the defendant failed to clear himself; for example, a man had either to produce an oath of 120 hides or pay twenty shillings fine. It seems to have been a simple and straightforward system without any of the gamble over damages there is to-day with our judge and jury system. The greater the wealth or the higher the status of the compurgators, the more chance there was of winning! The compensation system for torts or civil wrongs worked on a basis of wealth and status: an earl received ten times the compensation awarded to a churl. These were the curious features of that old law. Apart from them, property was more sacred than human life; theft was a very grave crime. Executions were almost a commonplace, and thieving was one of the commonest crimes for which the penalty could be death. There were several forms of execution, in accordance with the crime and circumstances: beheading, drowning, stoning and burning—but most in use was the time-honoured and still most-favoured English method: hanging. The bodies of hanged criminals were left dangling from gallows-trees to mark the boundary between settlements; a fact often recorded in old lists of boundaries of estates. In all this we can see the early phase of a ferocity which was to characterize English penal law until well into the 19th century.

There was little trading in those days, although there was an admirable coinage. London was the great central mart, the clearing-place for export and import and internal exchange of goods. Sufficient evidence does not exist for us to form a clear idea of town and city life, the dominating factor being that the Anglo-Saxons preferred to live on the land and disliked towns. The great age of trading had not yet begun. But London was already well ordered and had its aldermen; then as now its wards, boroughs and parishes; and it is from Anglo-Saxon times that we derive the custom of giving streets names to indicate the occupations of the men who lived in them. In our London to-day we have, for example, two Tanner's Streets, a Tanner's Lane and Tanner's Hill. If Anglo-Saxon vernacular literature has not been mentioned, the reason is that, apart from the one great (and pagan) saga in the national literature—*Beowulf*, which dates from the 8th century—a hymn of the Christian poet Cædmon, and Cynewulf's prose and verse, little of significance survives. Latin and not English was still the language of letters. It is possible that King Alfred's prose is of more importance than all the surviving Anglo-Saxon poetry. Alfred was not only a fine translator, he was also an original thinker and writer, a great educator, the father of English prose. His writings provided a stimulus to culture, and had influence among those who preferred their own language to Latin. How important that was we now realize, though little has survived of his works.

The pattern of the England which we know was forming. But there was still something missing from the ingredients required to make a great nation.

CHAPTER IV

THE NORMAN INVASION: 1066 TO 1200

1

The Normans at Home

THE word 'Norman' is merely another form of the word 'Northmen' often given to the Vikings—Scandinavians, that is —who in the year A.D. 911 invaded northern France in the area around the mouth of the Seine and, by a succession of brilliant conquests, seized a fine piece of territory, founded 'Normandy' and settled there permanently. This was a very different kind of conquest from that achieved by the Scandinavians in England, where they had to deal with a kindred Germanic people whose language and institutions were very similar to their own. In northern France the fierce Vikings found a Celtic population that had long been under Roman domination, and had become, in terms of politics, civilization, language and culture, a thoroughly Latinized people. The significance of this fact can hardly be over-estimated. The Northmen, intelligent, vigorous and efficient in war, suddenly found themselves overlords of a people defensively weak but otherwise far in advance of themselves. A less intelligent people than the Scandinavians might have been content with conquest and exploitation. Not so the conquerors of this part of northern France. Their conquest was completed and consolidated in the 10th century. By the end of that century they had wholeheartedly adopted and assimilated the French language, manners and customs, the Roman Catholic religion, and the principles of law and government surviving from Roman times. This was a miracle of assimilation in a slow-moving epoch. From Northmen they changed—in a matter of half a century —into a people so very different from their forefathers that they had completely forgotten their own old language, their paganism and almost everything else connecting them with their homeland, except perhaps some of the old Viking ferocity in battle.

What deeply concerns us here is the character of this new people that had so strongly established themselves just across the English Channel. The more we contemplate those people, the more there seems to have been something magical in the changes which had taken place when Northmen became Normans. A contemporary historian, Geoffrey Malaterra, tells us that the Normans were "a race specially noteworthy for cunning", people who would "despise their own inheritance in favour of a greater one"—which they did in northern France—and *"avid for gain and domination"*. He goes on to say that they were given to imitation of all kinds—a statement which might be explained by saying that they had a very keen sense for anything better than what they themselves possessed, and did not hesitate to appropriate to their own use any seemingly beneficial idea. Unlike the Anglo-Saxons, they were eloquent and good orators, and they were consummate in flattery. Above all, they were a race "altogether unbridled unless held down by the yoke of justice". As warriors they were formidable: fierce and unyielding in battle, strong to withstand hunger and cold, and with great powers of endurance. Curiously enough, they loved to deck themselves out in the panoply of war—we would say that they were 'great exhibitionists'—and they loved horses, hunting and hawking. To these qualities one may add some others equally important: they had a strange, indefinable quality of improving the national life of peoples with whom they came into contact, by modifying it and strengthening it. That is, they could start where other people had left off, and give a new impetus to progress. For example, when they adopted French as their language, they were soon practising the art of literature in French, and immediately became pioneers in making it known abroad. One of the most important things they did in the way of adaptation was to take from northern Italy a style of architecture, which they developed to a remarkably high standard at home in Normandy and later in England. They abandoned the sea and became landlubbers, like the Gauls and Romans. In land warfare they took over every new idea they found, in some cases adding the new idea to their own; as, for example, when they took to the Celto-Roman idea of cavalry and used their own battle-axe from the saddle. Their

Fingle Bridge, Devonshire
BTHA

Buttermere Village, Cumberland
BTHA

natural aptitude for war, and their great skill in handling weapons generally, added to the old natural Viking ferocity, usually enabled them to sweep all before them. They had one other quality which hardly seems reconcilable with all this: they loved law, legal forms, processes and litigiousness! The Norman seems to have been 'born' to many things: he was a born soldier, a born lawyer, a born bureaucrat and administrator, and born with the strange ability to make a full, speedy and fruitful union with any nation or people from the moment he had made up his mind to do so.

In considering what happened in England after 1066, one has to keep in mind not only the existing conditions at that date in that country, but understand the reasons for the change in the English politico-social atmosphere brought about by the fact of conquest by those remarkable Normans. Behind both the existing conditions in England and the changes introduced by the Normans was a dominating idea relating to political power: that of feudalism. The word has been defined as "a polity based on the relation of vassal and superior arising from the holding of lands in feud"—lands, that is, which could be passed on to a successor. This was not a new idea. It can be traced fairly clearly to later Roman times, but it probably dates back much earlier and was certainly not limited to the Roman empire. It has been found all over the world; and still exists in some countries. The system of feudalism, wherever it has existed, is said to have arisen from the prevailing need of society for 'protection'—protection against marauding bands, hostile tribes, peasants in revolt, oppressive neighbours, oppressions by officers of State; or even against oppressive exactions by the government itself. Similar conditions in widely separated countries and periods of history have produced a similar system. In the England of the Heptarchy it already existed, as it existed in a similar half-developed form in northern France when the Vikings first landed there. But whereas in England it continued in its rather loose and free-and-easy forms, the Scandinavians who became Normans took the system in hand and quickly brought it to a high standard of organization and efficiency. This enormously increased the power of those people in the higher ranks of society, and, as is usually the case in the matter

Godshill, Isle of Wight
BTHA

of power, the achievement of more power brought with it an appetite for still more. From which point it is not far to the power-State, especially with a people so "avid for gain and domination" as the Normans. In comparison with the great power-States which we know to-day, the Norman achievement in this respect was modest. The Roman Empire and its power had declined, and it was for Norman political ingenuity and dynamism to set the pattern and evolve the first principles in the general idea of the State which we now know in Western civilization.

One aspect of Norman life was so important that it deserves special attention. When the heathen worshippers of Odin had time to settle down in France and pay attention to such things, they found an advanced and sophisticated Roman Catholic Church that was in every way different from the rumbustious paganism observed by their race from time immemorial. Without the slightest hesitation they dropped their hale-and-hearty old religion and became Christians overnight!—just one more flash of Norman political genius. They became not just lukewarm Christians, observing the rules of the Church and paying lip-service to its doctrines. The Normans were strict observers of forms in all matters, secular and religious, but in regard to their Church they were genuinely enthusiastic, very bountiful and extremely proud of their religious foundations. Yet in one respect they showed a characteristic touch of the old Viking spirit: the Norman dukes would not submit to encroachments by the ecclesiastical power. This may seem a small point to us, but it was not unimportant if we bear in mind that unwillingness to submit to political domination by some other power—the political Church in particular—has existed in England ever since the Norman Conquest. It became an English characteristic, and not unrelated to those other English characteristics variously called empiricism, expediency, opportunism or just an immediate sense of relevant values. For the Normans to drop paganism and, so to speak, become Catholics overnight, but with a political qualification in regard to *power*, was a remarkable piece of expediency. And it was soon to be followed by what many would regard as an equally remarkable stroke of empiricism —or, shall we say, an immediate sense of relevant values?

When William had his eyes turned towards England, he thought of a conquest which should bring to the benighted islanders the benefits of enlightened Norman Christianity. This he would take there, so to speak, under his command, and as a very necessary unit of the governmental machinery he would establish there. It is not to be inferred from this that William was acting cynically. He had a sincere regard for his religion, and saw himself as a religious reformer in his duchy at home and as a potential missionary for backward England. But political power springing from the Church must take its place with military power springing from feudalism: both must help him.

This William (*b.* 1027, *d.* 1087), who became William the Conqueror, King William I of England, was the natural son of Duke Robert the Magnificent of Normandy (also called 'the Devil') by a girl named Arletta, who was the daughter of a tanner at Falaise named Fulbert. The fact explains why he is called *Guillaume le Bâtard* by French historians. In 1034 Robert decided to go on a pilgrimage to Jerusalem and, having no legitimate son, he persuaded his barons to accept William as his successor. When Robert died on his pilgrimage the barons held to their word, though duke-elect William was still a mere boy. From his youth onwards William's life was exciting. He soon found that he had to fight his cousin Gui de Bourgogne, whom he crushed in 1047, at Val des Dunes near Caen, with the help of the French king. Next he found himself fighting the king, his former ally. He defeated the French at Montemer in two battles, and then allied himself with his father-in-law Beaudoin (Baldwin) Count of Flanders, whose daughter Matilda he had married. On the death of Edward the Confessor, William claimed the succession of England, and in this he was supported by Pope Alexander II. He based his demand on Matilda's contention that she was able to trace her descent in the female line from Alfred the Great. The union of William and Matilda had been prohibited on grounds of affinity by the Papal Council at Rheims. William defied the prohibition. He must have felt that the Pope would support him, as his own political importance was growing daily. He was, in fact, granted a dispensation in 1059. During this time the energetic duke was not idle in either the military, the diplomatic or the administrative fields. Such was his all-round success that by 1062 he had advanced the Norman frontier as far as the Loire, isolated Brittany, and formed for himself a well-governed and powerful Duchy which grew stronger every day. In 1064 his court was visited by Earl Harold of England, who, it seems—for there is much mystery about what happened behind the scenes—promised to support William's claim to the English succession. From the confusions and contradictions in the history of those events, one fact emerges very clearly: that William was intent upon the conquest of England and had long been making plans to that end. He had made a friend and ally of Tostig, Harold's banished brother, and when the time came for invading England, it was very largely due to Tostig's invasion of northern England that Duke William and his compact and highly efficient Norman Army were able to land at Pevensey on September 28th, 1066.

2

Invasion and Conquest

The story of the Norman Conquest is so well known that the only justification for its inclusion here is to throw light upon some of its aspects, and to emphasize others which will help us to understand our modern England and the English. William Duke of Normandy's claim to the English throne was so flimsy that it would not be upheld by any reasonable and independent tribunal. It was, nevertheless, supported by the Papacy, for Normandy was now a 'Great Power' in Europe, and William held many good cards. The Anglo-Saxon system of king-making was elective and the Witenagemote, the 'Council of Wise Men'—an assembly of bishops, earls, royal officials and other potentates—had by custom the right to fill the throne by their own choice. They chose Harold, Earl of East Anglia and son of the powerful Earl Godwin, a man who by sheer ability had become master of the realm though never king. Edward the Confessor, it was said, also wished Harold to be king, although the nearest heir was Edgar the Atheling, grandson of Edmund Ironside, and a mere boy. Nothing in English history is more obscure than what went on behind the scenes from the moment it was known that the Confessor had not long to live. The historical fact remains that, the moment he died, the Council of Wise Men at once proceeded —very quietly!—to elect and crown Harold. That was in January 1066. His coronation was a signal for Harald Hardrada, King of Norway, to launch an attack on England without any excuse other than ambition, but obviously impelled by the thought that England was now weak and disunited, and that this would be an opportune moment to invade. Just at this moment William's invasion, which was well prepared, suffered some weeks of delay due to the weather which kept his ships in port. Meanwhile Harald Hardrada landed in the north with a very strong force. And so, in the summer and autumn of 1066, King Harold of England found himself confronted with the double task of dealing with a horde of Norse invaders in the north, and then with the Norman Duke William's highly efficient army in the south. Both invasions appear to us as plain attempts at daylight robbery. Our sympathies go to King Harold.

If there was a composite quality which above all others the Normans had acquired during their 150 years in France, it was of the discipline and orderliness which the Romanized Gauls had inherited from their Roman governors and administrators. William had applied and developed it with advantageous modifications, especially in regard to his fighting forces. He was an intelligent man of strong character, and he had organized for the invasion of England a first-rate expeditionary force. Its strength did not depend upon its size—there were not more than 12,000 men, half of them cavalry, in it—but in the nature of its organization, armaments, training and discipline. For its size, it was probably the strongest striking force in that world. This explains two things: the lightning speed of the Conquest, and its complete acceptance by the rulers and most of the people of Anglo-Saxon England, to whom the speed and effectiveness of William's army were little short of miraculous. His military campaign was simple —and ingenious—as nearly all successful campaigns are. At the mouth of the River Seine he first assembled a large fleet, and then looked about him for those feudal lords far and near who could be persuaded to join him with the promise of military adventure, immediate loot and considerable rewards later in the form of lands, which he said would follow success.

Here is a bald modern French statement of William's career: "On the death of Edward the Confessor, William claimed the succession. He obtained the support of Pope Alexander II, landed in England with an army of Normans and adventurers from every country, killed Harold near Hastings (1066), and had himself crowned in London. He confirmed his Conquest by repressing numerous revolts, took Exeter and York (1067), purchased the withdrawal of a Danish invader, and imposed his suzerainty on Malcolm King of Scotland (1072). On the Continent he had to give Maine to his son Robert, and then fight the latter who had the support of the King of France. He was defeated and wounded near Gerberoi (1079). He died as a consequence of a fall from a horse at Mantes in an expedition against Philip I. His body was buried in the Abbey of Saint-Etienne, Caen." [14]

William's military campaign in England was a model of efficiency and ingenuity. The ingenuity consisted in forming an alliance with Tostig, Harold's exiled brother, who was leader of the Danish invasion of northern England; this enabled the Norman duke to launch his invasion in the south and land unopposed at Pevensey on September 28th. He was unopposed because King Harold was compelled by sheer military necessity to abandon his watch on the south coast and rush off to the north to face Tostig, whose great army the Anglo-Saxons defeated in a hand-to-hand, 'no quarter given' battle at Stamford Bridge. Harold's victory was largely due to his wonderful force of 'housecarls', an organized, well-trained body of professional mounted infantry in the king's pay. The idea of having such a 'king's guard' had originated before King Cnut's time and was essentially Viking. Many of its Scandinavian members were to be replaced by Anglo-Saxons, and by Harold's time it was almost entirely Anglo-Saxon—the cream of England's fighting forces. The mere fact of compelling Harold to leave the south coast in order to fight that battle was the first reward of William's ingenuity. The second was equally great: Harold's victory had annihilated a potential enemy in the north. For although there was an understanding between William and those Scandinavian invaders, the intelligent Norman took it for granted that, if they were successful against the Anglo-Saxons, he in turn would have to fight Tostig. And now Tostig and his army had been wiped out of existence by Harold. There was even a third reward: Harold's victory at Stamford Bridge had greatly weakened the whole English army. Nevertheless, when news came to him of William's landing at Pevensey, Harold put himself at the head of the housecarls (who were regarded as the finest mounted infantry in Europe), and they set off at the gallop to meet the Norman invasion. At the same time he sent out a rallying call to the thanes and 'fyrds' (local groups consisting of all men liable for military service), and especially to those within reasonable march of the invasion area. But now he made what seems to us a bad though a pardonable mistake. Instead of waiting until he had a strong enough force at his command, he decided to engage William immediately, and took up his position on an isolated spur of hill a few miles north of Hastings. Military historians regard the famous Battle of Hastings as interesting from the purely military point of view. That need hardly concern us here, more than to say that William's success over Harold was mainly due to two factors, and, perhaps one should add—if there is sense in such post-mortem comment—that but for those factors Harold would probably have won the day. The English (mixed Anglo-Saxons and Scandinavians) fought their battle on foot in their own traditional way—and they used the old Viking battle-axe. The Normans fought from the saddle, using spear and sword, but their best efforts were shattered against the wall of shields which faced them. And so the battle raged for a time, neither side making great headway. Harold's position was well chosen; the fighting qualities of his men were excellent. There was a brief period of almost deadlock, and then the Norman leader, having taken good measure of the situation, fell back upon the use of archery, a military art which the Normans had carefully preserved and developed, but which the Anglo-Saxons had lost by neglect. The battle was thus reduced to a contest between Harold's solid mass of infantry, armed with striking weapons only, and a Norman force of mobile cavalry armed with better striking weapons and supported by archers who sent their missiles into the air to fall downwards on the men who had to fight in shield-rings to hold off the cavalry. These two factors—archery and cavalry—quickly decided the issue. By nightfall the one-day battle which decided the whole future course of England's history was at an end. Harold himself, and with him the great body of his housecarls, lay dead on the hill of battle (as it is called to this day), and the exhausted and battle-weary men of his quickly raised levies straggled off homewards, sad in defeat, but feeling that their bravery had not wilted and that their defeat was due to the superior tactics of Duke William. Had there been a great leader among them at that moment, someone who might have said to them: "We have lost a battle, but we have not lost the war. Let us rally together and we shall drive out the enemy"—then the Norman Conquest could never have succeeded. Instead, the rulers of Anglo-Saxon England had only one thought after the shock of the Battle of Hastings: peace with the Conqueror. Not a collective peace, formally signed. Each potentate wished to make his own private peace with William. There was some resistance here and there, but none to cause William great loss of sleep. He encircled London, which soon showed a willingness to accept him as king, and even invited him to come and be crowned at Westminster. And so, on Christmas Day in 1066, he was crowned as lawful heir to Edward the Confessor. This event proved to be a landmark, a turning-point in England's history.

William's method of consolidating his conquest was as cynical as might be expected from such a man; though some might object to the word cynical and prefer the word realistic to describe it. He took a lenient view of those of the Anglo-Saxon ruling class who wholeheartedly submitted to him *and* proved by something more than mere lip-service that they would give him their full support. To all others in that class he gave short shrift. He took their lands, everything they possessed. He waged a campaign against the Earls of Mercia and 'Northumberland' (who apparently suffered from the delusion that they could continue their independent rule as hitherto), which for cruelty, atrocities and devastation bears comparison with any war ever waged by a savage and ruthless military leader. In parts of the country, says Trevelyan,[8] "he left no house standing and no human beings alive that his horsemen could search out. As Domesday testifies, many scores of villages were still without inhabitants seventeen years later." [15] It was during this period of consolidation and the ruthless suppression of regional rebellions that a brave Saxon resister arose in the person of one Hereward, called the Wake or 'watchful'. He is a romantic figure in the national history. Hereward's territory was in the swampy Fenland area, the part south of the Wash between our present Peterborough and Norfolk and extending down to the Isle of Ely, north of Cambridge. When the rest of England had been conquered he waged brilliant guerilla warfare in that almost impossible swampy country. But he too failed, like all the other rebels, and for the same reason that the others failed: the absence of a collective resistance movement in his support.

William subdued England piecemeal. Almost everywhere he went he erected 'castles', military forts with picked garrisons, built with the forced labour of Anglo-Saxon slaves. Each castle had a keep standing in a courtyard surrounded by a high wall, often with turrets, and with a gatehouse opening. The castle was surrounded by a moat, which was crossed by a drawbridge beyond which there might be other walls. These Norman castles, established in well-chosen strategic sites, were at first built of timber and were usually set up on earthwork mounds. Later, in the reign of Henry I, William's successor, the most important were built of stone, many to survive into our own time as historic national monuments. Their original object was to serve as bases for the occupying forces, as refuges, depots and obstacles against possible rebels. That so astute a leader as William deemed them to be necessary is an indication of his caution and of the thoroughness of his consolidations. It also indicates that he must have had good reason to fear revolts. We see now that his caution may have been overdone, for the general disunity, the absence of collective effort and leadership among the Anglo-Saxons, faced with the Conqueror's well co-ordinated forces and ruthlessly definite policy, guaranteed an all-round success for the Norman invaders. England was made a Norman country, and, during the years which followed, there was established in it a much more rigorous and efficient feudal system than the Scandinavians and Anglo-Saxons had ever known, although William had sworn to observe the old English laws as well as the customs of feudalism. It was from the fusion of these two systems—Anglo-Saxon customary law and continental feudalism in its Norman aspect—that arose the English governmental and legal systems which exist to-day. This dual origin and happy marriage helps to explain many things which puzzle not only foreigners but even English people. The astonishing strength of the English governmental system with its powerful ruling class, both of which sprang originally from the Norman-English union, has often proved to be a complete enigma to friend and foe of England. But the English accepted it, and accept the enigma as just one aspect of the many benefits conferred by a mysterious but beneficent Providence on a people who do not deserve less.

3

The Norman Contribution

The Norman contribution to English civilization can be summed up very briefly as follows: it provided an education in discipline and orderliness. One immediately asks: for what purpose? And the answer is: chiefly for the benefits of the new Norman rulers and their friends among the Anglo-Saxon ruling class who had wholeheartedly come over to their side and were to be trusted. The common people—Saxons and Celts—were there to serve this end. A delicate calculation had to be made by the rulers of how much exploitation the common people would submit to without rebelling. In the year 1085 William therefore ordered the first close survey or inquest of the population and general wealth of the country to be made. In the short period of one year the work was completed, and the findings published in 1086 in the famous Domesday Book. Every village and estate throughout the land was visited by the king's commissioners; the principal inhabitants were everywhere interviewed. Manors and their extent were listed. So also were the numbers of tenants, their status and holdings; the nature and quantity of different kinds of ground, whether forest, pasture or arable land, etc.; the numbers of plough teams, mills, quarries, fisheries; the value of the manor (*a*) in the Confessor's time, (*b*) when bestowed upon its new owner by William immediately after the Conquest and (*c*) in 1085–1086.

This was a very remarkable survey in more senses than one. It was by its very nature so unpopular that, if the entire population had not been completely subdued, it could not have been possible to complete it. We read that so narrowly did the Conqueror cause the survey to be made that "there was not one single hide nor rood of land, nor—it is shameful to tell but he thought it no shame to do—was there an ox, cow or swine that was not set down in writ". What it all signified was that the chief feudal lord—the king—was now fully cognizant of the power and resources of all his feudatories and all their vassals in the 'shires', the old administrative areas. With Domesday Book the new government could cleverly overhaul all local administration, and establish new and more efficient feudal bodies for purposes not only of taxation but for the complete reorganization of the judiciary, the police and the army. In the new reorganization the township became a manor, the unit in the feudal system. There was "no land without its lord", who was the "lord of the manor"; which had its own manor court, with other private feudal courts to supplement it. The Anglo-Saxon idea of the 'shire' was retained, this being another name for the Norman *counté*, which became 'county'. The English counties are still called shires on the map. Inside the shire there were smaller units—in terms of feudal holdings.

The whole system was merely authoritarian feudalism. It was admirable for the rulers and 'free tenants', but it weighed heavily on the far larger class of 'unfree' villeins, cottars and serfs. What is really remarkable is how long this system endured. England still has many manors, lords of the manor, and a complicated system of property law which derives directly from that feudal system, though shorn of some of its most oppressive abuses. In this respect it is not nearly so advanced as, say, the Republic of Ireland with its present population of free small-holders, where for generations the population rebelled against the feudalistic land-holding system imposed on them by the English occupation. But it seems to be recognized that, thanks to this solid economic basis and the ingenious and efficient power-system which William established on it, the English State and the English nation was able to progress from strength to strength. The full strength and potentialities of the system were not to show themselves until much later, and by then the basic elements were overgrown by others though not killed.

The Norman contribution in terms of race must have been comparatively small. Apart from the rank and file of military units, most of the immigrants would form part of the ruling class. But if that class was not great in numbers, it had the final say in almost everything: not only in all matters of law, administration, taxation, land-holding and so forth, but in the steady imposition from above of Norman-French, the language of the conquerors. This language was never fully imposed. What happened was again the English miracle of compromise: Norman-French and Anglo-Saxon began to fuse together, and a new language to evolve—the beginnings of the very wonderful analytic Latin-Germanic language which has developed, matured, and become disseminated to the four corners of the globe, and is now evolving along two main lines: Standard English and American English. All these developments, it will be noticed, relate to the cultural superstructure, and not to race. For we must not allow ourselves to forget that the Normans were reformed Vikings of Scandinavian-Germanic race, and any racial admixture they may have received in Normandy would be Celtic, no doubt with an occasional drop of Latin blood here and there. And so, after the Norman Conquest, the population of England remained basically Celto-Germanic, the Germanics dominating in the lowland regions, the Celts in the uplands and to the west. The physical map of England (facing p. 14) is a rough guide to the distribution of that population. But one must make generous allowance for the simple biological factor that intermarriage between the Saxon and Celtic elements would not only take place but in all probability steadily increase. A marriage of Saxon and Celt would lead to a commingling of feudal units or families, from which would spring further acquaintanceships and intermarriages. And it seems reasonably certain that the Norman Conquest gave impetus to this process. It has continued ever since then, and still goes on under our eyes to this very day; but the descendants of the Celts, Normans, Anglo-Saxons or Scandinavians no longer care and often know nothing about such origins. They just marry and take in marriage, thus achieving further racial fusions—until it is often impossible even to guess the origins of millions of the people to-day. It is sometimes said that in the process the Normans maintained their place in the ruling class. This is true, as names show, but it does not mean that they did not often take wives from important families of Saxon origin, though the poor Celts would generally be outside their circle of acquaintances. All we can be really sure of is that, for a period of anything up to four or five hundred years, the melting-pot was steadily simmering to produce the modern Englishman.

The reformed pirates who thus established themselves to become a part of England had an air of their own, a peculiar form of pride and a jaunty personality which put the stolid Anglo-Saxons in the shade and entirely overshadowed the untamed Celts. Their power, wealth, land and Latin culture gave them a distinctive social superiority: and so to-day one often meets the Englishman who boasts of his Norman ancestry. This is a curious and harmless form of snobbery, and simply means that our Englishman would rather trace his origin to a pirate who made a successful job of conquest than to a defeated and exploited Saxon, or to a Celt who was driven to live in the mountains beyond the pale. Many of England's snobberies come from the Normans. That great heritage accounts for many English social characteristics.

CHAPTER V

THE TRUE-BORN ENGLISHMAN EMERGES: 1200 TO 1500

1

King's Government—Political Aristocracy—Church

THE period from the Conquest to about 1200 was one in which the new feudalism instituted by William the Norman settled itself in as the system by which England was governed, politically and economically, though not without some growing-pains which need no further mention here. The form of feudalism established in England was stricter and harsher than that existing in Norman territory in France, which was stricter than that of other continental countries. English society was now stratified in classes, with a rigid legal and social subordination of each class to that above it; questions of equality or of liberty concerned the members of the political aristocracy only in so far as their power or economic interests were affected. Under this effective feudalism some useful ideas for autocratic government were in the air whose object was to train and keep the 'lower orders' in their proper places, especially those on the land. The duty of these people consisted in working for a reward which gave them little more than a bare existence; all other products of their efforts went into the coffers of the barons, knights, bishops and abbots in elastic percentages, usually agreed upon and in accordance with the circumstances of each case. In this way the barons, knights, bishops and abbots rapidly accumulated great wealth; and the condition of the lowest orders—who formed the mass—went from bad to worse.

The keystone of the system was the King. He was not only its titular head. On his personal influence and activities its smooth working depended: peace or war, order or disorder, prosperity or poverty, progress or stagnation—all depended on him. Before the Normans the English monarchy was weak. But from the Conquest onwards—with some ups and downs depending upon the character of the occupant of the throne —the English monarchy grew in strength (not just in power alone) until it became one of the strongest in Europe, which meant the world. It acquired this enviable strength at a comparatively early date: by 1200 it was at least well established, as events proved. By then it had certainly lost some of the vitality shown under William the Conqueror, and especially under Henry II (*r.* 1154–1189), a great King with imaginative and expansive ideas. This Henry invaded Ireland and succeeded in acquiring that country as a doubtful asset of the English Crown. In the opinion of some historians it provided England with more trouble than it was worth throughout a period of almost 750 years.

By the 13th century the King's Household and Government were the peak of society and the principal repository of political power; and from the King and the King's Government was to come Parliament, the Common Law, and a host of equally distinctive English institutions. To-day England has a 'limited' monarchy; that is, one of which many powers have been shorn or curtailed. But in the 13th century the monarchy was absolute in theory, and in practice challenged only by the increased power and wealth of the barons and knights, who, with their harsh feudalism, had made for themselves a dangerously challenging position. There were abuses of power on both sides, especially on that of the Crown; for, as the great English Catholic, Lord Acton, crystallized it six centuries later: "Power tends to corrupt, absolute power corrupts absolutely." So it was with the Crown. It brought its reaction on the part of the barons.

It will be remembered that, when William the Conqueror came to England, he brought with him a number of Norman potentates whom he promised to reward with lands, and that there were also some Anglo-Saxons of similar status who threw in their lot with him. The Conqueror did not forget any of these people; they got their land, one condition being that they should supply from the villeins and serfs an army which they should equip and keep available for the King's service. It was precisely these factors which gave them their enormous power: the possession of wealth, the control of man-power, and the private armies which they created for collective use should occasion demand. As the years passed, the inevitable happened: the feudal lords, barons and knights became fully conscious of their power, and when the Crown began, as they thought and no doubt rightly, to encroach on their rights by raising aids and reliefs on their estates beyond what feudal custom permitted, they decided to act. In arms the barons made it clear to King John (*b.* 1167, *d.* 1216) that not only these but a number of other abuses of which the Crown was increasingly and constantly guilty should cease; and that a document should be drawn up in writing which would clarify beyond all doubt the relative powers of the Crown and barons. The barons had the support of the Church in the person of Archbishop Langton, a humanist of strong character, who in this power-clash showed his independence by acting contrary to the wishes of the Pope, Innocent III, to whom he had owed his election to the See of Canterbury. The document which resulted from what might easily have become a very disturbing state of affairs was the famous Magna Carta, the Great Charter, an historic national document which embodied as constitutional law the first steps towards that freedom from monarchical authoritarianism which the English people were to achieve.

Magna Carta was discussed, agreed to and signed by King John at Runnymede in one day—June 15th, 1215—a memorable date in the history of English liberty. It was revolutionary in spirit for that period and, as law, far ahead of anything in continental Europe. To-day English people can read some of those old clauses with justifiable pride, and a feeling that what they say represents national feeling and even national character. It struck at the roots of 'administrative law', at governmental tyranny, at the abuses of a King of whom a contemporary wrote: "Foul as it is, hell itself is defiled by the fouler presence of John." One feels that no praise can be too high for a law of 1215 which has such a clause as this: "No freeman shall be taken or imprisoned or disseised [that is, deprived of his land] or exiled or in any way destroyed, nor will we go upon him nor will we send upon him except by the lawful judgement of his peers or [and] the law of the land." Compare that with what is of daily occurrence in our world to-day. We must not forget that Magna Carta was the first of

Chapter Steps, Wells Cathedral, Somerset
BTHA

The Tower of London BTHA

The White Tower was built soon after the Norman Conquest

Troutbeck Village, Westmorland, in Winter BTHA

many campaigns for freedoms waged by a strange assortment of 'progressives' that were to continue for centuries through many battles against 'reactionaries' and replacing the Charter in men's minds. At one point the idea of Parliamentary Government arose from it. But the effects of it did not end there. Five hundred years later when, in the 18th century, tyrannous abuses arose, the spirit and letter of the Charter were invoked. In its name the colonies in America revolted and in 1781 won their independence. Magna Carta was important for the English barons and people in 1215; it was even more important for the whole English-speaking world in the ages which followed. Its spirit is not dead to-day in that world.

The King was the first of the three elements—King, Lords and Commons—which in time were to become the main pillars of the English governmental system. After Magna Carta the barons found their position strengthened. They had always regarded themselves as the King's proper councillors in matters of government. After the Charter, while it was still the King's right and duty to govern, the barons felt that they had a right to be consulted more often and to more effect, and that they had a duty to give advice. Long before the Charter they had been members of his Council. As yet, ordinary people had no say even in matters which deeply concerned them. The word *Parliamentum* (meaning 'parley' or 'discussion') had been used since the time of Henry III, but it applied only to the King's Council, the old *curia regis*. From the year 1215 until 1265 was a period of political fluctuations in which those local potentates, the knights of the shire, were elected in the local Shire Court to transact business with the officers of the Royal Household and the King's judges. At the same time it became more common for such meetings to be supplemented by the presence of other representatives of the shires and, something new, of the boroughs. On occasions the King himself would go to some centre to preside over his Court, consisting of not only the judges but of the knights of the shire and the other local representatives, from which it was no great step to the point at which they would all be summoned by the King to discuss some matter or matters of importance; in other words, to hold a parley or *Parliamentum*. The summonses increased in number until they became a burden, especially on the borough representatives. There was a falling off in attendance, which embarrassed the King and his government.

Henry III succeeded John in 1216, and proved himself to be a pious man whose first loyalty was to Rome, a fact which governed his political activities abroad and at home. One of the effects of this was that many Italian and other foreign priests were sent by the Pope—with Henry's approval—to cure the souls of the English, and at the same time to take over benefices in all parts of the country. England thus became a fruitful field for the Church. Some idea of the expansive generosity of papal ideas may be gathered from the fact that, on an occasion when the Pope felt that he must reward some of his shepherds with fresh and better pastures, he promised that they should have the next 300 benefices to become vacant in England.[8] The only protection which the English-born clergy had against this was the King; and here was a king who was on the side of their displacers—foreign displacers at that! It was not a situation which pleased either them or the laity in a country which by tradition prided itself on its independence of foreign encroachments of any sort. And, as usually has happened in such circumstances, a movement of protest began, this time under the leadership of the Earl of Leicester, one Simon de Montfort, a man of Norman origin who was completely anglicized and thought as an Englishman. Simon de Montfort was a man of strong character and an able leader; some say a man of the type to be known later as Cromwellian. He was also a man of liberal ideas. A civil war was the outcome of his movement of protest, one in which, after winning a battle at Lewes, he was defeated by the King's forces at Evesham in 1265. The most remarkable feature of de Montfort's movement was that the idea behind it conceived the law of England as something *above the King*; an idea even more revolutionary than any that had appeared with Magna Carta. Although he was defeated at Evesham, it could never be forgotten that Simon de Montfort had won at Lewes; and, after the Evesham defeat, it was clear to his enemies that his movement represented the feelings of so many people that, at any moment, it might again blossom into one which could shake the throne to its foundations. It was fully realized by the King and his advisers that they were sitting on a powder-barrel. The only policy possible to preserve the throne and the monarchy was to work for "government by consent".

One must pause here to note that two factors were at work in producing such a policy: the first, public opinion; and the second, the reaction of the King's government to that opinion. It was not guided or controlled or informed public opinion in our modern sense, but rather a widespread democratic feeling which, if not met by some kind of practical and convincing compromise, would quickly turn into revolution and civil war.

From the point of view of what followed these great events in the realm of political ideas—in a century often regarded as historically dull!—there was, soon after the battle of Lewes, what seemed at first to be an event of no great importance. Following his victory, de Montfort summoned two representatives of each of the chartered boroughs throughout England to be present with the knights of the shire in a *Parliamentum* that would deal with the pressing affairs of the whole country. All who were summoned, burghers and knights, were of Simon's anti-king, anti-papal and therefore revolutionary party; and they had been summoned to support him in a reformist policy for which the barons were only lukewarm. The practical achievements of Simon de Montfort's parliament—as this assembly was called—were in themselves unimportant, one might say almost negligible. What was of capital importance was that here, for the first time in European history, was the planting of the particular acorn from which grew the tree of representative government. In England the ground had been long in preparation. The important event occurred in an atmosphere of revolution, and it was an act of expediency. Yet it was natural and consistent with the progressive and reasonable feelings of the English people at that moment. It had their approval, because the idea of 'government by agreement' suited their temperament, even then. This was a step forward in ideas which were to be developed in succeeding ages—fairly quickly at first—into the system which we call Parliamentary government. That system was to spread over a great part of the civilized world. In England *it grew*. It was not the making of any one man or group but of generations. This fact need not blind us to the importance of Simon de Montfort's 'Summons to Parliament'; or that it took place in England nearly seven hundred years ago; or that the simple, practical system as then instituted became the one which ever since then has most appealed to the English; or that it still flourishes and continues to develop in our own time; or that it has had imitators, successful and otherwise, in every climate.

The 13th century was the age of merry monks and friars, of the Church of the medieval schoolmen, and also a period during which many serious churchmen were anxious to deal with the clerical abuses which every day were increasing in numbers and gravity. From the 8th century until now, the Church—the monks, that is, and not the centralized Church—had played a vital role in the spiritual and cultural life of the country. Many monks still continued to do so. And in spite of the abuses or, paradoxically, often because of them, this was a period in which some of England's most beautiful architectural gems were created almost entirely as a result of ecclesiastical influence, energy and imagination: Westminster Abbey, for example, was rebuilt in the form of which a part has endured until our own time. This is not the place, even if space permitted, for an account, however brief, of the momentous religious controversies of that period. Yet at least one aspect of those controversies was to have effects which are still with us and still play an important part in English life. In preceding ages men of substance had shown their appreciation of the good work done by the Church by their great gifts to the Orders. For this reason, combined with their own activities in exploiting the feudal system, the Orders had grown wealthy. Communities that were monastic towns increased, and those towns became centres of land-owning and property-owning corporations that were ordered and run like big business. In such circumstances the members of the Orders found their time fully occupied in dealing with worldly affairs. From that to living worldly lives was a short step: the affairs of the spirit were given a minor place in that struggle for wealth and earthly amenities. Little did the Church, either in its government and central power or in the Orders, realize the dragon's teeth its representatives were sowing. One would think that a lesson had been learnt from that ill-conceived papal experiment of sending foreign priests to England to replace those of English birth. Although not then apparent to the general public, it was clear enough to the politically conscious that from one incident had arisen Simon de Montfort's movement, of which the outcome fructified in the potent ideas of "Government by Consent" and the convening of a fairly representative Parliament for that age. The majority of the members of the Orders were English, but they were not capable of thinking in terms of their countrymen or, it now seems to us, of anything other than their own worldly interests. In that they made a fatal mistake, one which was to have far-reaching consequences. Their increasing interest in land and wealth, their harshly feudalistic methods of exploiting the lower orders of villeins and serfs, caused the growth of first resentment and then hostility. At the same time something equally important was happening. A churchman named John Wycliffe (or Wyclif: 1320–1384), a man of ancient Yorkshire lineage, a great scholar who in 1360 became master of Balliol College, Oxford, was attacking certain fundamental doctrines of the Church and calling for reforms in certain ideas which, he thought, were wrong and could never be wholly acceptable to the English. Papal power, he asserted, sprang from Cæsarism and was not related to Christ. He strongly supported the action of Parliament in its characteristic refusal to pay the tribute demanded by Pope Urban V. He said that the Church had grown corrupt and worldly, and that sincere men and women must return to a study of the true word of God, which was to be found in the Bible rather than in the teachings of those priests. To help them he made the first complete translation of the Bible into the vernacular, the English language which was now maturing out of the fusion of Anglo-Saxon and Norman-French: a wonderful medium already, this was the fine language of Langland's great poem *Piers Plowman* (1362), and was to prove its richly expressive vigour even more thoroughly in Chaucer's *Canterbury Tales* a little later (1391). Wycliffe's Bible was not only a highly important landmark in the development of English, but a monument of scholarship and great prose. Appearing just at that moment, when the general feeling of the people against the Orders was daily becoming more hostile, when good and sincere men such as Wycliffe himself were challenging ecclesiastical authoritarianism and (possibly a more cogent argument to many) when the Pope was demanding a tribute from that people which, from the advent of the Normans onwards, had shown no great liking for dogmatic religion (and especially for a Church which rapidly acquired their lands and wealth!), Wycliffe's Bible was to have revolutionary consequences. Those three factors—a Church in which abuses were blatant; the ideological challenge of English churchmen, especially Wycliffe himself; and the educative possibilities of the Bible in English—the lay, the reformist and the flexible as contrasted with the dogmatic in ideas, set the English on the path of seeking a religious way of their own. It would be one which they would work out for themselves, and it would be suitable to their traditions and temperament. There was little or no anti-clericalism in the continental sense in all this. Plain anti-clericalism has never been strong in England, and whenever there has been a sign or an act against the clergy or Church, it was nearly always due to economic, political or social rather than to religious promptings. English heresy arose from similar sources. But one thing is now clear: that, long before the continental Reformation began, the English Reformation was already in the air. And for purely English reasons.

2

Countrymen and Townsmen

While these important events were happening in the realm of ideas—and, as will be seen, were to have profound effects on the life of the people in the centuries to follow—the ordinary Englishman of that time, especially the man on the land, had a very poor existence by almost any standards. The Lord of the Manor and the Abbot were the power-factors between the King's Government and the people. "The villein, and the monk scarcely existed in the eye of the law," Trevelyan writes,[8] "except through the Lord of the Manor and the Abbott of the monastery. As a human being, or as an

English subject, no man had 'rights' either to employment or to the vote, or indeed to anything beyond a little Christian charity." There was no middle class outside the cities; only 'upper' and 'lower' classes existed. The upper class people were usually rich; the lower class always poor. Among the upper class there were strands of chivalry which had been strengthened by the crusades, and there was education and culture; among the lower classes the moral fibre was coarser, and the only education or culture possible came through contact with the religious communities. About nine-tenths of that England was illiterate. Custom ruled more than written law, and the Lord of the Manor was the lawgiver except in cases of murder or maiming, when serf or villein could appeal to the King's court. The Lord of the Manor was responsible only to himself—and to God. The life of the villein and serf was not very dissimilar from that of the domestic animal, and this notwithstanding the fact that by custom villeins had certain rights.

Life in the cities of medieval England was good for those with wealth, as indeed it was everywhere for everybody with wealth. One may say that this well-to-do aspect represents the early 'Merrie England' of the romantic historians. It was hale, hearty and colourful. The cities organized themselves under charters in which each city was granted certain rights and privileges, though always well within the framework of feudalism. The strata of city population were varied: in the cities there was every grade of society from great lords, who often had a city residence as well as their country demesne, down to a raggle-taggle of beggars who very often were fugitive bondmen trying to conceal themselves from their lords for the year and a day, after which period they automatically gained their freedom under the law. Between the lords and the raggle-taggle was a diversity of professional men, craftsmen, artisans, labourers, merchants great and small, shopkeepers, officials, ecclesiastics and, of course, the ubiquitous friars and monks. It is not easy to arrive at an estimate of the population of England in the 13th and 14th centuries. The most we can say is that the number lies somewhere between two and a half and four million, probably closer to the latter than to the former. And this number was reduced by almost half in an epidemic of bubonic plague known as the Black Death, a catastrophe which struck England (1349) after it had raged over a great part of the civilized world. London showed signs of becoming the metropolis, and was already 'cockneyfied'—that is, characteristically London in a sense to give it an atmosphere, a speech and way of life entirely its own. Although its merchants were increasing their wealth by trade with the rest of England and the Continent, it was still like most other big towns and cities in that it was not an agglomeration or conglomeration of citizens. Apart from a nondescript section of the population, it was made up of groups organized in accordance with their interests and for the furtherance of those interests. The Roman Catholic calendar provided generously for holy days, which became public holidays. Midsummer, and Christmas with its popular mummings, were lively celebrations. Yet it seems that the pagan Celtic survival of Nature-worship, long celebrated in Christianized festivities on May-day, was the liveliest holiday of all. Then city and countryside found release in song and dance in the squares on the greensward around gaily bedecked maypoles. There is not much of the brighter and more human aspects of life in that Merrie England which we cannot find beautifully described in Chaucer's *Canterbury Tales*.

That was one England. But, long before the 19th century when Disraeli wrote his novel *Sybil: The Two Nations*, there were two Englands. And next in importance to the affairs of the mind and spirit, with which the heretical Wycliffe and his friends were dealing, came the long-overdue and ominous rumblings of the other England—the England of the villeins and serfs, of the bondmen and small-holders and minor tenantry, of the poor and downtrodden. The first polemics of the religious revolution had stimulating effects far outside their immediate sphere. If the upper classes were uneasy about the abuses of the Church, the exploitations of the orders and religious corporations, and the unchristian behaviour of men who knew better but preferred the good worldly life, the peasantry—villeins, serfs, bondmen tied to the land, small-holders and minor tenantry—were in a state of suppressed rage against their conditions. "The luxury of the time," says John Richard Green,[15] "the splendour of pomp and chivalry, the cost of incessant campaigns, drained the purses of knight and baron, and the sale of freedom to the serf or exemption from services to the villein afforded an easy and tempting mode of refilling them." This process had the effect of setting free to go where they pleased thousands of poverty-stricken landworkers, who were now in the position of being able to demand a living wage. If the great landowners and Lords of the Manor did not meet their demands, there could be no harvests. And they did not meet the demands. Instead, they tried to have their distress relieved through legislation embodied in the Statute of Labourers in which: "Every man or woman of whatsoever condition, free or bond, able in body and within the age of threescore years . . . and not having his own whereof he may live, *shall be bound to serve the employer who shall require him to do so, and shall take only the wages which were accustomed to be taken in the neighbourhood where he is bound to serve.*" This law in effect represented a desire for the reintroduction of slave labour on a much greater scale than had existed hitherto. And so in 1350 Parliament tied the labourers to the soil. Refusal to obey was punishable by jail. Labourers who had bought their freedom were to be re-enslaved, and lawyers came forward to assist landowners in finding technical or other slips or loopholes in documents of emancipation so that every serf and villein could be swept into the net. The position of the labourer in England, one may say of the whole peasantry, was appalling. And then, to cap it all, in order to defray the cost of a series of disastrous military and naval adventures, in 1378 Parliament authorized a poll-tax on every person in the realm—the poorest man to contribute as large a sum as the wealthiest! The stupidity of such a measure seems incredible.

The reaction of the people was what might be expected. A revolt of the peasants began in June 1381, and spread like wildfire over England, with the Kentishmen round Wat Tyler, an ex-soldier, in the forefront of the movement. And then opened a new page in England's history: the first considerable blow for plain and simple justice and freedom to be struck by the poorest and most downtrodden in society. It was a violent blow, and it came in almost every district. The houses of landowners' stewards were set in flames and the records of the manor-courts fed the fires. The peasants marched from town to town, and were joined by the population as they converged on London. A curious feature of the rebellion was the fury shown by the insurgents towards lawyers in particular, as if the peasants believed that they were the real devils of the piece. Woe betide the lawyer who fell into their hands! Every lawyer who came the way of the Kentishmen as they marched on Blackheath was put to death. London's down-trodden rose and flung open the gates to the marchers. When the columns of peasants reached the metropolis, one of the first institutions they set ablaze was the new lawyers' 'Inn' at the Temple; and soon the flames of John of Gaunt's Palace at the Savoy and the houses of great merchants and other London potentates added to the conflagration.

In the end the Peasant's Revolt petered out. What was left of the movement was easily suppressed, which meant that their position was as bad as ever, and often worse. Nevertheless, that revolt had far-reaching consequences. It not only challenged feudalism but, in the preaching of a "mad priest of Kent", one John Ball, who had been declaiming doctrines akin to those of Wycliffe, Green[15] says: "*England first listened to the knell of feudalism and the declaration of the rights of man.*" As in the case of Parliament, of "Government by Consent" and of Representation, here again England was politically ahead of the rest of the world. For, if a long period was yet to elapse before those seeds bore full fruit, the soil had been well broken for them. The work of the English peasantry, of the yeomen of England, taught this lesson: that there was a limit of oppression beyond which they would not suffer; and that when that limit was passed they would strike —and strike in a way to make themselves felt. There was a moment in that revolt when the nobles were "paralysed with fear" and garrison knights "panic-stricken". It was never to be forgotten. The significance of these events lies even deeper. For, as Langland's humane and spirited poem *Piers Plowman* tells us in almost every line, the common people of England were beginning to find themselves imbued with a new spirit. In that spirit we can see the first signs of the emergence of a personality we can all recognize as truly English, distinct from

Celt, Saxon, Scandinavian or Norman, but with some of the qualities of each in a fusion of them all which produced something new: the true-born Englishman.

3

Impact of Renaissance and Reformation

While these movements, the growing-pains of a nation, were taking place in England—a country which at that time was a spectator of rather than a participant in the general current of continental civilization and culture and was developing along its own lines—the Renaissance and Revival of Learning which began in Italy in the 12th century was having profound effects of which some had important repercussions in the island kingdom. Little need be said here about the continental Renaissance, but the few aspects of it which deserve mention demand emphasis. First, it represented a completely new stage of vital energy, which was accompanied by a desire for liberation and expansion of the mind. Second, it represented a return to, a revival in, the study of Greek and Latin literature (especially the former) as the best means whereby man could learn to reconstitute himself as a free being outside the thraldom of theological despotism. Third, it embodied the spirit of 'humanism', which aimed at a just perception of the dignity of man as a rational, volitional and sentient being, born upon this earth with a right to use it and enjoy it. These are magnificent ideas, and the time was right and ripe for them not only on the Continent but, as we have seen in the last section, in England also. For, although their insular position and, indeed, the nature of the English people kept them well away from the immediate excitements of the continental Renaissance, they could feel its vibrations and learn much from their privileged position as spectators. What they were engaged in evolving for themselves, they saw, could benefit from a calm contemplation and study of continental developments. This was the unspectacular and again characteristically opportune way in which this country received the impact of one of the greatest movements in the history of Europe. And, as so often happened, there was not much which the English regarded as important that they missed!

The best reflection of this attitude can be found in the development of centres of learning, of which Oxford and Cambridge were already important in the 13th century. There is a record of organized teaching at Oxford so far back as 1133, and at Cambridge on a lesser scale in 1092. In the 13th century some important religious orders established themselves in Oxford, a pleasant market-town where, for reasons that are not clear, licensed clerks got together and gathered students around them. The Dominicans came in 1221; the Franciscans in 1224; the Carmelites about 1250; and there were others. In the later decades of that 13th century, the collegiate system was instituted with Balliol (1269), Merton (1274), and University (1280) Colleges as the earliest foundations. Something similar was taking place at Cambridge in the same periods: the Augustinians had been at Cambridge since the 11th century; the Franciscans came in 1224, and later in that century came the Dominicans, Carmelites and Gilbertines. Henry III in 1231 recognized Cambridge as a centre of learning by a writ of governance. The first Cambridge house was founded by Hugh de Balsham, Bishop of Ely, who drafted his statute on the model of that which Walter de Merton had drawn up for Merton College, Oxford. And in 1281–1284 he founded Peterhouse, the first of the Cambridge colleges. These foundations at Oxford and Cambridge were the beginnings of the English university system. They began modestly and grew in accordance with their own English ideas, and without any attempt to emulate continental institutions such as the University founded in Paris in 1200 by Philip Augustus, now the most famous and flourishing of its kind in Christendom.

Nobody has so far succeeded in explaining why these two market-towns rather than the great cathedral cities should have been chosen as centres for foundations of learning. It is less difficult to explain why they flourished, almost from the beginning. There was more freedom for scholarship, less immediate supervision in them than in the great cities where the Church held sway. That is one reason. But far more cogent is the fact that some of the most important work in Europe was being done in them, especially at Oxford in the 13th century. This gave them renown and attracted scholars not only from England but from the Continent. The stimulating influence and ideas of the Renaissance came to free scholars who were engaged in adventures of the mind, and their pupils, the young men who went out into life from those colleges, were intellectual enthusiasts equipped to play important parts not only in scholarship, if they should desire to pursue it for its own sake, but in what was equally esteemed: the governance and leadership of the realm—in ecclesiastical and political life, in the law, in commerce, or even as Lords of the Manor. The ruling families, at first a little wary of the new institutions, found that their sons were usually better all-round men for leadership after a period at Oxford or Cambridge. This they so fully realized that they were ready to help the colleges with gifts and endowments. Hence the new institutions flourished, and continued to prove their worth in many fields. One of the most important results was that, from then onwards, the Church no longer had a virtual monopoly of learning. A new educated class was being created, of men who had a 'university education' and were not tied to or by the Church.

If the Renaissance influence stimulated the advance of scholarship, literature and the arts in England, the revolutionary religious ideas which had originated with Wycliffe were now having important repercussions on the Continent. His ideas did not create the Protestant Reformation. But they contributed towards it, and greatly influenced some of its most important leaders. One of the most important of these was John Huss (*c.* 1374–1415), who inspired a movement for the reform of the Church in Bohemia and suffered at the stake as a consequence. From his vigorous movement, 'Hussite' ideas spread much farther than the frontiers of Bohemia. The 14th, 15th and 16th centuries were a period of crisis for the Church, with such men as Martin Luther in Germany, Zwingli and Calvin in Switzerland and France, and Cranmer (1489–1556) in England actively campaigning for a thorough reform of ideas and organization. In no country is it more difficult to weigh the various factors contributing to the reform than in England. On the Continent the Reformation took on the colours of a revolutionary movement. Not so in England. The

English are as capable as any other people of bringing about a revolution, but they much prefer to achieve the desired end—assuming that they really want it—by a process of adjustment and readjustment, one move, one stage at a time. The name 'gradualism' was later given to this English method, its great attraction for English people in general being that it avoids upheavals and makes for social stability, which they have long preferred to any other condition. Furthermore, it cannot be claimed for the English that they have ever been so deeply interested in theology—or in any abstract ideas—as continentals or their Scottish neighbours. But if theology or religion or any abstract thought or system of thought is in any way bound up with politics, economics or finance so as to affect his ordinary well-being, the Englishman, quickly as a rule, becomes alert to his vital interests, which are to him more important than any theology. The condition of the English Church, most men could see, was unhealthy, and that in itself was bad enough. When bishops and other important ecclesiastics were making careers as landlords, often as harsh landlords, and by their commercial acumen and organizing ability were acquiring vast fortunes and great properties—and thus power—and, at about the same time, the news was coming of the Reformation that was taking place on the Continent, then the English began to apply their principles of readjustment. The moves in all this kaleidoscope of history are often difficult to follow; yet they proceeded steadily. It was not until the 16th century that the Reformation in the fuller sense came to England. But already in the 14th and 15th centuries the 'gradualism' was at work from which came an Anglican communion free from Rome.

4

A Compact Nation with a Strong State

It has become fashionable for many writers, and even for a limited school of historians, to minimize the importance of monarchy (in England and elsewhere), and to decry that kind of history which is written "in terms of a list of kings" and their doings. Whatever one may feel about this, there can be no avoiding the simple fact that, in England, the King was the apex of the power-system which constituted the State, and that until comparatively modern times the influence on events of an intelligent ruling monarch with a strong personality could be almost paramount. No better example of this can be cited than the Welsh Tudor monarch Henry VII (*r.* 1485–1509). His worthy successors, Henry VIII and Elizabeth I, were to continue with success the very efficient work of the first of the Tudors, the dynasty which ruled in England for over a century from the accession of Henry VII to the death of Elizabeth I in 1603. Henry VII's highly important work must be summarized here in the most cursory manner. He found the State weak, its affairs almost chaotic and the decentralized system of administration and of society in need of 'pulling together', its various local units in need of being welded into a national whole. He had the vision to see that he had good material for the making of a compact nation and a strong State. Within the period of his reign, he used his considerable capacity towards this end with great success, and left the country very much stronger than he had found it. He did essential work at the right moment, and, in the making of the national State, he did the work brilliantly.

We must think of that England as a country of at most about three million people of which not more than one-tenth were town and city dwellers, with London as the great centre of business. It was a self-sufficient country with a lucrative overseas trade in wool and some other raw materials, especially tin and lead. Great areas of forest supplied the timber which then occupied the place in national economy later to be taken by coal; the abundance of oak for building ships was an important factor in the steady rise of English sea-power. Fifteenth-century England was already showing signs of a developing mercantilism: in 1486 the London merchants engaged in foreign trade were organized by the City magnates in a body known as the Fellowship of the Merchant Adventurers of London. The significant term 'adventurer' merely meant one who took part in commercial ventures or, as we would say, in speculative business.

The Tudors, having Welsh (Celtic) blood in their veins, were responsible for giving impetus to a new and stimulating movement: Welsh immigration into England. Without doubt this must have accelerated the process of intermarriage between Celts and other racial elements, of which the importance has been noted earlier. In regard to language, bilingualism had petered out: French, the language of polite intercourse and of the Court, was now a 'foreign' language; English—colloquial or in dialects—was the language spoken by the whole people, and English was now the language of all literature except certain technical treatises in theology and science; for these Latin was used, and it was still also the language of diplomacy. In innumerable other ways the country and people had all but completed a great series of changes, of fusions and weldings, of psychological adjustments, of mysterious and imponderable modifications, all of which can be summed up by saying that now this was the highly distinctive demographic entity which we can easily recognize as *England*.

First emerged the Englishman, the true-born Englishman; and then the nation. By 1500, the English people, from the rulers down to the raggle-taggle of beggars on the fringe of society, were thinking in an English way, in a way that is to us now nearly always unmistakably English. Those people, though still in the early stage of a remarkable evolution, are recognizably, and in spite of many superficial differences, the forebears of the people we know. The various institutions of monarchy, the King's Government, Parliament, the Law, the Church, the methods of commerce, literature, architecture, customs and habits and, indeed, the general way of life of the people, all had about them distinctive characteristics which can only be described as 'Englishness'. All these were already as different from anything on the European mainland as the characteristics of any continental country then were from one in the Orient. No doubt this was largely due to England's position as an island. That useful old sea-dyke was a wonderful protection during the formative period, the period when almost everything began that we now know as particularly English. The effect of this was highly beneficial: it enabled the English to concentrate on their own affairs without violent distractions from outside during a period when, intellectually and morally, the rest of the civilized world was in a state of

Anne Hathaway's Cottage, Shottery, near Stratford-on-Avon, Warwickshire
BTHA

upheaval. The nation had not yet reached full maturity. But it was growing in stature and strength in almost every way. The last phase of the period (1200–1500) considered in this chapter was one during which a transformation was taking place with politics, economics, religion and ideas generally all playing their parts. The main factors which, in this writer's opinion, most contributed to the wonderful 'Golden Age' which began about the middle of the next century were already actively at work. These were: (*a*) the general and solid social progress that was taking place in England; (*b*) the growth among imaginative and ambitious Englishmen of a feeling that the time was approaching when this strength would enable England to play a greater part in the world than hitherto; and (*c*) the stimulus from outside provided by the discoveries, explorations and conquests that were being achieved by the Portuguese and Spaniards. England was still outside the welter of the tremendous events that were taking place in the world beyond the Channel. But no book, no document, no treatise on the dialectics of religion, nothing in the realm of art, literature or scholarship, was attracting more attention on the part of the more spirited and adventurous Englishman than the ever-changing Map of the World. Here truly was food for the imagination!

The stories of those great navigations and discoveries have been well told and need no retelling here. But for a moment we must try to think as Englishmen must have been thinking in the 15th century as, one after another, the great achievements became known to them. The inspiration began in the study and may be said to have been one aspect of the Renaissance, for it was an early 'Renaissance man', Marco Polo (*c.* 1254–*c.* 1324), who was the first European to travel overland to Peking, and with his famous book of *Travels* to stir men's minds as they had never before been stirred. Pierre d'Ailly, a famous teacher who later became a cardinal, wrote in the *Imago Mundi* (1410) of the spherical form of the earth—hitherto regarded as flat—and discussed the means whereby the Far East could be reached by the western sea route. Prince Henry the Navigator of Portugal (1394–1460), during his lifetime and for long afterwards, inspired a crowd of cartographers, explorers and many

The Barn Museum, Warwickshire
The Barn Museum is at Mary Arden's Cottage, Wilmcote.
Mary Arden was the mother of William Shakespeare, the famous playwright
BTHA

great discoveries. Men happily found the way to use the polarity of the mariner's compass. The African coast was explored in 1462 and Sierra Leone was discovered; in 1484, the mouth of the Congo; and in 1486, Bartolomeo Diaz rounded the Cape of Good Hope, preparing the way for Vasco da Gama, who discovered India in 1498. The most spectacular and most far-reaching achievement was that of Columbus who, sailing in 1492 to find a way to the East, discovered the West Indies and America. But, as a feat of navigation, the palm has to be awarded to the Portuguese Ferdinand Magellan (*c.* 1480–1521), who first circumnavigated the globe.

From what we know of the English, can we imagine them being content merely to read about these breathtaking achievements without being deeply stirred? The printing-press, introduced by William Caxton in 1476, began to play its part in education, in the stimulation and expansion of the mind, and in the next century was to play its own revolutionary part in the outlook and attitude of the English towards the rest of the world. And so, together with good internal growth, in which, quite perceptibly, a country was changing into a great and strong nation, the events which were taking place outside the as yet somewhat circumscribed orbit of the English were to act as a tonic—a stimulus which came at the time when the true-born Englishman had come of age, and was in every way prepared for the major role which destiny held in store for him.

In 1933 Sir Stanley (later Lord) Baldwin, a true-born Englishman of our own epoch, broadcast his views on 'Our National Character'. He quotes A. L. Smith, Master of Balliol, who had mentioned the "twelve centuries of discipline" to which we owe the "peculiar English capacity for self-government, the enormous English development of the voluntary principle in all manner of institutions". Smith says that the English aptitude for colonization, politics, commercial enterprise and the Colonial Empire are all due to "the spirit of fair-play and give-and-take, the habit of working to a given purpose which tempered that *hard and grim individuality of the national character*". Baldwin dwelt on these last words which I have italicized, and went on to say, what I hope is emerging in these pages, that the English character is largely one of those contrasts: grim individuality and the spirit of co-operation. The contrasts make it so difficult to define briefly, to depict in fine lines. In dealing with it, we seem to be always dealing with something like quicksilver, which can split up into little units and, given the circumstances, can come together again in a solid mass. In nothing is it more dangerous to generalize than about English character; but do we not see, in what has been said up to now, that a distinctive character not very profoundly different from that of the modern English was already showing itself in those years between 1200 and 1500?

CHAPTER VI

THE UPSURGE OF A PEOPLE: 1500 TO 1603

1

The New Spirit of the Age

CERTAIN periods in the reign of Henry VIII, and nearly the whole of Elizabeth's reign, are breathtaking not only for their exciting events but for what these events represent in terms of human genius. A people which had hitherto jogged along steadily, applying itself with zeal and common sense to the solution of its many problems with a good measure of success, seems to have acquired seven-leagued boots at certain moments, and wings to fly and soar during the last phase of the Elizabethan age.

Perhaps, when all is said, the easiest way to convey some idea of this is by considering what happened in regard to the language and the use made of it in the national literature. The English language, a vigorous offspring of the felicitous marriage of two differing linguistic elements, had now reached a stage of perfect maturity. By the time of Elizabeth I, it was a magnificent literary medium, one of great richness, flexibility, expressiveness and power. What seems curious is that, until men's minds were stirred by the activating spirit of that great age, not many writers had appeared who used the wonderful medium to fullest advantage. The great inspiration came at about the time of the Spanish Armada. Before or since, no poet has used English as Shakespeare did, although there were some who ran him close. What is called Elizabethan literature—because of its distinctive characteristics—continued to be written after the Queen's death. Hers was, in terms of great literature, the most prolific period in the history of the language. A vast reservoir of excellent linguistic material was available. What was lacking was the inspiration to use that material to great advantage. Then the miracle happened, almost overnight. One may well ask why the inspiration came just at that time. This is one of those questions for which a score of answers is possible, and has been given, although none of them is entirely satisfying. None seems to touch the heart of the matter; and for a very good reason. It is impossible for 20th-century man to take upon himself, or to put himself inside, the mind of Elizabethan man. The externals, the great events of the time, the logical sequences of history, as well as its sometimes disconcerting vagaries, are all there in the records for us to study. The surface is brilliantly clear to us mortals of a later age, and we may often feel that we have penetrated below the surface of things. But in the end much of the mystery of that Elizabethan mind remains; we can only speculate about it. A commonplace answer is that environment and circumstances created the writers. That is too facile an explanation. It takes us no distance along a road different from any we know other than at second-hand from reading. It takes no account of the sunbursts that so often bemuse 20th-century beings who try to make their way along the road in their imagination. Nor can it account for the shoal of exuberantly creative writers who appeared in that Golden Age of English literature; nor for the continued vigour in almost every branch of letters after the death of Elizabeth. What has to be done is to catch at least something of the spirit of an age different from every other in English history; and spirits are notoriously elusive!

There was in the Tudor period a happy combination of events and circumstances, almost as if the Good Lord Himself had suddenly decided that the die of history must be loaded in favour of England. Most important was the delayed effect of the Renaissance, with which must now be counted the Protestant Reformation: a release of mental energy and a politico-religious liberation. With the release of energy, the imagination sought scope for activity, and found an outlet in the extension of ideas from the immediate, from the national and local arena, away from the parish pump into the realm of the universal. This was in no sense a political prompting. It was merely the manifestation of a desire to rise to a higher plane in an active mental and physical existence. Nor was there anything very religious about it; with a few exceptions, the great writers of the epoch are remarkably free from either political or religious ideology. Those writers, while fully aware of events around them, did not concentrate attention on them. Nor did they have great regard for the past. Their vision was almost entirely turned towards the future; for it was the future which held for them—and for the people of England—everything that could satisfy the yearnings of a young, vigorous, intelligent, prosperous and growing people that now had the kind of State desired, and seemed all set to have not only the nation that they wanted but a generous portion of the greater world outside. As if by the Grace of God they had in the person of Henry VIII an Englishman of a type they understood and really liked—and who liked and thoroughly understood them—and, in his successor Elizabeth, a very extraordinary woman who had the ability to respond imaginatively to and encourage their yearnings, and help them onwards towards the great future which they felt was awaiting them round the corner. When healthy men feel an optimism as they look towards the future, it can and usually does inspire them to fruitful activity. And even before Elizabeth the kingship of Henry VIII had helped the majority of English people to feel optimistic about their future—for they must have been saying to themselves: "Just look at what that man is doing!" When it came down to it, what was he doing but clearing the decks and building the power to meet enemies who might stand in the way of an England that now felt an urge to expand?

Hence, while potent environmental factors were present, what provided the leaven that was to begin that astounding fermentation which, in the age of Elizabeth, was to rise in an unprecedented exuberance manifesting itself in nearly every phase of life, was the personality and, one may use the term without hesitation, the creative genius shown by Henry VIII in the way he tackled two long lists of what may be called "important matters requiring attention". The first list consisted of matters that may for convenience be put under the heading of House Cleaning (one might almost say Spring Cleaning—for this was indeed England's early Spring). We quickly realize that what Henry did was much more than a mere tidying, for there was a constructive element in all that he did. He changed things for the better and brought about a bloodless revolution. Some of his achievements were momentous. He set about liberating the monarchy from its long-standing alliance with the Roman Catholic Church, for which he substituted Parliament. He initiated a new respect for the Common Law by sweeping reforms which not only totally abolished such extra-territorial rights as Benefit of Clergy and Sanctuary, but even made the nobility, the commoners, the whole laity and clergy equals before that law. He replaced the ideas of cosmopolitan feudalism and an international Church with those of a national State which would have a national Church as an appendage. He struck blow after blow at feudalism when it encroached on matters affecting the nation. He found a means of achieving law and order in the cheapest way imaginable by the appointment in every district of unpaid Justices of the Peace whose interests lay precisely in safeguarding law and order, and who took over a host of public functions hitherto regarded as personal rights of the feudal lords. With great vision he allied the monarchy to a number of rising forces within the realm: to the great London merchants, to shipowners and seafarers, to the rising tide of important Protestants, to the new squirearchy that arose on the lands he took from the corporations of monkish landowners. He cleared from the minds of the English the hitherto accepted idea that they must submit their souls to the discipline of an external Church, and instead substituted the new idea of liberty of conscience; and insisted that, if the faith of his subjects must needs be defined, it was for their own Parliament to do so. From this came the Anglican Communion, the Church of England. These are not all the items in this awe-inspiring list of his far-reaching reforms and clearances, but they will give some idea of the magnitude and sweep of this man's work. Henry VIII was a hale-and-hearty good fellow, a fine boisterous live man of the type the English love. Of course he was a playboy, but what of it? He was forgiven most things because, when it came to the point, he could be not merely destructive—always calculating and never wantonly—but also imaginatively constructive. Above all, he knew his people's thinking and, although he raised royal power almost to the point of being a despotism, his whole life and efforts were directed towards one goal: to make England strong and prosperous and capable of facing any future. From the time of his father, men of culture and learning had access to the Court, and were encouraged to come there. To Henry VIII's Court came the intellectual and cultural élite of England; he thoroughly enjoyed their conversation, in which he was well able to hold his own. When we look at the other list, for which a suitable heading would be National Interests, it is no less impressive than that already noted. Perhaps the most spectacular achievement in the list was this: Henry made England's Royal Navy the finest in the world: her great Senior Service. Furthermore, he contributed brilliant and, as later events were to demonstrate, far-sighted ideas in the construction of ships; and some excellent new ideas for the use of artillery at sea. He it was who first ordered the building of longer and more easily manœuvrable ships with portholes for a row of cannon which could be discharged as a 'broadside', thus avoiding the need to go alongside and board an enemy vessel. The importance of this was to be demonstrated later. His Welsh ancestry and sympathies enabled him to make Wales a willing and law-abiding part of his realm on a basis of equality with England. He saw in the 'Balance of Power' idea the key to England's foreign policy. He had more than a faint perception that his country's future was on the seven seas, and for this reason he was always encouraging to seafarers, to men of spirit who were ready to face any danger. In short, he had the intellectual stature and tough character to meet the circumstances of an age that was a vital prelude to the age which established England's greatness. Although his last phase was disastrous compared with the first, he had cleared the minds of his countrymen for the advantage of the future. With all his faults, Henry VIII represented the new spirit which was to fructify in an upsurge of the people during the reign of Elizabeth.

2

The Seamen

Those great events in the realm of navigation and discovery, of which some account was given in the previous chapter, made England more conscious of the sea than ever before.

In view of this country's later achievements, one is almost justified in feeling that there remained in the English far more of the old spirit of the Vikings than we have been inclined to suspect. There was this difference between the Vikings and the English seamen of the Tudor period: what first inspired the English was not so much a lust for conquest as a passion for merchant adventuring. This already existed in 15th-century England, but the adventures were not yet on a great scale nor far-flung. They had not yet reached the stage of the Elizabethan period when far-reaching and perilous expeditions on the sea were constantly being undertaken in a spirit of adventure that can be compared to prospectings in space in our own time. Many factors other than the Spanish and Portuguese achievements contributed to turn the eyes of the English towards the seven seas. Curiously enough, one was the Reformation. There was a growing body of Protestants who thought that Catholics were having too great a share of the world. When, in order to avoid disputes between Spaniards and Portuguese in the division of the world, the Pope in 1494 drew an imaginary line from pole to pole, allocating all lands west of it to the Spaniards and all east of it to the Portuguese, he can hardly have imagined that Protestant merchants sitting in London would not regard this as a cause for annoyance, even as an impertinence. Still less could he have foreseen that his 'line' might be taken as a challenge by the heretically inclined people living on their island beyond the edge of Christendom. The English had by now lost most of their desire for military adventures on the Continent, having had several unprofitable experiences in them. Henry VIII became much more interested in the security of the homeland than in any such adventures. But he was also deeply interested in furthering foreign trade. Hence, to his mind, England's foreign policy must be calculated to guarantee as far as possible the security of England and to advance overseas trade. The two great powers, Spain and France, were a constant preoccupation of the English; if one of these should defeat the other in war, England could be left at the mercy of that other. Clearly, the best thing for England to do would be to follow an opportunist policy so that, by throwing in her weight on the side which would serve her best at a given moment, her interests would be best safeguarded. Thus arose the famous 'Balance of Power' policy in foreign affairs, which England was to follow from then until our own time. Once this policy was evolved and applied, it would help greatly in regard to land-power. There was still the sea and the overseas interests. Henry realized that the sea deserved his closest attention; and the fine English Royal Navy which he created—itself the best then existing—was to be the progenitor of the navies which later were to win for England the title of mistress of the seas.

The navigations and discoveries of the Portuguese, the drawing of a new map of the world, and then the 'Pope's Line' brought home to the more thoughtful of the great London merchants, as well as to the sea-conscious people of other ports, that, if England did not do something, she would be left behind, while those others, especially the menacing Spaniards, would be growing in wealth and strength. Whoever cared to look at the new map of the world could not fail to grasp the importance on it of England's extremely favourable geographical position. That position on the fringe of the civilized world had helped England to evolve as she did. Now it could be regarded as potentially a central maritime base for world-wide activities at sea. There was already a good steady trade with the Netherlands and the Mediterranean, and from time to time an adventurous spirit would go much farther and return well rewarded. Across the Channel the Spaniards under Alva were holding down more than half the area which comprised the Low Countries, and in Elizabeth's reign the passing to and fro under their eyes of great Spanish ships loaded with interesting booty proved too great a temptation to English seamen and their masters. They began to raid the Spanish convoys, and were much encouraged by the Queen. In this way the crews of naval and merchant ships were able to train themselves for warfare in time of peace: an invaluable experience. Many of those 'sea-dogs', as they were called, turned across the Atlantic, and successfully pursued their piracy, freebooting and privateering in the West Indies. And then came the spectacular and daring adventure of Francis Drake (born in Tavistock, Devon, son of a Protestant vicar), a great sailor who, educated by his kinsman Sir John Hawkins, in character combined Puritanism with a genius for the sea and a dare-devil spirit which won the hearts of the English and of Elizabeth. He was aided and abetted by her in his wonderful adventure, in which she secretly took shares. It has been called the greatest piratical expedition in history.

The Pacific Ocean had never yet been sailed by an English ship, and Peru was one of the great treasure stores in the New World from which Spain still received every year at least one great galleon loaded with gold, silver, diamonds and other precious stones. Drake's plan was to sail to the Pacific via the Magellan Strait, raid the Chilean coast as he made his way northwards, and take as much precious booty as he could load into his ship from the Spanish galleon in Callao harbour that was being got ready to sail. He set out with five ships, none of them bigger than a coastal schooner, but before they reached the Pacific four were left behind in storms. With his own little vessel, the *Golden Hind,* and a crew of eighty, he sailed up the coast, raiding on the way. Among the Spanish settlers, the appearance of an English vessel in those waters and on that enterprise was terrifying; they regarded themselves as safe from all such molestations, and this threatened their security. They could never again feel at ease. Drake sailed into Callao harbour, the port of Lima, surprised the crew of the galleon, loaded his little bark with its treasure to the value of over half a million—much more than England's national revenue for a year—then boldly set out for the Moluccas, rounded the Cape of Good Hope, reached the home waters and dropped anchor in Plymouth harbour. In his little cockleshell vessel this extraordinary seaman on a piratical expedition had, as part of the day's work, circumnavigated the globe and, incidentally, robbed Spain of enough easily negotiable wealth to solve all the immediate problems of England's national exchequer and, furthermore, to pay for strengthening the Royal Navy. Philip II of Spain took Drake's adventure as an outrage; Elizabeth regarded it as a stroke of genius and knighted her sailor, thereby adding insult to injury in the eyes of Philip. Drake's was a great achievement. It stirred the imagination. From then, the new spirit of the sea in terms of Drake's achievement seized the English.

There was something more than accident or mere good

luck about the progress which England made in seafaring. As in so many other things, they evolved their own methods to suit their own particular circumstances. For example, Henry VIII's idea of long, easily manœuvrable ships, provided with a row of cannon on each side which fired through portholes, substituted the broadside for the old method of ships grappling one another and their crews fighting on the decks what amounted to a hand-to-hand soldier's battle. The English were intelligent enough to see that they could not stand up to the superior weight which Spain could use in such fighting. On all fighting ships in that age—except those of England—crews consisted of two distinct categories of men: a comparatively small section of sailormen who looked after the ship, manœuvring and so forth; and the fighting men, infantry and artillery taken from the land forces and put on board, no further training being considered necessary. Spain was still using for heavy units great top-heavy vessels rowed by slaves, with small crews of raggle-taggle seamen picked up anyhow in the ports, and contingents of artillery and infantry as their most important elements for fighting battles. The English had thought out something very different, something quite revolutionary, it proved to be, in naval warfare. The English idea was that every man on board a ship should be, above all else, a first-rate *seaman*. Seamanship in every branch must take precedence over everything, for their common sense told them that the training and experience required to make good sailors took longer and was more exacting that what was required to make fighters. But those English sailors were also trained as specialists in warfare at sea. On board ship they could use every kind of weapon, from cannons to small arms, from cutlasses to knuckledusters. Their artillery was the best in the world. Thus, the crew of every English ship was, in terms of sea warfare, homogeneous. There was even something more, and this a very English feature, about those crews: the comradeship, the brotherhood of the sea, which existed between officers and men. The English naval and mercantile officer began as a humble apprentice or midshipman, collaborating in every rough task that fell to the lot of the ordinary seaman, and made his way on the road to advancement in rank by years of close collaboration with ordinary and able seamen, quartermasters, boatswains, sailmakers and ships' carpenters, as well as with officers, sailing-masters and commanders. The English officer was a gentleman who took to the sea because he liked it; the sailors were volunteers. Officers and men worked together in a highly trained team. There was nothing that any able seaman could do or had to do which his officer could not do as well or better. In addition, Royal Navy and mercantile marine worked together as one force. All these things now seem commonplace. But in Elizabeth's time they were new ideas, English ideas, and startlingly different in their whole conception of life from those which prevailed on board any other nation's ships. The explanation is a simple one: among the English the feudal relationship had ceased to exist; on the ships of continental nations, stiff and often harsh feudal ideas governed the relationship between officers and men. On the English ships there was a free, adventurous and collaborating spirit, which was intensely patriotic just because England facilitated and encouraged the enjoyment of that spirit. In saying all this, I must not mislead the reader into believing that life on board an English ship in the age of Elizabeth was easy. It was harder than anything we can imagine. But it was governed by a strict code of law and traditional customs, which every man knew and accepted before he sailed with the feeling that, within the broad limits of that code, he could always be sure of fair play.

No part of England is more than seventy-five miles from the coast. The simple fact that the sea is never far away has its own effect. Long before Elizabeth's reign certain traditions relating to the sea had been growing. There were 'seafaring families' in which the father and at least one son took to the sea. There were areas in which seafarers made most of the population. Inland there were not many remote villages, nor any towns or cities, from which some men did not go to seek their fortune in the new adventures. After Drake's voyage, most young men wanted to try their luck. And they were encouraged. And so the Royal Navy grew, the mercantile marine increased. England became a seafaring nation.

When the fast, new, well-armed ships of the Royal Navy and mercantile marine collaborated in a series of brilliant actions to shatter the Invincible Armada which Philip II sent in 1588 to prepare the way for his planned invasion of England, this was more than a victory over Spain. Lord Howard of Effingham's achievement was certainly one of the decisive battles of history; for, although it was an early battle in a long war, its spectacular nature, apart altogether from its tragic consequences for the Spanish fleet, thrilled Elizabethan England from Land's End to John o' Groats. It was a feat after the hearts of the people. Until now the reign of Elizabeth had been colourful, interesting and progressive. But from 1588 onwards England experienced that tremendous exuberance, that great burst of vivacity and creativeness, which we normally associate with the word 'Elizabethan'. The little fire-ships which Drake sent among the great warships of Spain not only succeeded in their immediate task of setting the enemy warships on fire. It was as if the Almighty had wished, by the spectacular defeat of the Catholic king's great Armada, to demonstrate in an unmistakable manner that, from this moment onwards, England and the English were to be the favoured of the earth in His sight. The effects on them were tremendous. This was the real beginning, not only of England's long reign as mistress of the seas, but of her success in a hundred fields of endeavour.

3

The Golden Age of Elizabeth I

Although Elizabeth was more English than any monarch since Harold, she had Welsh and French as well as English blood in her veins. There are people who do not attach importance to a simple biological fact such as this, but it would be as difficult to explain that lady's temperament in any other terms as it would be to explain why breeding makes the difference between the temperaments, as well as between the physiques, of cart-horse and racer. In our age we are satisfied that genes are important. We see in the life of this Queen contrasts of temper and temperament which were curiously in tune with those of the people around her. The English can look back with gratitude to the Providence which just at that moment gave them a Queen who could, as she wished and as occasion demanded, fall back on great psychological resources to deal with the many problems of her reign: on her Welsh subtlety and imagination; on her French logic; and on her Saxon stolidity for a reserve of energy and balance. Like her father, Henry VIII, she instinctively knew her people's thinking; and she could respond in exactly the right way and in the right words to their thoughts and feelings. She had the courage of a lioness. As she was in more than name the apex of government, of the ruling class, of the important and growing middle class of wealthy merchants, of the intellectuals and, in short, of all the power-elements that mattered, the unique combination of qualities of that amazing woman were of great importance. Her reign was remarkable for the success with which, as it were like an expert juggler, she could toss these various human elements to and fro to make a political pattern as she kept them in the air; and no mere man could ever be sure of her next move. She was a lukewarm Protestant who could on occasion enjoy hearing a Mass. To her, religion meant politics and little more. Even in this respect she was in tune with her age, for the Elizabethans were not religious in the sense that their successors the Puritans were. A vigorous, cheerful and almost pagan mood dominated the country, which was in a transition stage from a Roman Catholicism fighting a rearguard action to a Bible-reading Protestantism that was to become aggressive in its religious intensity. She was a flirt and coquette who could banish, imprison or have beheaded the admirer who overstepped the mark of flattery and adulation which she so greatly loved. When presiding at councils of State, she was as shrewd and hard-headed as any of her ministers, and could be as unyielding as granite. Hers was an overpowering personality. Men feared and loved her. In matters of culture and of the intelligence, she was far above the ordinary: she had a complete mastery of French and Italian; she could read Latin with ease, and began every day not by saying her prayers but by reading a portion of Demosthenes. She was, indeed, an accomplished all-round scholar. She was also, like her father, a skilled musician: highly important in that England, "the country of music *par excellence*". She had all the accomplishments expected of a great lady in that age. She was a daring horsewoman and an excellent shot. When a monarchy is not far short of being absolute, the personality and temperament of the monarch is important. We can safely say of Elizabeth that she proved to be just the right Queen for her time. Like her father in his time, she personified her epoch.

What a time it was! On the credit side—which most concerns us here—its general events lead up to the Armada, with the release of energy which followed, and the establishment on a firm basis of a prosperous nation with a population that had increased to almost four millions. From the Armada onwards until the Queen's death, England throbbed with the joy of life. It was a period of restless spirit, of curiosity, of a quickening of the intelligence, of passion, creativeness and great breadth of feeling among people in most walks of life. The downtrodden were given a better deal than ever before. The peasantry now ate better than ever: they became regular meat-eaters for the first time in history. Elizabeth initiated the Poor Laws. The armies of urban beggars, deprived of charity previously given them by the monks, were not ignored by her. The prosperity of the merchants increased with the steady growth of a mercantile marine of which the ships, when not engaged in honest trading, would fill their time with lucrative piracy, freebooting or privateering, which brought grist to their mills and useful additions to the Queen's revenue. As the wealth and prosperity of England increased year by year, luxury and prodigality took wayward courses: the rich built those great 'Elizabethan mansions' of which many still adorn the English landscape. They indulged their fancy even in dress, for this was the greatest of all ages for richness of men's dress. Men often, it was said, "wore a manor on their backs". The slave-trade added its considerable profits in a world which had long been educated to believe in the usefulness of slavery. Before the later Elizabethan period, the English had few ideas of domestic comfort. The interiors of the houses were cold, the floors if covered at all were covered with rushes, chimneys were rare, chairs were hard, cushions were few and even pillows for beds were despised as namby-pamby. All this became transmogrified in a matter of less than twenty years—changed into luxurious furniture, gorgeous beds, and with everything to match the extravagant ideas of men and women

BTHA *Sulgrave Manor, Dining Room, Northamptonshire*

Sulgrave Manor, Kitchen, Northamptonshire

BTHA Ancestral home of the Washington family

MODERN ENGLAND
COUNTY BORDERS INDICATED
BORDERS INDICATED
0 10 20 30 40
statute miles
S. Hyrne Shepherd, 1954
SCOTLAND
NORTH
SEA
WALES
ENGLISH CHANNEL
ISLE OF MAN
ANGLESEY
ISLE OF WIGHT
NEWCASTLE
CARLISLE
MIDDLESBOROUGH
APPLEBY
RICHMOND
KENDAL
LANCASTER
LEEDS
BRADFORD
HULL
PRESTON
MANCHESTER
LIVERPOOL
SHEFFIELD
LINCOLN
CHESTER
STOKE ON TRENT
DERBY
NOTTINGHAM
STAFFORD
SHREWSBURY
LEICESTER
NORWICH
WOLVERHAMPTON
BIRMINGHAM
HUNTINGDON
WARWICK
NORTHAMPTON
CAMBRIDGE
IPSWICH
WORCESTER
BEDFORD
HEREFORD
COLCHESTER
GLOUCESTER
HERTFORD
MONMOUTH
OXFORD
ST ALBANS
LONDON
BRISTOL
SWINDON
READING
CROYDON
CANTERBURY
REIGATE
MAIDSTONE
SALISBURY
FOLKESTONE
TAUNTON
SOUTHAMPTON
LEWES
EXETER
DORCHESTER
PLYMOUTH
TRURO
R. North Tyne
R. South Tyne
R. Riddle
R. Ouse
R. Mersey
R. Trent
R. Welland
R. Yare
R. Waveney
R. Severn
R. Avon
R. Stour
R. Wye
R. Thames
R. Kennet
R. Taw
R. Exe
R. Tamar
R. Dart
COUNTIES
1 LONDON
2 MIDDLESEX
3 SURREY
4 KENT
5 ESSEX
6 HERTFORD
7 BUCKINGHAM
8 BERKS
9 EAST SUSSEX
10 WEST SUSSEX
11 HANTS
12 DORSET
13 DEVON
14 CORNWALL
15 SOMERSET
16 WILTS
17 GLOUCESTER
18 OXFORD
19 MONMOUTH
20 HEREFORD
21 WORCESTER
22 WARWICK
23 NORTHAMPTON
24 BEDFORD
25 HUNTINGDON
26 ISLE OF ELY (CAMBS)
27 CAMBRIDGE
28 WEST SUFFOLK
29 EAST SUFFOLK
30 NORFOLK
31 HOLLAND LINCOLN
32 KESTEVEN LINCOLN
33 LINDSEY LINCOLN
34 LEICESTER
35 STAFFORD
36 SHROPSHIRE
37 CHESHIRE
38 DERBY
39 NOTTINGHAM
40 LINDSEY LINCOLN
41 WEST RIDING YORK
42 LANCASHIRE
43 WESTMORLAND
44 CUMBERLAND
45 NORTHUMBERLAND
46 DURHAM
47 NORTH RIDING
48 EAST RIDING

in regard to their colourful clothing. Comfort has been an English ideal ever since then. Almost every form of craftsmanship throve and was encouraged. In that exuberant age the skilled craftsman found great scope for his work and joy in it. The machine-made articles of our age of science and engineering turn our hearts cold when we see them beside the gorgeous Elizabethan hand-made articles for similar purposes. Ours may work better; few if any of them look better than those old ones. In whatever direction we turn, we see that the Elizabethans 'did something new', something creative and progressive; and with imagination behind it. But among all their achievements, none excelled those of that period of miracle and magic which ran from 1588 until a decade or so after the great Queen's death in 1603. The reign of Elizabeth, regarded as a whole, was a Golden Age for England. Within a period of about a score of years we find the highest peaks in the great range of literature in the English language.

4

The English Language at its Best

Is it a coincidence that the great sunburst of Tudor English and Elizabethan literature should have shown its first dazzling rays about the time of the defeat of Philip of Spain's Invincible Armada, and that from then England should witness the appearance of a literary floodtide? What has already been said indicates that it was not entirely coincidence. If explanation is demanded, it may be found in the liberation of the pent-up spirit of a vigorous and expanding people by the impact on them of a tremendous event pointing to their destiny and providing reason for the highest optimism. The event was the brilliant achievement of the sailors in the English Channel. To the English mind of the period, there was something about it of the perfect combination of arts such as we find in a great ballet beautifully performed by individuals, groups and the whole body of sensitive, lively and highly talented people whose total of efforts are calculated to satisfy an audience which, expecting the best, is regaled to something that excels all expectations. The Armada provided a satisfaction plus a joyous element of surprise at what Englishmen could do when they put their minds to it; a fact which had never before been demonstrated in such comprehensible and unchallengeable terms and on such a national scale. The freedom of spirit which followed the Armada has no equal in English history before or since. It was such that one may well ask whether it has had its equal anywhere, and speculate whether it can ever again be recovered.

This free spirit showed itself powerfully in prose and poetry, but most effectively in the drama. The characteristic negative feature in the new works which began to appear was their lack of ideology. They were not inspired by religious or political motives; nor in the least by the didactic spirit. On the positive side there was in them a profound interest in human character and human behaviour, in human passions, good and bad—for in almost every work the bad received as much emphasis as the good—and, above all, there was a tremendous intensity behind the efforts of nearly every writer to see just how far his imagination could reach, and what perfection he could display, in reducing his flights and fancies to a form of words that others could understand, appreciate and enjoy. The exciting events of the age, the drawing of a new world map, the boundless possibilities opening before them, all these provided the writers with the inspiration, themes and scope they required. The greatly increased activities of the printing presses also encouraged them. The prologue to the great age had appeared worthily in Spenser's *Faerie Queen*. It provided a foretaste of the gorgeous word-painting and rich imagery which characterizes so great a part of Elizabethan literature. A veritable mountain of literature followed, a great crowd of writers of prose and poetry in every form, and a shoal of writers of lyrical poetry for that great age of music. Outside the drama, the writers included men of every class: noble lords tried their hands, the intellectuals and scholars of the middle class made their generous contribution in every field of literary endeavour. But something curious happened in regard to the drama, the most popular form of entertainment during a period when the temper of the nation was dramatic and the humblest beggar spoke in terms which in our rather cold, intellectually stream-lined age would be considered dramatic. The Elizabethan drama rose suddenly. One public theatre served London in the middle of the reign, but before its end there were eighteen theatres in London and one in nearly every important town. Fifty dramatic poets, many of the highest excellence, appeared in the next half-century, and have left us a hundred plays from which we can choose a score of supreme masterpieces, another score of near-masterpieces, and another score in which each play is not far short of being as good as the best known in our 20th century. English drama very quickly rose from small, groping beginnings to a height comparable to the highest reached in the great period of ancient Greek drama. The general run of the playwrights consisted at first of middle-class writers who had been to good schools, many of them to Oxford or Cambridge. But, as the drama steadily made its way to the masses, it attracted the poor literates of that doubtful and rather despised section of society which respectable people regard as Bohemian raggle-taggle. They are worth looking at, those poor literates—poor in worldly wealth but not in art—for they, more than any others, created Elizabethan drama. The historian Green comments that, instead of "courtly singers of the Sidney and Spenser sort", we see the advent of the poor scholar. He says: "The early dramatists, such as Nash, Peele, Kyd, Greene or Marlowe, were for the most part poor and reckless in their poverty; wild livers, defiant of law or common fame, in revolt against the usages and religion of their day, 'atheists' in general repute, 'holding Moses for a juggler', haunting the brothel and the alehouse, and dying starved or in tavern brawls. *But with their appearance began the Elizabethan drama.*" (The italics are mine.) The moment of miracle in this richly creative work came in the year before the triumph over the Armada: Marlowe's *Tamburlaine* represented at the same time a revolt against the old drama and all the elements of imaginative daring that were to be used by the playwrights which followed him. Green adds: "In the higher qualities of imagination, as in the majesty and sweetness of his 'mighty line', he [Marlowe] is inferior to Shakespeare alone."

If the literary achievement of this rumbustious poet living on the fringe of respectable society rises to defeat explanation by the conventional analysts and critics, the life and achievement of one of his contemporaries, William Shakespeare, provide equally insoluble mysteries. For, in spite of the attention devoted to the subject by generations of scholars, very little has been discovered about this man. Of few great poets and national figures do we know less. It is supposed that he had at best a school education. But he never went near to a university. His father was a glover and small farmer who lived in Stratford-on-Avon in Warwickshire, one of the most English of all the English counties. He married a wife older than himself, went to London, became an actor, took to play-writing: and very quickly developed into the greatest glory of the Golden Age of English literature. There is no explaining how he did it. At the age of 47 he retired to Stratford with enough money to support himself comfortably, wrote a few more plays, and died at the age of 52. That is about all we know of the greatest poet in the language, perhaps the greatest poet in all literature. His work needs no comment; Shakespeare is too great a theme for any man less than himself. For our purpose here it must be recorded that this inspired man found the English language at its peak of development. His own genius, encouraged by the spirit of the age, did the rest. But let us not forget that such a playwright could never have flourished in any age but one of great literary freedom; one in which the creator could—as Shakespeare did—keep so clear of religion, politics and 'ideologies' that, from his whole works, so teeming in ideas, we cannot extract a line which will give us the faintest idea of his personal attitude to religion or politics. He is the perfect mirror of the spirit of the age in which he lived—and its greatest reflector.

One must pass on to a very different aspect of the final phase of Elizabethan literature, for something of great importance was happening on a very different plane from that of the poets. The English Reformation, started by Wycliffe, implemented by Henry VIII in his great raid on Catholic property-holding corporations, suffered ups and downs which, with the excitements of Elizabeth's reign, had the effect of causing many English people to lose interest in religion itself. Elizabeth's Parliament in 1559 passed the Act of Supremacy, which abolished the power of the Papacy in England, thereby giving a political finish to Henry's economic onslaught on the

Catholic Church. That enabled the Anglican Communion to offer its attractions without serious opposition. In the same year the Act of Uniformity was passed, which made the Prayer Book of the Anglican Communion the only form of worship legally permitted. These in themselves were powerful factors in the subsequent history of the English people, but they might not have been half as effective as they proved to be but for another. This was William Tyndale's magnificent translation of the Bible, a noble work of literature which was later to be taken as the basis of the Authorized Version. About ten years later Miles Coverdale published his version of the Bible; and then Thomas Matthew produced still another translation, which combined the labours of Tyndale and Coverdale; and a literary pirate named Richard Tavener 'edited' a skilfully made-up version. All this activity in Biblical translation came within the years 1525–1539, the point which most matters being that, from then onwards England had the Bible in the magnificent language of the period. And then the Bible was ordered to be set up and read in the churches of the Anglican Communion. If Shakespeare's *Works* represent the greatest glory of Elizabethan literature, the Bible in English was the single book which was to have greatest influence on the character and further progress of the English people. From then onwards there is hardly an aspect of English life which was not in some way affected by the influence of Bible reading.

CHAPTER VII

THE EXPANSION OF ENGLAND: 1610 TO 1814

1

Puritanism and the Puritans

NOBODY could claim that religion was in a satisfactory state during the reign of Elizabeth in spite of attempts to bring order out of chaos. The Church of England was established in law by her royal injunctions of 1559. The Church itself must do the rest. In 1563 Convocation passed the Thirty-nine Articles representing its fundamental doctrines, which eight years later were given legal sanction. For all that, the Queen's heart was not in religion as such. To her it was a branch of State power, just then an unimportant one. She thought much more of other things: of trade and prosperity; and, above all, of the possibilities for development and expansion which sea-power and the new map of the world offered. Although the Church of England was now well buttressed with legal measures and firm doctrines which, if competently used, could solve many problems, it was not a favourable period for action on the part of churchmen. Like the Queen, her subjects were interested in life more than in religious observances, for which there seemed to be no great enthusiasm except among the small sections of devout. Catholicism had been yielding ground to Protestantism: at the death of Elizabeth there were about three Protestants to one Roman Catholic. Towards the end of the 16th century the Catholics had little or no influence in England, and in the Anglican Church there was not yet either the calm or the orderliness which could give a basis for strength. It is not necessary here to enter into the details of the religious unrest or the widespread heart-searchings that were taking place. The clergy hardly knew where they stood, and many priests embraced both communions. No man could then see where this would lead. There is, however, one aspect of that uneasy period of such tremendous importance for the subsequent history of the English-speaking peoples that it cannot be ignored. It comes under the broad heading of Puritanism.

Few religions have been without their strict doctrinaires and their latitudinarians; the Anglican was no exception. Such was the lax interpretation given to religious duties during Elizabeth's reign that strict observers and those who favoured greater discipline became alarmed for the future. Besides, there were many things in the recently established doctrines of which many did not approve. The public now had access to the translations of the Bible by Tyndale and Coverdale; and the Bible in English was ordered to be set up and read in churches. Crowds flocked to the churches to hear the inspiring words of the Scriptures, hitherto denied to them, but now presented in their own tongue and in noble diction. From the religious laxity of Elizabeth's reign the temper of England changed during the decade after her death. From their semi-paganism of Shakespeare's hey-day the English were inspired by *The Book* to think seriously of God, of the great problems of life and death, of their individual responsibilities to their conscience, and of their attitude towards their fellow-men. Religious indifference died and was replaced by religious enthusiasm, and, as the change took place, one of the most important results was the increase in the number of 'precisians' and perfectionists, of men and women who believed that the Word of God as presented in the Bible demanded a much higher respect and a closer, narrower observance than ever before accorded. From this began a movement within the Church of England for greater strictness in life and a greater simplicity of worship. The movement had many followers among a population that, year in and year out, Sunday after Sunday, had been listening to or reading the Bible, especially among those who, from the words of the Bible itself, were convinced that there had not been a sufficient divergence from the Roman Church. The rigid doctrines of the French Reformer Calvin (*d.* 1564) also had a powerful appeal. This was the beginning of English Puritanism, though the term had been used at least fifty years earlier. From the rapidly increasing movement arose separatism and nonconformity. There were various breaks with the Church of England, accompanied by the independent growth, at first tentatively and later firmly, of vigorous offshoots which took their final forms in Presbyterianism, Congregationalism, Quakerism, the Baptists and other independent sects of English Protestant nonconformists.

As it is impossible for us now to appreciate fully the mind of Elizabethan Man, it is almost as difficult for us to realize to the full the extraordinary passion and driving-force which inspired the early Puritans of the 17th century. The first thing that strikes us as we read about those people is that they included not only some of the most alert and cultured minds in England from the nobility downwards, but that now for the first time the common man, with as much natural intelligence as his social superiors, having heard the message of the Holy Scriptures in the impressive beauty of the new translations—to which the Authorized Version of 1611 had been added—was able to add his own voice and efforts. John Bunyan, a tinker, contributed in *The Pilgrim's Progress* a work of literature with qualities as enduring as those in the works of his great contemporary Puritan, John Milton. The literature produced by Puritan writers is impressive. It is strong, direct and mostly written in the unpretentious plain prose which appealed to the Puritan mind. What a contrast this is to Elizabethan literature! So it was in every field of endeavour: vigour, direct honest thinking, an attempt to solve fundamental problems and an austere attitude to life. A sense of direction had evolved. The common purpose of these people was to free themselves from the fog of mysticism inherited from Rome in the Church of England Communion Service, to assert and assure the right of the individual to interpret the Holy Scriptures for himself, and to achieve freedom from spiritual governance by bishops claiming to rule by divine right. Simple as these aims may appear, when the Puritans tried to achieve them by campaigning and agitation from platform and pulpit, it meant a frontal attack on the established Church. Dangerous as this was, the Puritans did not hesitate. They were the first of many English Nonconformists.

2

Civil War—Cromwell—Execution of Charles I

When religious passion enters the hearts of men, they are not easily deterred from pursuing the call of their faith. On the side of the Puritans there was this driving force; there was nothing comparable to it on the side of those who stood in their way. On the other side there was the power of the monarchy, the inner bastions of the Church of England, a small number of keen representatives of the Church of Rome, and a solid nucleus of people who resented the activities of those ardent and often fanatical reformers. The clash which came was inevitable, and the details thereof make so great a story that here it must be dealt with summarily. After a tyrannous period, in which King Charles I (*r.* 1625–1649) did everything he could to wreck the efforts of the Puritans, a man arose among them who, believing himself to be the appointed of God for this task, set about making an army to face that of the King: Oliver Cromwell. It meant Civil War from 1642 to 1648. His was the Parliamentary party which favoured reform. The men of his New Model Army were called 'Roundheads'; the King's forces were called 'Cavaliers'. It was a struggle between the old and the new, the old in this case being full of dangers for England; its success would mean the undoing of the work of the Reformation, the return of Catholic power; reaction all round. But with his New Model Army fortified by his 'Ironsides', mostly Puritans of the Eastern Counties, Cromwell won the war for the Parliamentarians against the Royalists. The real bitterness of the war came after it had ended. For the new House of Commons assembled in an aggressive and unreasonable mood, into which toleration, especially religious toleration, did not enter. The Cromwellian Army pressed Parliament to try the King, Charles Stuart, for treason. Resolutions in the House of Commons declared the people to be the origin of all just power in the land, and its laws binding without consent of King or Lords. An Act of Parliament was passed on January 6th, 1649, setting forth that Charles Stuart had wickedly designed totally to subvert the ancient and fundamental laws of the nation, and in their place to introduce an arbitrary and tyrannical government; that he had levied a cruel war against Parliament and kingdom; and that new commotions had arisen from the remissness of Parliament to prosecute him: wherefore that, for the future "no chief officer or magistrate whatsoever may presume to imagine or to contrive the enslaving or destroying of the English nation, and to expect impunity for trying or doing the same". A commission was appointed to try the King. Before the trial they decided that, if he should ask by what authority they tried him, the answer must be: "In the name of the Commons in Parliament assembled and the good people of England." At his trial Charles I refused to plead. "Princes", he had said, "are not bound to give an account of their actions but to God alone." And at his trial he maintained repeatedly that "a King cannot be tried by any superior jurisdiction on earth". The trial proceeded coldly and systematically, evidence was called to prove the various charges, and documents were produced to prove the King's invitation to foreign forces to enter England. He was sentenced to death by beheading. Having refused to plead during the trial, Charles now wished to make a statement. "Sir, you are not to be heard after sentence," he was told and, when he struggled to make himself heard, the president of the commission said coldly: "Guard, withdraw your prisoner." The execution was a dignified ceremony which took place in Whitehall. Charles died bravely, and never at any time renounced his ideas of absolute monarchy. The event not only ended absolute monarchy in England: it asserted Parliamentary supremacy. The execution of Charles I was followed by the abolition of the monarchy, and by a vote in the Commons that the House of Lords was both useless and dangerous and that it also ought to be abolished. On May 3rd, 1649, an Act of Parliament established the English Republic. "England", it said, "shall henceforth be governed as a Commonwealth or Free State, by the supreme authority of this nation, the representatives of the people in Parliament, and by such as they shall appoint as ministers under them for the good of the people." It was a salutary lesson, one never forgotten.

The Puritans had won. True, there were reactions afterwards, and by agreement the monarchy was to be re-established—but on new terms. All that is an intensely interesting story. What we are concerned with here is that Cromwell and his Roundheads and Ironsides—the Puritans—had asserted for all time the supremacy of Parliament, and had begun the process of curtailing royal power that was to end in the limited constitutional monarchy which, since then, has found favour in the eyes of the English people. Even more important, he and his revolutionaries established the great principle of liberty of conscience, which meant that from then a man had the right to practise any religion of his choice, or no religion, without let or hindrance. This was a new freedom in the world. The English Revolution had done its work: at the cost of a Civil War and the King's head. This law-abiding people which, perhaps more than any other among civilized nations, detests disorder or unrest of any kind that is liable to shake stability of government, public life and commerce, had demonstrated that, rather than submit to royal absolutism, rather than have liberty of conscience suppressed, they would stop at nothing; not even at fratricidal strife or the execution of a monarch, the last an act deeply regretted by all but a few, though considered by the majority, and by succeeding generations, to have been the only course expedient at the time. The political act engendered a public confidence which was to carry the English a long way.

3

The Pilgrim Fathers: Colonization and Independence of North America

The Puritan movement had other far-reaching effects as important as those just noted. English seamen, by the beginning of the century during which the events recorded above took place, were still doing good work following the great period of Drake, Hawkins and the others. In his voyagings Sir Walter Raleigh discovered on the coast of North America a paradisaical territory where, it was said, men lived after the manner of the Golden Age of legend. It was named Virginia, after the Virgin Queen Elizabeth, and there, on the shore of Chesapeake Bay, was established in 1606 the first permanent settlement of 150 English colonists. They were steadfast men, mostly Puritans, 48 of them free spirits from upper-class families, and all were inspired by simple, honest and democratic ideals. In five years the settlement had grown to 5,000 under the austere leadership of brave John Smith. Here, for the first time, the laws and customs of old England were planted in the New World. That was the first Puritan exodus from the mother country, but it was only a beginning.

Under political and religious pressure a little community of Puritans known as Brownists, who had strict and independent ideas of their own, had left England in Elizabeth's reign and taken refuge in Holland. They heard of John Smith's settlement, and were not in the least dismayed by tales of the hard life and sufferings of the pioneering settlers. They returned to England, and in two vessels set out for the land in which they could be sure of freedom of conscience. One vessel had to put back. The other, the *Mayflower*, a little bark of 180 tons with 41 emigrants and their families, reached the coast of Massachusetts at a place which they named Plymouth after the port from which they had sailed. They were the famous Pilgrim Fathers of North American history. From then onwards the Puritans in England realized that on the other side of the Atlantic was a great new territory which offered them freedom to practise their religion and to establish themselves in accordance with their own ideas of life, far from the turmoils, molestations and oppressions experienced in the mother country. As troubles at home increased, migration to the land of the free also increased. It became a great movement resembling that of the Celts from the Continent into Britain, or that of the Angles, Saxons, Jutes and Norsemen before the Norman Conquest. A dominating spirit demanding freedom of conscience now inspired the great migration of Puritans to America. By 1640 some 25,000 English people had settled, mostly in New England. About half of them came from the Anglo-Saxon counties of Suffolk, Essex and Hertfordshire, one-quarter from Sussex, Surrey, Middlesex, Nottingham, Yorkshire, Lincolnshire and Norfolk, and the remainder from various parts of England, with a few from the Welsh and Scottish borders. Trevelyan[8] writes: "The tree whose branches were destined to cover the continent from sea to sea, had its deepest roots in the close-settled, democratic, Puritan land of the New England townships." Those people left behind them in England what remained of their feudal ideas. They had no class of gentry, no squirearchy. They were all equal, and all of them Puritans in regard to dogmatic religion based on divine authority. But, even as Puritans, they divided themselves into groups representing the rigid disciplinarians and the more liberal sort, dissent from 'Puritanical' authoritarianism being common and allowed to pass unmolested. By 1700 the coastal colonies of North America had a quarter of a million inhabitants. Here was English overseas expansion in earnest!

It seems a pity to interrupt this tale of human progress with a tale of woe. But there is no other word to describe the almost incredible succession of stupidities on the part of English leading men which brought about the loss of the American Colonies, the population of which had risen to over two millions by 1770. It was now a very mixed population, consisting of Americans born, Lutheran Germans, French Huguenots, Irish, Dutch, and there was a sprinkling of many other races including many Negroes and, of course, the native Red Indians. Among the descendants of the English Puritans there was not only a traditional feeling of independence, but this was now mixed with a strong feeling of resentment against England for methods of mercantilism which, in 1760, caused the colonists to have an adverse trade balance of nearly $10 million. The taxation which the English government exacted was another and a sore factor. At a time when England was deeply involved in a struggle with France, Americans began to think that their economic difficulties might be solved by complete political independence of the home country. From their point of view, the moment could hardly be more opportune. The English Prime Minister, Lord Grenville, devised a series of measures to reduce the appalling national debt of £130 million caused by the war with France. His measures included some which would mean little less than economic slavery for the Americans. And that was something to which those sturdy descendants of Puritans—and the others—would not submit. There were in England men who saw what must be the inevitable outcome of pursuing so short-sighted, so stupid a policy as Grenville's (to which Lord North was to add aggravations). But war came. On July 4th, 1776, a group of representative men in America signed the document which symbolized the will of those colonies: the Declaration of Independence. And one of the most heartbreaking and incompetent wars in history continued to be fought by both sides. It came to an ignominious military end for England with the surrender of Lord Cornwallis at Yorktown in 1781, and in November of the same year, in the Treaties of Paris and Versailles, England acknowledged without reserve the complete Independence of America.

No event in English history has caused greater heart-burnings than this. The immediate home and European problems which England had to face just then were such that there was no time for grief over even so great a loss. The American crisis came at a time when events in France (to be followed later by the Revolution in that country) demanded greater attention than ever. With the rise of Napoleon to a point at which he threatened England's security and even existence, there was something else to think of. The American colonies were free. They were inhabited by vigorous people with strong English, Irish and Scottish elements dominating the social ideas of which they all approved in principle. Those people had everything on that northern part of the American continent that men need. It was a country of incalculable resources. The possibilities were boundless, and the men were to justify the possibilities. Meanwhile in England another kind of revolution was taking place.

4

Prosperity and Empire

From the time of the Cromwellian upheaval onwards, the England that developed out of the Puritan Revolution was a country entirely remarkable for innumerable important movements and activities which arose spontaneously. Behind them all was the rise of the powerful system which, very largely, was to replace feudalism not only in England but in most of Europe, in European overseas possessions, and in the world:

Capitalism. It now seems to be agreed that the speed with which Capitalism then developed in England was one of the principal results of the Puritan Revolution, though the idea of Capitalism was already as old as the hills. In the 17th and 18th centuries England laid the solid foundations of the system by which she steadily rose to wealth and power in the world. In its major aspects it represented a collaboration between the centralized power state and private enterprise; in nearly all other respects, it was private enterprise alone. There is still much research to be done for that period before it will be possible to clarify the various influences that were at work. Tawney says: "In the triple reconstruction, political, ecclesiastical and economic, through which England passed between the Armada (1588) and the Revolution (1649), every ingredient in the cauldron worked a subtle change on every other. There was action and reaction.... Puritanism helped to mould the social order, but it was also itself increasingly moulded by it."[16] This complex and as yet uncharted 'gradualism' continued for nearly a century, and with remarkable results.

Expansion of foreign trade helped to increase prosperity at home. The English discovered that colonization, encouraged and supported by an efficient mercantile marine and protected by a strong Royal Navy, could be *profitable*. The now powerful London merchants, helped by the State, did not allow grass to grow under their feet. The North American colonies were working, though some time was to pass before they showed a profit; but the French and Dutch were now proving that it paid to acquire possessions overseas, as Spain had demonstrated already. The first overseas possession to be openly seized by the English State was Jamaica, which Cromwell colonized. A trade in slaves, who were transported from Africa to the English possessions in the West Indies and to the colonies in North America, brought much wealth to England, and laid the foundation of the fortune of many merchant families whose offspring moved into the landed aristocracy. In 1635 the easy-going Portuguese conceded to the English the rights to trade in all Indian ports; a small seed from which was to grow British India. Meanwhile, the East India Company became one of the first 'joint-stock' companies in London and the world. English merchants settled in Madras, which began exporting to England. In 1672 a Royal Africa Company was established for slave dealing, but was put out of the business by the activities of a swarm of private slavers. The Hudson's Bay Company was formed, and survives to flourish in our own time. The Bank of England, established in 1694, helped in all this. The system of granting charters to companies for some enterprise had long existed—from the time of the Merchants of the Staple and the flourishing Merchant Adventurers; but now it grew with the discovery and development of new trading routes. Charters were given to companies trading with many parts of the world, but the enterprises tended to develop into monopolies and become obnoxious to merchants and colonists who wished to have absolute freedom in trading; and little by little the merchants and colonists found ways to drive out of business the companies which unreasonably exploited their advantages. The system almost died out, though it was later to be revived with modifications and to greater advantage. The old chartered companies were not only monopolists, they were, abroad, almost a law unto themselves. They were the vanguard of the new British imperialism.

America, Africa and Asia as suppliers of materials and products. At home: an England with a rapidly developing industrialism. That is the pattern of the increasing prosperity of the country, which, notwithstanding all this commercial activity, continued to fight and win wars which it deemed necessary in the interests of balance of power. And what was this balance of power other than a way of guaranteeing to England her own security, stability and freedom to develop along the lines which she was finding congenial and beneficial? That in itself was always worth a war! From Puritanism had arisen a seemingly unrelated idea, but one which, in fact, was closely related. It was an unwritten tenet of many Puritans that a godly, righteous, sober and industrious life got its reward on this earth from Almighty Providence in the form of success. Thus, if the aim was commercial, success proved that God approved. Then, as strict and sincerely religious Puritanism grew lax—which it often did—it changed to something that was believed in sincerely enough but had not

Blenheim Palace, Oxfordshire
Settled by Parliament 1704 on the first Duke of Marlborough, John Churchill, ancestor of Sir Winston Spencer Churchill, who was born there in 1874
BTHA

Photo: Courtesy of J. C. Berrangé

Netley Castle, Hampshire

Built in 1540 by Henry VIII. Now a convalescent home

in its inner core the objectively rigid, the unyielding morality of the early Puritans' code. In the age succeeding the monarchical Restoration which followed Cromwell, the new statesmen conceived an ideal of England as the centre of a great trading empire, herself to be the rich, governing nucleus. England was to be the lake into which all imperial rivers bearing wealth should flow. If that dream seems a little fantastic, the reality which the English experienced for a period of about two hundred years did not fall far short of the ideal.

Wars helped to increase prosperity at home, even the disastrous American war. The old sea-dyke and the Royal Navy kept at a safe distance enemies who had not forgotten what happened to the Invincible Armada. When a war came, it meant great bulk purchases by the State from private manufacturers and merchants: of weapons, clothing, boots, commissariat supplies, of everything required by soldiers in the field and sailors at sea. Then many new and profitable industries were established. Already in this period an idea was developing which, in the 19th century, was to be generally accepted in most corners of English free enterprise: "Trade is one thing, religion is another." The idea, though not expressed in those words when it first began to have effect, was a comforting one. It enabled the great organizers of that rising period to keep their religion strictly apart from their business. And this helped to avoid many embarrassments and discomforts of the human conscience. The balance-sheets of the counting-houses became the charts to success in both worlds. The boiling cauldrons and the whirlpools of religion and politics had gradually settled as a calm lake on which the bark of private enterprise in commercial and industrial undertakings could sail without risk of being overturned. As if by a natural process, Scotland became a part of England with the Act of Union passed in 1707. Even that difficult country, Ireland, looked better from London in most of the 18th century.

The Whig and Tory political parties—Liberals and Conservatives, grandparents of those now existing in England—appeared before the end of the 17th century. In 1679 a General Election was fought on party lines for the first time. In almost every sphere of activity the clear pattern of modern

Jacobean House, Clockwork Spit, Hereford
BTHA

England was being formed. It was a country different in almost every way from other European nations. By the 18th century there had come to this prosperous England an epoch which has been compared with the great age of the Emperor Augustus in Roman history. No country could be more different from the England of Elizabeth. From this fact there is a lesson to be learnt, if it had not been taught by the history of England before Elizabeth: the extraordinary quality which the English have of being able to change themselves from one distinctive type into another equally distinctive. The picture which John Dover Wilson gives us in his *Life in Shakespeare's England* is so strange to most of us that we think we should feel ourselves lost in that extraordinary country. The picture which the 18th-century writer Daniel Defoe gives us in his *Tour through the Whole Island of Great Britain* makes us feel that this is *our* England. These two books are studies in such amazing contrasts that one can hardly believe in any relationship between the earlier and the later people. Yet there it is. Those people were to change again in the 19th and 20th centuries, but the later changes represent a straight line in progressive development from the condition existing in the 18th century. There is no great difficulty in following it, for the English were no longer groping or feeling their way.

Finally, we must glance at the classes of society in 18th-century England. Rank had long, perhaps always, been related to wealth. Now rank could be achieved from wealth, and often quickly. The gentry no longer lost caste by being associated with trade, for "if a gentleman be bound an apprentice to a merchant or other trade, he hath not thereby lost his degree of gentility". This meant the disappearance of one more coloured ribbon of surviving feudalism. In the 18th century there was a well-beaten track leading from the commonalty to the upper ranks of middle-class society, from which a slight hop could land a sensible man among the higher aristocracy. The retail shopkeeper, always a grade below the foreign merchant (who raised his hat to the banker), could educate his son for a liberal profession which, if it was the Law or the Church of England, could lead to the House of Lords. The complex stratification of classes gradually became a part of the English way of life. "In 1760 the stratification was not like a system of caste, but it roughly blocked out the division of functions between the different groups of the community, and it did so by a division of opportunities. Inheritance was the foundation of the higher ranks and of the whole system of ownership in land and business, so that, once risen, a man had a lasting advantage, and his family with him." [17]

It was now that England evolved what has ever since been one of her characteristics and great strengths: a governing class with a feeling of community of interest not only within itself but with the people in general. This ruling class was made up in grades descending from the great nobles and bankers to members of the squirearchy and the learned professions. It was only partly hereditary, for its success depended on ability. Successful lawyer-politicians made their way into the ruling class which, from generation to generation, renewed itself and developed a sense of government. Education at a great public school and at one of the Colleges of Oxford or Cambridge, or at an Inn of Court, was a good preparation for all this. English public schools offered a first-rate education and training for those who wished to take advantage of it. To all their pupils they imparted a knowledge and a training which experience showed to be fruitful in leadership. The bulk of the population accepted the words of the Book of Common Prayer—"To honour and obey the King, and all that are put in authority under him: To submit myself to all my governors, teachers, spiritual pastors and masters: To order myself lowly and reverently to all my betters. . . ."

It was a remarkable system that was being evolved, all the more remarkable because it was based on "government by consent" and "freedom of conscience". If England did nothing else but evolve this system and make it work as smoothly as it worked for over two centuries, the achievement would be a landmark in the history of government.

From the outset, the new ruling class grew powerful and its members seldom grossly abused power; never in the way those of the continental ruling classes abused it, for the English ruling class disciplined itself severely. Those of the next, which we should call the 'middle' class, were growing in numbers, but did not until the 19th century reach their full strength. Employers were the backbone of that class in the

18th century. One might perhaps add to its upper ranks the professionals—churchmen, lawyers, great merchants—but not actors, who were vagabonds; nor doctors, who were little regarded as yet; nor writers and artists, who were regarded as nondescripts unless highly successful, as to-day. And then, below all these were the workers and wage-earners of whom it must be recorded that, even then, in England they had strong excellent organizations and, on the whole, lived better than workers in most parts of Europe.

Not one-hundredth part of the activities and movements of those two hundred years can be mentioned here. The seamen never stopped from adding new overseas possessions, which included Australia. But in what has been said there is an inkling of the England that, with increasing overseas possessions, was already an Empire in the making; one with a rich and increasingly powerful nation as its centre, on an island beautifully situated on the new map of the world that had been sketched but remained to be filled in.

5

Rivalry for Power: Napoleon Defeated

Across the Channel, France had not been as successful as England in emerging from decaying feudalism into a new way of life. The French Revolution which broke out in 1789 was the culmination of years of unrest and the demands of the people for an entirely new governmental and social system. The Revolution was to give new directions to political and social ideas in many parts of the world, but the protective shell which England had created for herself, though slightly penetrated in a few places, stood firmly against ideas representing French solutions for problems which the English felt they had solved for themselves in their own way long before. What interested their rulers far more than ideas of liberty, equality and fraternity was the fact that, almost on their doorstep, was a potentially great nation which was also a rival for world power. For England the threat of real danger appeared in the period of revolutionary wars (1792–1800) which followed the Revolution, and especially with the emergence of a formidable leader in the person of Napoleon Buonaparte. It was again a question of 'Balance of Power' for England: France must not be permitted to dominate Europe. It began to look very much as if the French, under the inspiration of Napoleon's leadership, would succeed in helping that ambitious man to achieve a peak of power which might threaten everything that mattered to the English, from the immediate security of their island to their wealth, future security and possibly existence as a nation. Never since the time of Philip II of Spain had there been such a threat. Napoleon's success in arms was taking him to all parts of the Continent. It became quite clear to English statesmen that the sword, and the sword alone, could decide his fate, and the English were anxious to see it settled in both internal and in international affairs. The island home and an Empire were now at stake. The diplomatists set to work and, by 1815, Great Britain, Russia, Austria and Prussia bound themselves to end the rule of Napoleon, for which goal they would put into the field a joint army of 150,000 men. On the English side, two Anglo-Irish aristocrats prepared the way for, and brought about, the defeat of Napoleon at the Battle of Waterloo on June 18th, 1815. Not only that. Wellington's brilliant tactics at Waterloo enabled him, with a force inferior in numbers to that of his allies, to play a decisive role in a battle that would settle the fate of Europe for years to come. Hence, when Castlereagh and Wellington arrived at Vienna for a peace conference, they spoke with a voice of authority which could hardly be challenged by the Great Powers present.

The resultant Treaties of Vienna may not have been perfect. But there is this much to be said for them: they were followed by a long period of peace—one which lasted for forty years. The principal reason for this—it has been reasonably claimed—was that both Castlereagh and Wellington, in everything they said or did at the conference, were inspired by a spirit of leniency to the conquered—or call it long-term foresight, in marked contrast to that of the very reactionary German representatives, and even to the clamour of a vengeful part of the English public. The two Anglo-Irishmen would not listen to anything which savoured of the spirit of revenge. In the end, the treaties were signed, the national delegations returned home—in Europe to foment troubles based on the fears of ruling classes, in England to proceed with what now mattered most to Great Britain: a consolidation of interests at home and abroad. Of the two sets of interests, those abroad are perhaps of most interest to us here. The treaties had given power to England to settle how many would be returned or retained of the overseas possessions that had been taken in the struggle. France and Denmark were given back their most valuable islands; to the Dutch were returned their East Indian possessions, Java and other rich islands. But England retained Ceylon, the Cape of Good Hope and Singapore; and purchased a stretch of Guiana for a song of three million pounds. England also retained Mauritius, Heligoland and Malta (Gibraltar had been retained as a British possession since 1704). With Australia and Canada and a list of other possessions which would almost fill a page, the Empire began to assume the shape and proportions we now know. For England, the Napoleonic War was not merely a military victory, it was equally an economic victory. On the new map of the world that had been drawn by the Portuguese, Spanish, Italian, English and French navigators and explorers, the colour which from now appeared most often was red.

CHAPTER VIII

EXPANSION INTO EMPIRE: 1814 TO 1914

1

The Age of Peace and Prosperity

EVERYTHING that happened in English history before the defeat of Napoleon (which removed a major obstacle to progress) seems to have been a mere preparation, a setting of the stage, for England's Age of Peace and Prosperity. We need not be concerned with philosophical discussion of what constitutes 'success' or 'progress'. The dominant classes, the rulers and the merchants, the landowners and the new industrialists of the 19th century, had fixed ideas about what progress and success meant to them: peace for expansion, order and stability at home for manufacturing and export. All could be summed up in the result desired: continuous and increasing prosperity. No need here to look too closely at the other side of the medal. But it must not be imagined that England achieved her world supremacy in the Victorian period without appalling human misery among her working classes. That other side of the medal represents a tale of misery and distress, slum growth, sweated labour, and often social unrest and agitation because of such conditions. From the new and independent United States of America, and as a result of the French Revolution, the English workers received ideas which stimulated them to organize themselves for protection against harsh and greedy employers. Coal-mining, the manufacture of cotton and other goods, the working of blast furnaces and all such activities, attracted into urban areas thousands of men and women who had hitherto worked on the land. The population of England's industrial areas was at first made up of people who had abandoned agriculture in favour of 'more money' and town conditions. With steam power and an inexhaustible amount of coal to make it, raw materials of all sorts coming from the farthermost parts of the growing Empire, plus a world of almost completely undeveloped markets, a boundless horizon of wealth and prosperity opened itself to the eager eyes of the ever-increasing manufacturing and merchant classes. Those busy, acquisitive Englishmen may not have realized to the full the economics in which they were involved or that they were the leaders in a revolution —the Industrial Revolution—which was to have a greater influence on humanity than the French Revolution. The economy was based on scarcity: so long as there was a scarcity of what England could produce from her ready access to raw materials and her manufacturing ability, the world was at her feet and the sky the limit. Full advantage was taken of an extremely favourable state of affairs. For all this peace was an absolutely essential condition, and it is noteworthy that, in the century from 1814 to 1914, England was engaged in only two wars (the Crimean and the Boer), and her unrest at home was negligible in comparison with the upheavals which took place in continental countries, not to mention the wars in which many of them were involved. Indeed, the contrast between English and continental, or even American, history during the 19th century is astonishing. One wonders how it was achieved. There was a fair element of luck in it. During the first part of the century the countries of Latin America were fighting their wars of independence to sever the political bonds with Spain. In the United States there was a bitter civil war (1861–1865). Eleven southern states seceded from the Union and formed the Confederate States of America. The struggle between the Union and the Confederacy was severe. In the end the Union was reasserted. But the war, with its long prelude and epilogue of uneasiness and unrest, worked to England's advantage. All wars and upheavals in other countries then were to the advantage of England. The ideas of the French Revolution sprouted weakly in England and, apart from their effects on the workers, helped to encourage liberalism and radicalism.

Meanwhile the population was rapidly increasing. In 1750 it was (with Wales) 6½ millions, and in 1801 (the year of the first census, before which statistics are guesswork) 8,892,526. By 1851 it had increased to 17·9 millions and by 1901 to 32 millions. The increase was due to many factors other than prosperity: mortality was reduced by progress in medical knowledge (by vaccination, for example) and by such advances as the introduction of the turnip family into the rotation of crops, which enabled farmers to feed cattle in winter and thus produce meat and fresh milk in that hitherto difficult season. This increase in population, the increasing production of coal for power and export, together with an astonishing dynamism in invention and scientific progress, all helped in the development of industrialism; and it all took place while other countries were, for one reason or another, unable to compete. That, very briefly and roughly, is the explanation of Victorian prestige, power and prosperity; prosperity on such a scale that, before the middle of the 19th century, England had become the wealthiest country in the world as well as the most powerful, and with prestige which stood higher than ever before. Economists are not agreed as to the year which should represent the peak point of this country's prosperity. Most of them put it at about the middle of the 19th century, which may be correct if statistics only are considered. But other things must count in any estimate of prosperity and, all things considered, it seems to me that the peak year must be somewhere between 1850 and 1875. My estimate would be 1860.

A generation of writers in the 20th century devoted their talents to 'debunking' Victorian England, a permissible, salutary and often highly entertaining literary exercise. There is no need to challenge the pictures they produced, for the period was one with many facets, and some of them displease us to-day. But we must not forget that if there was much ridiculous and hypocritical pontificating by the smug and the moneyed, and an absurd and unjustified complacency among the new social thrusters who believed that England and the English had reached the top of the world and would remain there for ever, in few countries can there ever have been a comparable period of such useful endeavour and strenuous activity. In mechanical inventiveness alone the Victorians were far ahead of all others, as they were in science generally and, above all, in the fine art of adjusting a democratic system of government to suit the new way of life which Industrial Man was evolving for himself. It is useful for us to remind ourselves that England first produced Industrial Man, and first evolved a system in which he became content to live without need for violent upheavals. This is not to say that he had no reason for protests against injustices, or no need to agitate for better conditions or to organize to achieve them. The Englishman had learnt his lesson in politics: that violence to redress wrongs must be the last resort and when all else had failed. Whoever thinks that for this reason the Englishman is always willing to submit to injustice makes a profound mistake. He is usually much more patient than most; but when his limit of endurance has been passed, he can be more dangerous than most. Field-Marshal Sir William Slim once said: "The British are no braver than anyone else, but they can be braver for longer. Courage is a long-term virtue." So it is in this matter of patience in the face of wrongs. It becomes a long-term virtue for the English, who will protest, agitate, organize and try to achieve a fair settlement by peaceful means. It is their preferred method. In major internal affairs their record of successes in these terms is formidable, for they became past-masters in the art of evolving workable formulas, and in the equally subtle arts of compromise and face-saving. Their attitude in this respect is based on an innate desire for peace and stability, which in the Victorian age again and again has proved to be highly beneficial to the people in general. To the English the Revolution of 1688 was and is little more than the memory of something which sensible and politically conscious men and women need not repeat. In the Victorian age the idea of 'self-government' replaced 'government by consent'; the idea that government, however good, if imposed by authority and without the consent of the governed, was relegated to the scrap-heap of obsolete politics. And so, consciously or unconsciously pursuing this line of thought, the Victorian workers organized their Trade Union and Co-operative Movements, and governments, one after another, stimulated by the works of such men as John Stuart Mill, felt themselves compelled to adopt the principle of gradualism: to encourage among other things popular education. Often under popular pressure, often by virtue of the enlightenment and political foresight of a few men of liberal ideas, the leaders of the age initiated innumerable reforms that have since been developed and become a part of the English way of life, and have been copied in many countries. In no other age had there been so many reforms or so many suggestions for reforms. With the growth of industrialism, the traditional way of life was at first thrown out of balance. A new social balance was necessary, and long before the century had ended it was achieved. The initial phase of social revolution took place with hardly any violence. Where it differed from most other social revolutions was that it took place during a period of peace and prosperity.

2

Social Reforms and Peaceful Social Revolution

Before the 19th century, the English 'way of life', as we now call it, evolved of itself unplanned and empirically. Every step in that evolution was based on action and experience, not on theorizing, dogmatic assumptions or preconceived ideas. The rational Englishman, it seems, tends to favour the mental attitude which demands of every new idea put to him: what is the use of this? If he can be quite satisfied that there is something in the new idea, he will next ask: will it work? If it works, he will judge its final utility by results. In this attitude, which seems to be a second nature to him, he will be impatient of abstractions, side-issues and frills, however interesting they may be. He is always suspicious of logical systems of thought which do not conform to his own empirical way of thinking. He makes no great claims for this attitude. He regards it as merely common sense: English common sense, if you will. It may appear strange that such an attitude should be used by an English thinker—Jeremy Bentham (1748–1832)—as the principal element in a social philosophy, and even of a whole system of thought. Perhaps even more remarkable is the fact that much of this particular philosophy has since then become "so far part of the common thought of the time, that there is hardly an educated man who does not accept as too clear for argument truths which were invisible until Bentham pointed them out." [18] The influence of this one man was so great in 19th-century England, and still continues to be so effective, that it is worth while to pause for a moment and consider what it has meant to the English people.

Jeremy Bentham was born in Red Lion Street, London, just off the main thoroughfare of Holborn. His father and grandfather were successful attorneys, and he inherited a considerable fortune which enabled him to settle down peacefully as a barrister to discover, among other things, "the principles upon which all sound legislation must proceed". In 1789, he published his *Principles of Morals and Legislation,* a work which brought him such widespread fame that he was made a citizen of France in 1792. From then onwards his advice was welcomed by leading men of Europe and America, with whom he maintained an active correspondence. Nevertheless, Bentham was not exactly a public figure. He was a shy, retiring man, almost a recluse, a rather eccentric character who lived in a secluded blind-alley, where he had a house in which he received and entertained those few friends who interested him and no others. His speech was as unimpressive as his appearance, but if ever man proved that the pen is mightier than the sword, it was Jeremy Bentham. Ideas of all kinds radiated from him; he it was, for instance, who first propounded schemes for making the Suez and Panama Canals. He added many new words to the language: 'codify', 'codification', 'minimize', 'international', 'utilitarian', and others that are now in every dictionary. Incidentally, he designed the Tate Gallery. His final act of pure reason was to leave his body to be dissected and the skeleton preserved. It is in University College, London.

The formula adopted by Bentham is "the greatest happiness of the greatest number". That is the essence of Benthamism or, as it is also called, Utilitarianism. It meant, in the first instance, the rigorous application of common sense to the facts of society, of which it embraced every aspect, especially the legislative. Never before had accepted English institutions been subjected to such a comprehensive and dispassionate survey by so logical a mind. No serious politician, legislator or statesman could afford to ignore Bentham's writings, of which the effects can be seen not only in the gradual and progressive overhauling of the laws of England, but in innumerable other directions and in other countries, especially the United States of America. Law and politics, he proclaimed, are perpetual experiments in the means of promoting happiness; this he regarded as 'utility'. We have not yet reached the end of Bentham's influence. In the 19th century, this 'utilitarian philosophy' not only dominated the writings of such men as John Stuart Mill and the liberal reformers in general, it guided movements for economic, political, parliamentary, municipal, educational, legislative, prison, and even ecclesiastical reforms. It also had a salutary effect on governmental corruption and inefficiency surviving from the rather lax and easy-going 18th century; it swept away innumerable abuses. Democratic individualism grew from it, the exponents of *laissez faire* seized on it to further their doctrine of "as little official interference as possible in private business"—only in the end to abuse it. It also helped to inspire the beginnings of the movement which later blossomed into English Socialism. Reformist and even revolutionary writers all over Europe turned the pages of Bentham's works to find logical arguments to define or support doctrines which they very often propounded as their own. The position is that Benthamism has been accepted as the common-sense solution for so many previously existing problems that it is now difficult and at times impossible for us to say where it begins or ends. The plagiarism has been immense. "Bentham is pillaged by everybody," said Tallyrand, "but he still remains rich in ideas." It is not the function of this book to criticize such philosophies as Benthamism, but merely to record what has deeply affected the English people and their way of life. It may well be that in the 19th century the influence of Benthamism on the general reform of institutions, and the resultant steady improvements in so many directions, was so great that England was saved by it from violent social revolution.

In that 19th century, England became more than ever a country of classes, but the balance of the complex stratification of society was being changed by a rise to greatness on the part of the middle class which stood between the other two classes, the upper and lower. (Yes, the term in common use for all who worked with their hands was 'lower class', later modified to 'working class' or workers', who are called 'operatives' in the United States.) Rise to greatness is here meant in terms of wealth, influence and power. From the increasingly important middle class and the landed aristocracy was drawn the ruling class, into which no lower-class man had yet entered.

For the moment we must look at the working or, as Victorians would have it, the lower class—almost 90 per cent. of the population. Theirs was at best a hand-to-mouth existence; at worst an existence little better than that of poor slaves. Lord Beaconsfield (Benjamin Disraeli), in his novel *Sybil: The Two Nations* (1845), told England that industrialism had created in it a new 'nation' that was separated, cut off from the upper and governing class. He puts the point of view of those who under the new industrialism had abandoned the land to work in factories:

"Why are we, after manfully struggling for years and each year sinking lower in the scale, why are we driven from our innocent and happy homes, our country cottages that we loved, first to bide in close terms without comforts, and gradually to crouch in cellars, or find a squalid lair, without even the common necessities of existence; first the ordinary conveniences of life, then raiment, and at length our very livelihood vanishing from us?

"It is that the capitalist has found a slave that has supplanted the labour and ingenuity of man. Once he was an artisan; at the best, he now only watches machines; and even that occupation slips from his grasp, to the woman and the child. The capitalist flourishes, he amasses immense wealth; we sink, lower and lower; lower than the beasts of burden—for they are fed better than we, for according to the present system they are more precious. And yet they tell us that the interests of Capital and Labour are identical!"

The condition of the working class was such that early in the century one Robert Owen, possibly influenced by Bentham's ideas, tried an experiment by applying the doctrine of 'self-help' to a very bad factory at New Lanark of which he had taken over the management. In less than fifteen years it was not only flourishing—it was a model of good, healthy conditions in the factory itself, with excellent amenities for the workers, and all sorts of facilities in the village, including educational, for their families. Pay and general conditions were better than in the average English factory. Owen was proving to the world that the worst evils of industrialism could be avoided—without a lowering of production or earnings—if only the simple, social aspects of life were attended to. Thousands came to see for themselves the happy and flourishing community of New Lanark mills. Investigators were sent by foreign governments to see whether the stories told about it were true. Owen appealed to the Government in London for attention to be given to his experiment, at first without success. The only legislation which then existed to help the working class was an Act of 1802, and its provisions were limited to the protection of pauper apprentices. In 1815, Owen and a Lancashire millowner, Sir Robert Peel (father of the great Prime Minister of that name), drew up the first Factory Bill, which applied to all factories, forbade employment of children under 10 years of age or, after that, for more than 10 hours a day; and provided for paid inspectors to enforce the law. Manufacturers hastened to London to protest against a measure which would strike hard at abuses existing all over industrial England. They began their case before a Committee of Inquiry by personal attack on Owen, in which they established the quite irrelevant point that he was an infidel. From that they went on to argue the real point with less success: claiming rather absurdly that children in mills had a healthy and happy existence. But as a result of the 'smear' on Owen, the provisions of the Bill were whittled down to the point at which they were harmless. And so Owen's efforts failed. But only for a time. He had provided a lesson which was not lost on either legislators or the workers. From Owen's 'failure' began a struggle for State control in the interests of men and women employed in industrial organizations. The struggle lasted well into the 20th century, and at last gave the English factory workers all the protection they needed against the bad type of employer. But that was not all that sprang from Owen's activities. Later, in the 1830s and 1840s, came the movements in favour of Trade Unionism, and then, in 1844, the beginning of the Co-operative Movement: to sell goods at market prices and divide the profits among purchasers in the form of a dividend. Both these movements were, in essence, to protect those engaged in production from exploitation. Their progress was slow; the new ideas were opposed and fought at every step. But by the end of the century they were so firmly established that they had become a part of English life. What was even more important, they now provided a solid and interested body of voters on which a general Labour Movement with parliamentary representation could be based.

Meanwhile, the question of votes and voters had to be settled, for in the early part of the century the lower class was unrepresented in Parliament because it did not have the vote. To achieve a reasonable suffrage meant reforms in many directions, not least in the parliamentary system itself—a very tall order! It is impossible to record in this brief sketch the widespread and varied activities that were organized for and against Parliamentary Reform. One aspect of this general movement demands attention if only because it is so characteristically English, so perfect an example of the way English people set about achieving new social measures which evoke strong opposition, that it can serve as an example of the common-sense quasi-Benthamite 'utilitarianism' that seems to come into play in this country almost spontaneously when great problems arise. As is usually the case, it began in a very simple way. A prominent and popular business-man named Thomas Attwood (1783–1856) in January of 1830 inspired the foundation in Birmingham of a 'Political Union' whose general object was to work for a generous measure of Parliamentary Reform with undefined limits. A well-to-do middle-class man himself, Attwood saw that unity of the middle and working classes would mean strength; and that the question of Parliamentary Reform interested the middle class as much as it did the workers, and appealed to supporters of both Whig (Liberal) and Tory (Conservative) Parties. His idea caught on. Branches of the Political Union sprang up throughout England. A most important plank in Attwood's platform was that there should never be in this agitation for reform any act of violence or any form of illegality. Vast crowds assembled to hear him speak; everybody saw how reasonable his demands were. In December 1831 a Reform Bill was introduced in Parliament, passed by the House of Commons and accepted by the Lords. But the

Durham Cathedral, Durham
BTHA

Lords attempted to take the Bill out of the hands of Ministers and amend it in their own way. Whereupon the Cabinet resigned. The country was very agitated during this period, and in a few places there was rioting by the Chartists, as those in favour of reform were called. But now the Political Unions took the matter in hand. They existed in most towns, included all classes, and were mostly led by middle-class business-men; though in the industrial north there were purely working-class unions, and in some places middle-class and working-class unions functioned side by side and in friendly co-operation. Some of the unions began to arm themselves and to drill. It was a perfect example of English spontaneity and self-help on the part of these improvised people's organizations, which not only showed their strength but a wonderful sense of discipline, especially in view of the events which followed. King and Tories called for their suppression, though their agitation was constitutional apart from the drilling and arming; Whig Ministers tolerated them on condition that they would cease to arm and drill. King William IV was prepared to do anything—except create more peers—to get the Bill through in the modified form to which the Lords had reduced it. He requested the Duke of Wellington to form a Ministry to carry the Bill through. The country immediately suspected that this was an attempt at dictatorship, and feelings began to rise alarmingly. The Political Unions were ready to lead resistance if it should prove necessary. The Tories sensed grave danger, and refused to rally round the Duke, who withdrew from what he saw to be a thankless and perilous task. The King now called upon Charles, Earl Grey, to form a Ministry, but the latter did so only on condition in writing that the King would create sufficient peers to pass the Bill in a constitutional manner. The lesson had been learnt. The threat of more peers persuaded the House of Lords to pass the modified Reform Bill (1832), which became law. It was the first step towards the universal suffrage which England now enjoys.

It would not be difficult to continue almost indefinitely exemplifying the steady progress of reforms in that fruitful century. It is hoped that sufficient has been said to show in broad outline the working of the English mind in the field of politics. Every class in England hates and fears instability and

Clovelly Harbour, Devonshire
BTHA
Chipping Campden, Gloucestershire
An ancient town in the Cotswolds
BTHA

unrest, and violence—which very rarely shows itself—is not only disliked but regarded by many as a sign of either wicked influences which must be eliminated or of last-stage exasperation for wrongs which must be given immediate attention. The English system and way of life has not, since Cromwell's time, provided a favourable climate for violent movements. In that 19th century, especially during its first half, England achieved wonders in the way of social reform almost without violence or serious interruption in general progress and prosperity. To judge the achievement fairly, one must think of a population rapidly increasing; then think for a moment of the total number of people who lived and died in that century, and finally of those moments of unrest in which there were casualties or fatalities due to violence on one side or the other. The violence, in comparison with the peaceful achievement, appears as little more than an odd grain of sand in an hour-glass. The French had their Age of Reason. Did they achieve more reasonable results in terms of human welfare than the English achieved in that 19th century?

3

Victorian England: Country and People

England was moving towards the full tide of prosperity when Queen Victoria came to the throne in 1837. The face of the land was changing rapidly; with the growth of industrialism the countryside lost many of its beauties. The Victorians never learned to build factories or industrial towns of good appearance or passable amenities. Whatever was touched by industrialism became drab. Urban areas increased; the countryside shrank accordingly. In the north and in the Midlands the growth of urban areas transformed everything, including life itself. Writing in 1848, Macaulay records some of the changes in the people. "It is pleasing to reflect", he says, "that the public mind of England has softened while it has ripened, and that we have in the course of ages become, not only a wiser, but a kindlier people. There is scarcely a page of history or lighter literature of the 17th century which does not contain some proof that our ancestors were less human than their posterity. The discipline of workshops, of schools, of private families, though not more efficient than at present, was infinitely harsher. Masters, well born and bred, were in the habit of beating their servants. Pedagogues knew no way of imparting knowledge but by beating the pupils. Husbands, of decent station, were not ashamed to beat their wives. The implacability of hostile factions was such as we can scarcely conceive. . . . Nowhere could be found that sensitive and restless compassion which has in our time extended a powerful protection to the factory child . . . the more we study the annals of the past, the more shall we rejoice that we live in a merciful age in which cruelty is abhorred, and in which pain, even when deserved, is inflicted reluctantly and from a sense of duty."

How smug that last statement seems to us! Yet it is representative of intelligent thinking at that time. That discerning American, Ralph Waldo Emerson, wrote in 1856: "In the island, they never let out all the length of all the reins, there is no berserker rage, no abandonment or ecstasy of will or intellect, like that of the Arabs in the time of Mahomet, or like that which intoxicated France in 1789. But who would see the uncoiling of that tremendous spring, the explosion of their well-husbanded forces, must follow the swarms which, pouring now for two hundred years from the British islands, have sailed, and rode, and traded, and planted, through all climates, mainly following the belt of Empire, the temperate zones, carrying the Saxon seed, with its instinct for liberty and law, for arts and thought—acquiring under some skies a more electric energy than the native air allows—to the conquest of the globe." Later in the century came the writings of Samuel Smiles and Martin Tupper. The first wrote a series of uplifting books which seem to have penetrated into every Victorian middle-class household. One of them was the famous *Self-Help* (1859), a most curious work to us now, and an extreme example of Utilitarian propaganda written in a manner so full of smugness, secular unction and self-complacency that we just laugh at it. The sales of this book were phenomenal. More curious still, it was translated into a score of languages as a Key to English Success. It is the fountain-head of a branch of literature which, with modifications to suit each generation, has flourished in the English-speaking world ever since. Tupper's works were less materialistic and strongly flavoured with religious sentiment. He wrote a long series of moralizings in blank verse called *Proverbial Philosophy* (1838–1867), and they proved to be precisely what was required at the time. The Queen herself thought highly of the genuine moral and religious feeling in these works, and of the author, whose conversation she is said to have enjoyed. The majority of Victorian readers were uncritical of such naïve works as those of Smiles and Tupper; they just loved them. It is not difficult for us to appreciate the appeal of such writings if we bear in mind the spirit of that prosperous and stable epoch, in which a good-hearted, well-ordered but rather puritanical Protestantism provided a basis of morality for business and pleasure as well as for the general spiritual comfort of the great and growing middle class. Tupper's *Proverbial Philosophy* and Smiles's *Self-Help* have evoked satire, but, if we feel inclined to smile over them now, we must not allow ourselves to forget that they are documents which contain the essence of Victorian middle-class morality.

While life at home was chiefly concerned with commercial prosperity and reforms, British possessions abroad continued to expand. Of these India was the most important. Fifty years of conquest had followed more than a hundred of commerce. In the early 19th century the conquered area of India was about one-third of the whole country, which, little by little, was to fall under the British Raj until only Nepal and a few smaller areas remained independent. The year 1876 marked a great event in the life of Queen Victoria. In that year a Bill was passed by Parliament which conferred on her the title of 'Empress of India'. It was said at the time that the Prime Minister—Disraeli—was merely ministering to a whim of the sovereign, but there is reason to believe that the title represented a calculated act of political expediency. Britain's advisers in India were of opinion that the title 'Empress' would "impress on the minds of native princes the idea of British suzerainty". There was opposition in Parliament to the measure, but it went through. No doubt it pleased the Indian Princes as well as Victoria. She was henceforth not only Queen of the United Kingdom of Great Britain and Ireland and of

Britain's Possessions Overseas, but Empress of India. Her Majesty, until her death, showed great interest in the magnificent dependency, "fairest jewel in the crown". At her death nearly all of the map of India was coloured red.

Queen Victoria proved to be an ideal monarch during her long reign (1837–1901). Like Elizabeth I, she reflected the spirit of her time. When she came to the throne, the popular faith in monarchy was declining. Her sincerity, her desire to further England's interests, her happy and fruitful marriage, and the close attention which she gave to all her tasks as ruler of the Empire—by the end of her reign it represented about one-quarter of the globe—revived popular faith. It is noteworthy that the Queen-Empress, the 'eminent Victorians', and one might say almost that whole epoch, appealed enormously to a succeeding generation chiefly as fruitful subjects for satire or irony. This in itself indicates the chasm between life in the 19th and 20th centuries: the later writers failed to enter into the spirit of that age or to understand the motives which activated its great personalities. If it is difficult for us to enter into and appreciate the Elizabethan Age to the full, it is quite impossible for us to detach ourselves far enough from the much nearer Victorian Age to be able to view it clearly and dispassionately. Criticism becomes futile; gentle satire and well-informed irony or humorous writing at the expense of the Victorians can provide the succeeding generation with entertainment; but even the best of it does not wear well. It is, perhaps, in the works of the great Victorian novelists that we find the best and truest documentation of the epoch, the best pictures of country and people. Victorian novels, because of their turbulent disorder, do not appeal greatly to mid-20th-century readers who are accustomed to the tidy, well-constructed and streamlined novels which cater for a more impatient, a more scientifically exacting age. For all that, the Victorian novelists usually tell better stories, and they certainly provide less tortured, more authentic pictures. All the great novelists of that reign were creatively alive; they regarded themselves first and foremost as entertainers who, if they did not tell a good story—and tell it well—must fail in their task; and that story had to be written with a background which almost any reader could recognize as authentic. Hence their value as documents. There is an intense individualism about those writers, and a genuinely artistic sense of the pictorial and panoramic. Furthermore, most of them tended to specialize. And so we go to Disraeli for his illuminating works dealing with political life and the ruling class, especially the middle-class section of it that was steadily creeping into the higher stratum of society. Whatever his three works, *Coningsby, Sybil* and *Tancred,* may be as novels, they are invaluable to us as panoramas of the very important section of society that was to dominate England for over half a century. We go to Dickens—the greatest Victorian novelist—for other aspects of life, especially of low life in London. For us the novel is to that age what the drama was to the Elizabethans: the characteristic medium of expression. The vignettes in Thackeray comprise Victorian life in almost every phase. Here he is at Brighton, then a favourite seaside resort of the people, as it is to-day: "In Steyne Gardens . . . the lodging-houses are among the most frequented in that city of lodging-houses. These mansions have bow-windows in front, bulging out with prominences, and ornamented with neat verandas, from which you can behold the tide of human kind as it flows up and down the Steyne, and that blue ocean over which Britannia is said to rule, stretching brightly away eastward and westward. . . . One of the best of physicians our city has ever known is kind, cheerful, merry Doctor Brighton. Hail, thou purveyor of shrimps and honest prescriber of South Down mutton! There is no mutton so good as Brighton mutton; no flys [light carriages] so pleasant as Brighton flys, nor any cliff so pleasant to ride on; no shops so beautiful to look at as the Brighton gimcrack shops, and the fruit shops, and the market. I fancy myself in Mrs. Honeyman's lodgings in Steyne Gardens, and in enjoyment of all these things."

In those Victorian novels one never finds any rude or crude treatment of sex; the passions were treated in accordance with the teachings of the pulpit and always kept well under control. Succeeding generations of Victorian writers, editors, publishers and printers were highly competent in the work of expurgating any obscene word which might shock, or any passage which might titillate, never mind inflame, the passions, all of them following the tenets of literary morality laid down early in the century by the highly approved Dr. Thomas Bowdler who expurgated Shakespeare—so that the works of the greatest poet could be permitted into respectable homes and even to take their place beside those of the great Martin Tupper, which were usually more deeply appreciated and their author considered by many good Victorians to be the better poet. There was not much in the way of literary criticism or judgment outside the romantic—Coleridge is the great exception—for the great new middle class had no deep traditions of culture or taste; and ordinary readers did not want literature which imposed a strain on the intellect. Yet it would be a grave mistake to imagine from this that great works of the intellect were not being produced; Darwin's *Origin of Species* (1859) and many other major works came as intellectual bombshells which shook comforting and accepted ideas to their roots.

The new prosperity and the quick upward climb into a higher rank of society had inevitable consequences which showed themselves most strikingly in matters of taste appertaining to many things which remain for us to see. Vulgarity began to touch most of them. Victorian architecture, for example, though occasionally good, is seen by the 20th-century critic as too often a mere perversion of historic styles. Clothes became showy, often eccentric by our ideas, and usually very ugly. It was a vigorous and self-confident vulgarity that did little harm at home but, when manifested by English travellers in the older and longer established civilizations of France and Italy, often evoked derision and disgust. The newly rich English traveller too often appeared as a disagreeably high-handed egoist with a complete contempt for all values that were not his. His wealth gave him the feeling that, whatever those foreigners may have been in the past, *he* was now their superior—and in everything. This obtuseness did not endear him to those whose way of life, because it differed from his, he regarded as nonsense. In this way a comparatively small number of robust, self-confident wandering vulgarians did much harm to English prestige on the Continent and elsewhere. This sort of thing is not unusual when the *nouveaux riches* of one country are let loose in another. In the case of the English, it was very often redeemed by the work of some Englishman, inevitably regarded at home as an eccentric, who seriously and sympathetically studied a foreign people and, in a masterly book, showed their qualities in a favourable light. George Borrow did this in his *The Bible in Spain* for the humble muleteers and gypsies of the Peninsula. The Victorian Age produced innumerable 'eccentrics', men and women who are so called because they did something extraordinary. They are high-lights of the Victorian panorama.

Not through mere tricks of history, but far more often by hard work and high endeavour, England achieved her supremacy: mistress of the seas, the richest nation on earth, ruler of islands and great lands in every climate, owner of a quarter of the globe. Her men of science were in the vanguard of progress, her engineers, technicians and inventors second to none, her doctors and chemists and physicists among the best, her commercial products regarded everywhere as of higher quality and better value than those of other countries. . . . The chronicle of achievement by the English on their little island in the 19th century represents the greatest advance mankind had hitherto achieved in so short a period. It was not only a new England that the English made. *What they did*—at home and abroad—changed the fortunes, in reality or by example, of whole countries and even of continents. The English led or pointed the way in that amazing 19th century.

The Diamond Jubilee of the Great Queen was celebrated in 1897 and was made a Festival of Empire. The Queen's representatives came from every part of the earth, and there were troops from every colony and dependency. The procession through London was unique. Never before was there anything to equal it in colour and variety in this country of great pageants. The Queen, a frail little lady of seventy-eight, was four hours in her carriage. What were her emotions as she acknowledged the cheers from the crowds which lined the way for one of the most remarkable processions in history?—one with representatives of every race and colour. Tall serious Irishmen in their saffron kilts, green cloaks with torcs, playing haunting airs which had come down from their remote Goidelic ancestors, whose origin lay somewhere between Switzerland and the Black Sea; the more flamboyant Scots, descendants of Celts and Picts, whose inspiring bagpipe music rose above the cheering and floated on the air to be heard miles away; Welshmen from the mountains and valleys, vigorous survivors of the ancient Britons. And Englishmen: the blend of Celt with Saxon or Scandinavian Viking or Norman, or with all these—the ruling race which had arisen from the fortunate mixture. And the sailors—bearers of a tradition which began in the time of that other Great Queen, Elizabeth. From Canada and Australia came magnificent men mounted on magnificent horses. These were the main part of the procession. But there were also Hausas from Africa; and coloured men from the West Indies, descendants of the slaves of an earlier age; and Cypriot Zaptiehs and Chinese soldiers from Hong Kong; and Dyaks from Borneo, many of them ex-head-hunters transformed by civilization into military police. Most colourful of all were the detachments of Imperial Service troops sent by the Indian Princes; they, and especially the tall dignified Sikhs, were acclaimed by the populace. An important reminder is necessary. All these men were volunteers. There were no conscripts among them. They were accepted as proven supporters of the Empire, as loyal subjects of the Queen. What a tribute that fact is to Victorian statesmanship! Where else in history had there been anything to equal it? From Land's End to John o' Groats that evening the hills were crowned with bonfires which, as they burned themselves out, symbolized the passing of a mighty epoch. One more episode, representing one more acquisition to the Empire, must be mentioned: the Boer War (1899–1902), from which came the Union of South Africa and the greatest diamond mines in the world.

Queen Victoria died in 1901. She had made the monarchy a much firmer, a better and a more greatly beloved institution than it had ever been. She made the English monarchy known where it had never before been heard of.

4

The Shadows begin to Fall

With the Reform Bill of 1832 (followed by a greater one in 1867) the centre of political gravity passed from the aristocracy, and land-owning class to the great middle class, especially its richer members. Even before the first Reform Bill ideas had been fomenting to challenge the political power of the middle and upper classes. The ideas then and later came mostly from the minds of middle-class people: John Stuart Mill, for example, who in his *Political Economy* (1848) thought that the workers were not getting a fair deal and that the part they played in the country's prosperity—they being over 75 per cent. of the population—deserved and needed political representation. Socialist ideas were still strange and suspect to the English people, accustomed as they were to an old system ordered for them by Whigs and Tories and supported by the Church of England. The very word Socialism frightened many. In the 1880s and 1890s works were written with the object of making the new ideas known: Edward Bellamy's *Looking Backwards* (1887), for example, and the poet William Morris's *News from Nowhere* (1891). In 1894, from the pen of a working-class writer, Robert Blatchford, came a little book with the title *Merrie England*, written in strong simple prose akin to that of Defoe or John Bunyan which could be understood by anybody. Blatchford edited the *Clarion*, which, from then onwards, was the popular forum of the English Labour Movement. The growth of popular education towards the end of the century, the propaganda of such men as Keir Hardie, the dissemination of ideas propounded by Karl Marx and the general condition of the working class —all contributed towards the formation in 1893 of an Independent Labour Party. In 1894 a Fabian Society was formed with the object of achieving social reforms and the *gradual spread of Socialism by peaceful means.* This society was almost entirely middle class, and little by little attracted the support of such people as Bernard Shaw, Beatrice and Sidney Webb, H. G. Wells and other intellectuals whose combined efforts made remarkable propaganda with an increasingly popular appeal. In 1900 the very important Labour Representation Committee was formed. From it came the fusion of the Socialist and Trade Union Movements, a development which resulted in the election to Parliament of a number of 'Labour' members pledged to work independently of the two older parties. This new Labour Party was determined to work constitutionally, and in terms of reason rather than of emotion, to achieve political power. It is a great testimony to its 'Englishness' that never once, from then until now, has it been associated with any form of violence in the achievement of its aims. It was precisely this reasonable attitude which made its progress slow but steady and a growing challenge to the Liberal and Conservative Parties. The growth of the Labour Movement from those small beginnings to the enjoyment of full political power (which did not come until 1945) was to be the most noteworthy political development of 20th-century England. Long before political power was achieved, the mere existence of this potentially great and growing element in political life, and the realism of the old parties in recognizing its potentialities, enabled the English people to face and live through the two greatest crises in their history, and in each case to emerge—greatly weakened, of course—without social upheavals, and able to reconstruct, readjust and to evolve new ideas to meet new circumstances. When crises came, all classes worked together like a good football team. If this is mentioned now, there is a reason. In the decade before the First World War, England's enemies were already proclaiming that she was finished, that she had shot her bolt. Had they but known the extraordinary resilience and philosophical flexibility of the islanders, they might have hesitated to go to war. The great paradox is that what often appear to others as English weaknesses are often England's strength.

From the death of Victoria in 1901 to the outbreak of the First World War in 1914, England enjoyed, under King Edward VII and (from 1911) King George V, the last phase of the great peace which had begun nearly a century before, and had continued until then with only two interruptions that were hardly felt by the people. Socially, the pre-1914 period was still at heart Victorian. I am old enough to remember the England of those days, and the memory is a very pleasant one.

Life was at least as good as elsewhere (and in many ways better than it is now, apart from the medical advances which since then have increased longevity). The fact that England was still the greatest world power, still prosperous and busy, even flourishing, gave a gusto to John Bull's existence which he has not experienced since then. The ordinary young person—myself, for example—was almost unaware of the terrible threat to England's comfort that was looming up across the North Sea. No doubt our wise elders knew of the menace; some popular newspapers constantly harped on it. Youth did not care, for youth is blind and carefree, and we were enjoying a good world that was to vanish and never reappear. When four of us could, by clubbing together, make up ten shillings (say $1·50), we knew that we could finance a glorious evening. This was our usual programme:

Beer (two pints each) . .	total cost	1*s*.
Three-course meal . . .	,,	5*s*.
Cigars	,,	1*s*.
Music-hall	,,	2*s*.
More beer	,,	1*s*.

And everything was *good*. The music-hall of those days had risen to its highest peak of its art and exuberance, providing great value in return for very little money. It was a healthy national institution whose rumbustious vigour overshadowed the theatre, the opera, the ballet and the still primitive cinematograph. Its superb vulgarity suited us all. Audiences knew the artistes, and the artistes knew exactly what the audiences enjoyed. Those were the days of giants in the English music-hall, and the power of the artistes for creating goodwill and happiness was enormous. For it was not only in the halls that one heard the jokes and quips, the comic songs and catchy airs: they were carried everywhere, and might be heard at any hour of the day or night. I remember a cold January morning dark as pitch, the hour about six o'clock, when I had to make my way to a ship in the London Docks. I felt as cold as a frog, and as miserable as sin is said to be. Suddenly, as I turned a corner, I heard a cheerful masculine voice singing:

I'm 'Enery the Eighth I am,
'Enery the Eighth I am, I am:
I got married to the widda nex' door,
She's bin married seven times beefoh'a:
Every one was a 'Enery,
There ain't bin a Willy or a Sam;
I'm the eighth ole man cawlled 'Enery,
'E-n-e-r-y the Eighth I a-m.

—the last line sung in a mock-operatic voice. My misery vanished on hearing the first line. When the verse came to its dramatic, ironically lugubrious end, I had warmed up and the world appeared in a new light. The singer was a Cockney milkman going his round of those poor dockland streets on a morning to make angels weep. But in his head and heart was the lively measure of a music-hall classic that has survived into our own time. It was simple things with a strong tang such as this which made that age, and gave it its particular flavour. There was about it the indolent happiness of a people who had not known war, who were reasonably comfortable, and who had evolved for themselves a healthy way of life which, when not interrupted by economic troubles, was as good as could be found anywhere on earth.

The German Menace! King Edward VII was called The Peacemaker because (no doubt realizing what his cousin Kaiser Wilhelm II was up to) he used his influence to bring about the signature of treaties, with first France and then Russia, to help England in safeguarding the Balance of Power in Europe. The Germans took these moves to mean their strategic encirclement. Whereupon began the armaments race which precedes war. In 1904 Germany was conciliatory in the highest degree to England, an attitude which changed as her power grew. That Germany was already a formidable power: her peace-time land army was the strongest in the world, perfectly trained and equipped. Her Navy increased in strength with such speed from 1909 onwards that English experts thought that the German naval-building programme begun about then would be achieved long before 1917, the date fixed for completion; and that equality with the British Navy might be established. In less than a generation Germany's merchant shipping had increased by 234 per cent. From 1894 to 1904, her foreign trade had increased from £365 to £610 millions. No country in the world was making more rapid strides to overtake England in manufacturing. It was obvious to everybody that the German Empire of 60 million people, with a further 30 million German-speaking allies, would not, because of the temperament of her leaders and the nature of those tremendously energetic people, content themselves with mere commercial progress. The German State and the English State prepared for war, which they no doubt believed to be the only possible way of solving their serious problems. When the preparations had reached a certain point in the summer of 1914, all that was required—to justify States in joining in a European conflagration which developed into the First World War—was a lunatic to throw a bomb! In one respect only was England well prepared: on sea. Her Navy was stronger and better than the German Navy. Her land forces were minute in comparison with Germany's. Air power was in its infancy, but the old sea-dyke was still effective as a protection against an invader so long as the Channel and North Sea were dominated by the British Navy. Although England was not invaded, not even threatened with invasion, that German challenge, lasting from August 1914 until November 1918, when it was defeated, cost the English and their Empire more in suffering and general loss than they had ever before known.

CHAPTER IX

ENGLAND AND THE TWO WORLD WARS: 1914 TO 1945

1

The Tide ebbs in Blood and Treasure

THE England of 1914 was a liberal democracy with an old conservative background and a rising labour movement. English people were, on the whole, satisfied with their way of life, but most of them still thought in terms of the great peace and security of the 19th century. The suffragettes had been causing a ripple on the surface which dyed-in-the-wool conservatives regarded as not only revolutionary but preposterous. In the rest of the population, those who thought at all of 'Votes for Women' believed them necessary. The ordinary man in the street looked on good-humouredly. Before the war ended almost full suffrage for men, and a first instalment for women, had become the law. Far more serious in 1914 was the dark cloud over Ireland, which had been promised a measure of Home Rule that was being strongly opposed in Ulster and by a threat of mutiny on the part of some officers in the English garrison on the Curragh. The danger of civil war in Ireland—a grave one at that moment—was averted by the attitude of the Irish Nationalists who, in the moment of England's crisis, agreed to accept postponement of the Home Rule promises until a better day for England. Until war suddenly broke out the prospect of such a calamity had hardly any place in the mind of ordinary people; and when it came, it came to most as the kind of overpowering shock which is not understood until long afterwards. It is difficult for those who were not adults at that time to realize how innocent, how simple-minded and how gallant that generation of young men was. They did not need and were not given a period of "conditioning for war" such as is now prescribed. There was no conscription, no National Registration in which every citizen is numbered and indexed from cradle to grave, and no direction of labour. In fact, nothing of the highly ingenious net which the modern State has since then woven around the individual existed. From August 1914 until the spring of 1916, every man was a volunteer. 'Your King and Country need you!' a famous poster shouted from every wall, and the young men went in their thousands to the recruiting offices to become soldiers in Kitchener's Army. There was an enthusiasm in their hearts such as no 'psychological conditioning' could induce. The great issues of the war were reduced for everybody to a simple formula based on the German violation of Belgium's neutrality; and that was enough. We look back now and are astonished at the naïveté of the ideas used. But behind them was John Bull's fear of a powerful rival who had been "going a bit too far" and must now be dealt with at any cost. The deeper reality was that Europe, for half a century peaceful on the surface, had been gestating explosiveness. We know now that, if there ever was a moment in history when the European scene was set for war and the players ready to act, even if all of them were not fully prepared, it was in that fateful month of August 1914. A mere spark sufficed to detonate that heap of explosive material. Britain and her Empire faced the most dangerous challenge in her history.

England had two major allies: Russia and France; the former not too calculable but essential, the second vital and, as it proved, well able to fight. Since her disastrous war with Germany in 1870, France had gone through a period of fear of fresh aggression, and then, especially after the treaties with Britain and Russia, had lost that fear and regained her old confidence as a fighting nation. In 1870 she had fought alone; now she had Russia and England on her side, and England meant the British Empire and its resources. Besides, England had powerful friends, among them the United States, whose people had as little desire as the English to see Germany dominate Europe. The very small British Army of 1914 was a highly trained professional one, but by the end of the war it numbered over five millions and became as efficient in the field as any German Army had ever been.

The outlook of the nations then was very different from that of to-day, when in time of war civilians run as many risks as soldiers. For England—because of the Navy—it meant that

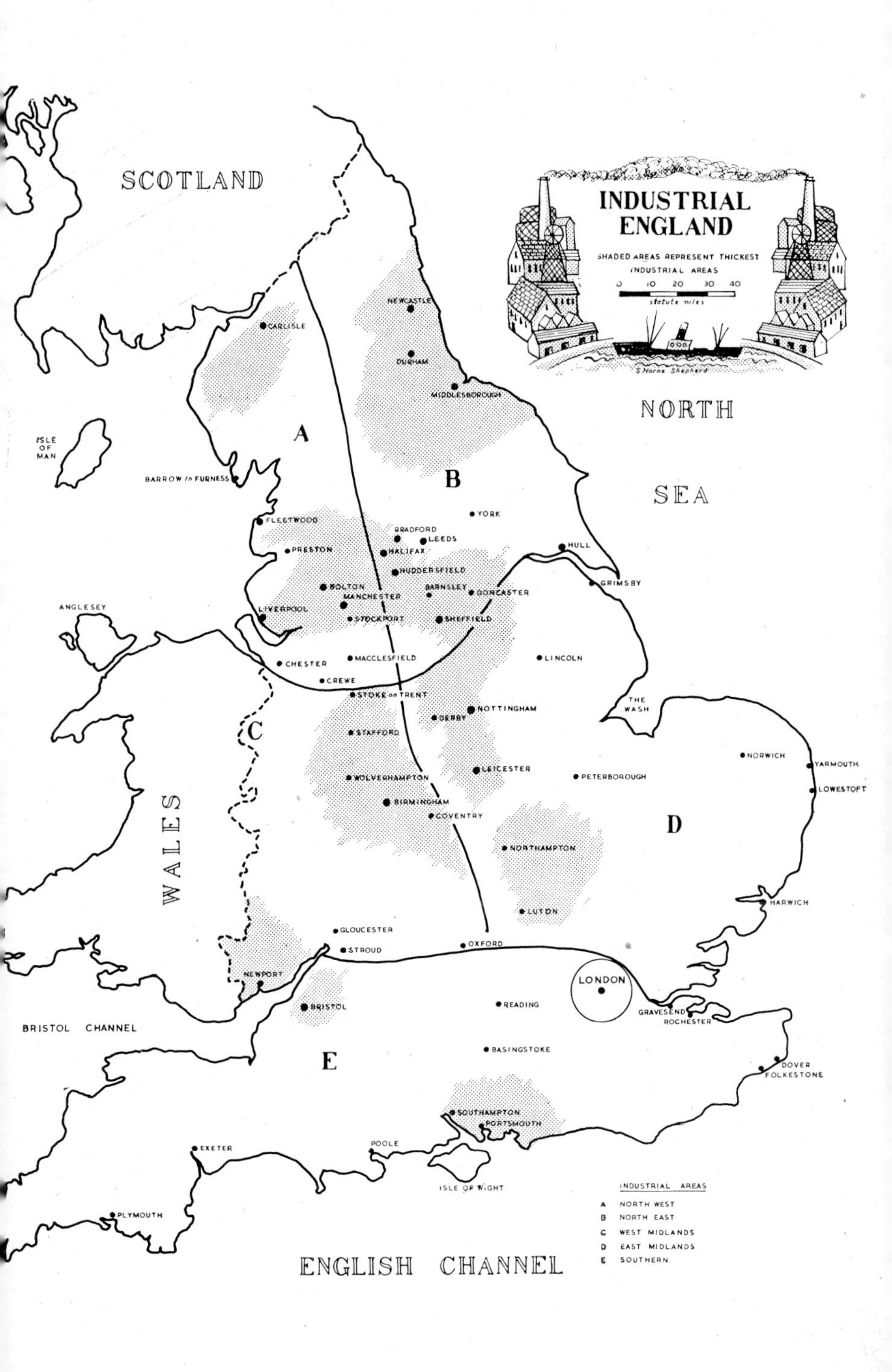
INDUSTRIAL ENGLAND
SHADED AREAS REPRESENT THICKEST INDUSTRIAL AREAS
0 10 20 30 40
statute miles
S. Horne Shepherd
SCOTLAND
NORTH
SEA
WALES
ENGLISH CHANNEL
BRISTOL CHANNEL
ISLE OF MAN
ANGLESEY
ISLE OF WIGHT
THE WASH
A
B
C
D
E
CARLISLE
NEWCASTLE
DURHAM
MIDDLESBOROUGH
BARROW in FURNESS
YORK
FLEETWOOD
BRADFORD
LEEDS
PRESTON
HALIFAX
HULL
HUDDERSFIELD
GRIMSBY
BOLTON
BARNSLEY
DONCASTER
MANCHESTER
LIVERPOOL
STOCKPORT
SHEFFIELD
CHESTER
MACCLESFIELD
LINCOLN
CREWE
STOKE on TRENT
NOTTINGHAM
DERBY
STAFFORD
NORWICH
YARMOUTH
LEICESTER
PETERBOROUGH
LOWESTOFT
WOLVERHAMPTON
BIRMINGHAM
COVENTRY
NORTHAMPTON
HARWICH
LUTON
GLOUCESTER
STROUD
OXFORD
LONDON
NEWPORT
BRISTOL
READING
GRAVESEND
ROCHESTER
BASINGSTOKE
DOVER
FOLKESTONE
SOUTHAMPTON
PORTSMOUTH
EXETER
POOLE
PLYMOUTH
INDUSTRIAL AREAS
A NORTH WEST
B NORTH EAST
C WEST MIDLANDS
D EAST MIDLANDS
E SOUTHERN

the English people were able to contemplate the achievements of their armed forces as if from seats in an amphitheatre. On sea the war was in every way ruthless: the submarines of the German Navy attacked and sank English and even neutral ships that brought materials and food to England, culminating with the sinking in 1917 of the huge Cunarder *Lusitania.* Submarine warfare, as waged by Germany, was 'unrestricted'; that is, sinking at sight without warning—against all accepted rules of warfare. The struggle on the Western Front—where English forces were most deeply involved—after some manœuvring and open warfare in the first weeks, settled into trench warfare, which meant a war of attrition. It was this long-drawn-out process which made it so appalling for the front-line fighters: often weeks of immobility with intermittent sharp episodes, occasionally a grand-scale attack with perhaps thousands of casualties on each side; but all the time, day and night, week in and week out—for years—the masses of infantrymen lived like troglodytes constantly harrowed by shell fire, trench-mortar fire, machine-gun and rifle fire and, from 1915 on, attacks of poison-gas or flame-throwers. And as those English troops dragged their feet wearily along the cobbled roads of France, they would keep up their spirits with a song:

When this bloody war is over
Oh, how happy we shall be!

Behind the lines in France every suitable building was turned into a hospital, and those hospitals were filled with wounded who were moved to England if permanently 'out' or if long treatment was needed. For the first time in history peaceful England became accustomed to seeing hospital trains at all hours of the day and night, and to a landscape on which every town and village had its significant tale of convalescing soldiers in their unmistakable light blue uniform. The old country had also become a factory, a hive of industry, and women were working beside men to produce everything required for the war. Never had there been such adaptability, such spontaneity, in rising to every occasion. The Germans tried air-raids; balloon aprons then appeared to protect vital centres. They caused excitement, those raids, but little

Bibury, Arlington Row, Gloucestershire
BTHA

damage; aeroplanes were still in the primitive stage. Airships devised by Count Zeppelin, having a longer range than aeroplanes, were able to raid London and many parts of England; at first almost with immunity, in the end with almost equal certainty of being brought down by fighting planes; and finally to be disposed of in a thrilling episode which all but wiped out the whole fleet of German airships. Although the civil population at home hardly felt the wrath of war, those Zeppelin attacks and the sporadic raids by aeroplanes meant the birth over England of a new form of war: one which then made known to a horrified world that a war of armies could become a war of peoples, for the Zeppelin bombs generally killed civilians, not soldiers. Writing of this in 1922, Liddell Hart said: "The difficulty of distinguishing from the air between military and civil objectives smoothed the path for a development which, beginning with excuses, ended in a frank avowal that in a war for existence the will of the enemy nation, not merely the bodies of their soldiers, is the inevitable target." That seems to have been one of the important long-term lessons of the First World War. The other: that as machines advance in efficiency, there need not be such heavy expenditure in casualties among the infantry and land forces generally. The military casualties in that First World War were appalling. In just over four years Great Britain alone suffered the loss of 744,000 of her best men. Furthermore, "the fall of the birth-rate during the same period—and later owing to the deaths of so many potential fathers—represented a greater loss of unborn casualties: a loss which by the four years following the war equalled the whole of the war losses".[19] The casualties in wounded and disabled were nearly three times the number of killed. Only France, in proportion to the number of her population, suffered more severely than this.

In 1914, England was a rich country with profitable investments all over the world. During the war she did not count the cost of anything which would help to win it, and a great hole was made in her foreign investments. In those days they had not learnt many ways of economizing which ingenuity, driven by necessity, has since then made possible. Apart from this, there was a great lavishness about the 1914 war. In the factories and in the mines wages rose to hitherto unheard-of heights, with inflation all-round. Blood and treasure were fed without stint into the gaping maw of Moloch. The misery and suffering of the men in the trenches during the terrible winter of 1917–1918 was a fierce test of morale for all armies on the Western Front, but the English troops came through it well . . . cursing and grumbling like the others, yet emerging still capable of fight. The main events of 1917 were the entry of the United States into the war and the complete collapse of Russia. Early in 1918 the Germans mounted a great offensive in which they swept the British back at St. Quentin and the French almost to the outskirts of Paris, as in 1914. The last phase of the war was dramatic. Under the brilliant leadership of Foch the allied armies, now supported by battle-fresh American troops, drove the Germans back steadily until their retreat developed into a rout.

On November 11th an Armistice was signed.

The above is a bare and inadequate summary of the events responsible for stripping England of a great part of her monetary wealth, which meant that a very different England was left in 1918 from that of August 1914. At the risk of boring some readers (who, like myself, may dislike or even suspect statistics), a few figures may help to tell that tale more eloquently for others. The 1914–1918 War cost Britain in hard cash the sum of £10,112,000,000—a colossal amount of money for a little island which, throughout that war, could not trade profitably with the rest of the world. England did not borrow much money during the 1914–1918 War: £865 m. from the United States, £184 m. from Canada and £136 m. from France, Russia and Italy. And against this lent £1,665 m. to Allies and Dominions. Her mercantile marine was reduced by enemy submarines—in spite of great war-time building—from 44·81 per cent. of the world's total shipping before 1914 to 35·09 per cent. when the war ended.

No other statistics need be quoted, for, as everybody knows, the very existence of England depended (and still depends) on her mercantile marine, which was not only reduced by the war but during the war outstripped by that of the United States, whose ships were now everywhere. Bad as all these material losses were—most of them irrecoverable—the real loss went deeper. The victory achieved was certainly a great one: a powerful rival had been defeated on land, on sea and in the air.

On July 19th, 1919, an impressive column of nearly 20,000 allied troops marched through London. It represented the fourteen nations whose combined efforts had won the war. The people of England who lined that long route cheered through their tears. There were so many cases of fainting among the often allegedly unemotional English that the ambulance services could not keep count of the number. King George V, in a gay pavilion near the Albert Memorial, took the salute. His Majesty and all who saw were delighted when Foch, Generalissimo of the victorious Armies of the West, rode forward proudly flourishing his Marshal's baton as he came near the saluting-point. That night the sky was filled with fireworks, and there was an enormous illuminated device:

VICTORY: THANKS TO THE BOYS

Victory! It was a sweetly sad victory for England, a sort of Pyrrhic victory. The island and its people had survived. But the cost of survival had been appalling. The England which survived was different from that confident, cheerful England of 1914 before the lights went out over Europe.

2

Interlude between the Two Wars

In spite of the enthusiasm, the great spirit shown by the young men of England, and the determination of the rest of the population, the outbreak of war in 1914 was to most people the negation of everything in which English people had grown to believe. When the war ended, in spite of the appalling losses in blood and treasure, those people manifested an immediate and healthy resilience: they wanted to draw a blind on the whole filthy business and begin afresh to live a life of sanity—one in which the carnage and horrors could be forgotten. Most people felt that they could and must play their part in reconstruction. There was in that post-war

England something of the spirit of a violently disturbed ant-heap, when one sees every member of the insect community rushing to tackle some task which will contribute to the well-being of the whole. It seems to us now that there was surprisingly little of war-weariness. In many directions progress was often slow, but everybody, and even the government, was impatient to get on with the job. The record indicates that, all things considered, fair progress was made. Life resumed an even beat, a quicker one than before 1914, though not quite so hectic as during the war. It was during the early post-war period that a number of sterling platitudes were launched—many by statesmen—which, in one form or another, have proved to be of perennial recurrence since those days of their pristine glory. Some of them related to Soviet Russia, the new and mysterious home of a cult called Bolshevism which nobody then could or would understand, but which, ever since the Russian Revolution of 1917—obscured for the West by the war—had been causing deep misgivings. In April 1919 the brilliant Lloyd George, Prime Minister of Britain, uttered this comforting statement: "Bolshevism is rapidly on the wane. It is breaking down before the relentless pressure of economic facts. You cannot carry on a great country upon rude and wild principles such as those which are inculcated by the Bolsheviks. . . . We cannot interfere, according to any canon of good government, to impose any form of government on another people, however bad we may consider their present form of government to be"; adding that, besides, it would cost too much. How generous were the illusions of that period! At the Peace Conference in Paris the Europeans, with the support of President Woodrow Wilson of the United States, a sincere and high-minded idealist among those leathery cynics, were drawing up what was to be called the Treaty of Versailles: a document which was to sow the dragon's teeth for 1939. In India all sorts of disquieting things were happening, and in Ireland things were going from bad to worse. . . . Well, the less said about that the better!

London suddenly brightened up. It had been a dark and gloomy place during the war, with its black-out and a great decrease in traffic after sundown, not in the least like its own old self. Someone invented the slogan 'Brighter London'; a newspaper made a stunt of it, and the idea caught on. The brightening up of lamp-posts, streets, shops and restaurants changed into something better, something that had long been missing: the spirit of gaiety. And so London became a gay city! Not in the Parisian sense, for London gaiety could not be quite so light as that of Paris, and could hardly be expected to appeal to delicate or highly sensitive souls in search of the more ethereal pleasures. But for the hale-and-hearty good eaters and drinkers who, after a blow-out, liked to see a leg-show with music, that London was your city. And so London filled with visitors from the provinces and from overseas, money was spent lavishly, and if Victorian respectability received shock after shock, some of them shattering, what took its place was often little better than crude vulgarity. It was some years before that phase passed; but it did some good and necessary work, for, really, most people felt that the old country had become too stuffy.

That was the period when the Cassandras wailed that morals were in the melting-pot; as if morals are not always thrown into the melting-pot from the moment war begins, and float on the surface when it ends. It was the period of the Bright Young Things, so delightfully drawn by Aldous Huxley in *Antic Hay* and later by Evelyn Waugh in *Decline and Fall* and *Vile Bodies* which, like some of the Victorian novels, are the best documents for those who would know something of that time and its cheerful seamy side of upper middle-class life. Mr. Stanley Baldwin, an idealized pipe-smoking John Bull, solid, cautious and seemingly naïve, was now the right kind of Prime Minister to cool the political atmosphere after the pyrotechnics of Mr. Lloyd George. The Bright Young Things and modern youth were given a good Press, and, if they scandalized some of their elders, those elders were made to pay for their criticisms by men with literary talent who had survived the trenches. When these writers returned to find themselves forestalled in every sort of compensation by stay-at-homes who had done well out of the war, their bitterness rose in fierce indignation and they flayed their elders unmercifully. This was something new in England, something unheard of for her young men. It rather frightened the elderly, but it gave courage to the young. For a difficult problem had to be faced: the rehabilitation in civil life of five million disillusioned men from the Services.

The return of the soldiers, following the social upheaval caused by the war, meant so great an increase in the Labour vote that the Liberals (whose stock had long been falling) and the Conservatives, who were bewildered by the mass of post-war problems to be tackled, found their strength crumbling. The Labour Party had taken the lead in the Opposition, and Stanley Baldwin's rather somnolent government was not doing too well. In the autumn of 1923 he thought that an election would strengthen the Conservatives, but when it was held on December 6th, he was defeated. His office must go to the Opposition. The Press, nearly all owned by Conservatives, expressed horror. One great daily openly declared that a Labour Government would undermine the Constitution, and failed to see the humour in its demand that King George should on this occasion *ignore the Constitution* and call for the Liberal Mr. Asquith, instead of Labour's Ramsay MacDonald! The British Constitution may be fluid and unwritten, but it is not fickle. The King called for MacDonald, who took office as Prime Minister of the first Labour Government. That was on January 22nd, 1924, a notable date in English history. From then onwards Labour's voting strength steadily increased. The two great political parties from then onwards were Conservative and Labour. They have been so well balanced in numbers that elections usually became exciting political bouts, the electoral system having an element which in certain circumstances resembles pure chance, thus introducing a sporting flavour into English political life.

An important feature of the first Labour Government was that, although it was in office, it was not in power. The gradualness of change had been carefully calculated and arranged beforehand, so it seemed; but there is no convincing evidence of such Machiavellism. Far from proving to be the frightful red revolutionaries some of them were said to be by the Press, the new Labour Ministers, if sometimes lacking in style and as yet inexperienced, proved themselves to be as staunch supporters of King, Constitution, Country and Empire as the best models among the Conservatives. The spirit of England is stronger than any social doctrine.

The repercussions in England of the Wall Street slump in stock prices in the autumn of 1929—part of a general world slump—came at a time when England had recovered a fair measure of prosperity. The economic situation was, to all appearances, much better than it had been for years. Now, world conditions, and especially American conditions, caused an acceleration in the lowering of wholesale prices and production, with great unemployment in Britain. It was a time of serious financial crisis, and England tackled it by forming, in August 1931, a National Government consisting of members of the three political parties, whose main task would be to balance the Budget and save the pound. Events were too great for them: on September 21st the gold standard was suspended and the pound sterling dropped to about 80 per cent. of its par value—a catastrophe which cast a shadow of gloom over the whole country. But the Government, by a series of Draconic measures which struck at everybody, avoided recourse to borrowing; and the pound recovered to steady itself, though well below parity. The powerful national Press, and the news broadcast on the radio, added to the gloom. There could be no disguising the fact that England was again living in a time of crisis.

In the 1930s there was not only the general feeling of economic crisis—a feeling impossible to avoid, what with all kinds of stringencies and a vast and growing mass of unemployed—but once again came a touch of the feeling which some had felt in the pre-1914 period. The fragmentary chronicle need not be continued. One may state baldly that, perhaps for the first time in a century and a half, England felt *unsure* of herself, worried and suffering from a lack of clear and vigorous leadership. To cap everything, there was the disaster of the R101, which was wrecked with fifty-one people aboard fully representing the talents and experience which England had in the construction and navigation of airships. All except three were killed. The largest airship ever made set out from Cardigan on October 4th, 1930, for India by way of France, the Mediterranean and Ismailia. A few hours later she was a mass of twisted metal on a French hillside. In the perspective of war, it was a very minor disaster. In time of peace, and in those circumstances, it shocked the nation and added curiously to the general feeling of depression. . . .

We are still too close to those events to be able to analyse them with detachment. Did we or did we note in the 1930s realize the significance of the rise of Hitler? No doubt the experts did. But the man in the street? Hitler was still rather a joke to him; Mussolini was a clown. Not until the Spanish War of 1936–1938 clarified the position—and gave more than an inkling that from the point of view of Hitler and Mussolini it was the prelude to another world war—did the English begin to realize that they must face another great trial. It came in 1939. That story is so well known and so exhaustively recorded that we shall leap from 1939 to 1945, and look briefly at some of the changes that were caused or hastened by the Second World War, and most deeply affected country and people.

CHAPTER X

THE CONTEMPORARY SCENE: FROM 1945 ONWARDS

1

Austerity Britain: The Welfare State

WHEN the Second World War ended in 1945, the population of England was about 40 millions which, for an area of about 51,500 square miles, means that English people live on a smaller square mileage than any other white community of comparable size in the world. That population is increasing at the rate of nearly half a million a year. The growth of industrialism—and with it of population—in the 19th century brought about a heavy decline in agriculture, so that England ceased to be a country which lived on itself. It paid better to purchase abroad what was required to make up the deficiency in home production of food, and the system worked in the piping days of the great peace which lasted until 1914. The first shock to the system came in the First World War, when the German submarine campaign wrought havoc with British shipping. The second came in the Second World War, when a greatly increased submarine fleet plus a strong air force enabled the Germans to do even greater damage. How Britain survived is a brave story which need not be retold more than to say that, without the help in foodstuffs received from the United States under the Lease-Lend system, it would be a different one. It must suffice to record that when Lease-Lend came to an end, Britain, once again survivor after a life and death struggle, had to face the problem of feeding herself, this time in a world with Europe prostrate and in which prices were rising, shortages increasing, and everything was becoming every day more difficult. It was not long before life had changed from the strict but adequate war-time rationing of food and other commodities to a condition which justified the name 'Austerity Britain'. John Bull had lost flesh; but, if he now had to tighten his belt, he still kept fit and well, and never once showed signs of losing heart.

A Coalition Government—England's political recourse in time of grave crisis—under the inspired leadership of Winston Churchill (1940), with Mr. Attlee (Labour) as Lord President of the Council (Deputy Prime Minister and a sort of political 'Chief of Staff'), had worked together with exemplary smoothness and efficiency during the critical war years. No sooner had hostilities ended (1945) than Mr. Churchill resigned and, in accordance with custom, the country faced a General Election. The electorate voted under an almost universal suffrage. People entitled to vote in modern England are those resident in a constituency on a qualifying date, who, at that date and on the date of the poll, are British subjects of full age and not subject to any defined legal incapacity to vote. All the three great parties—Conservative, Liberal, Labour—fought the election to the full capacity of their resources. This was the first General Election since 1935, and it was highly important for everybody to know how, and how far, opinion had changed throughout the country since the pre-war era. This was the result:

Labour	11,985,733 votes
Conservative . . .	8,693,858 ,,
Liberal	2,253,197 ,,
Others	2,085,605 ,,

These votes returned to Parliament:

Labour Members . . .	393
Conservatives . . .	189
Liberals	25
Others	33

Now, for the first time in history, England had a Labour Government not merely in office but *in power,* and with a generous working majority. It was the most important political event since the first Reform Bill of 1832. A notable feature of the electioneering was that the great Conservative and national leader, Mr. Winston Churchill, showed the energy of a man half his age in a remarkable campaign during which he visited most places of political importance and, with his unbeatable oratory, good humour and his immense personal appeal, besought the people to vote Conservative. He was himself returned to Parliament as Member for Epping, to become Leader of His Majesty's Opposition. The Labour majority surprised a good many people in England, though it was widely recognized that almost inevitably there must be "a swing of the pendulum", the Englishman's philosophical way of regarding a change in political fortune. "The Conservatives have had a good run. Let us see what the other fellows can do." That was the way the result was received, apart from the usual mourning of the losers and their supporters, and the cheering of the winners and theirs. The die was cast. Here was steady old England under a Socialist régime! Foreigners were most surprised by the electoral results. In the United States, where England and the English, I am told, are very often found to be incredibly difficult to understand, the surprise seems to have been greater than elsewhere. The rationale of it all need not be pursued. The supreme importance of that 1945 election and its result was that it prepared the way for an entirely new political experiment: the Welfare State, an essentially English phenomenon. For some years the country was to go its way—at all events in certain directions—in accordance with planning. *Laisser faire* had virtually ended. It was the beginning of a new era in circumstances of great difficulty; and with great handicaps in a topsy-turvy world. It betokened a new phase in England's political evolution.

It was a new era in more senses than one. From the news of the atomic bomb dropped on Hiroshima on August 6th, 1945, the common man learnt something of the meaning of, to him, a hitherto unknown or mysterious power called nuclear physics. In the spate of popular writing on the subject which has since then appeared, it has been quite usual to overlook or gloss the rather important fact that the foundation of the nuclear theory of the atom (the basis of modern atomic physics and the real starting-point of all modern developments in the field, including the bomb) was the work of Ernest Rutherford (1871–1937), a New Zealander who was created an English peer for his great achievement. From the brilliant researches and experiments of Rutherford, Thompson, Soddy and others, in the modest little Cavendish Laboratory at Cambridge, came a corpus of unspectacular discoveries which, in the spirit of Victorian scientists, were freely given to the world: to change the destiny of man. What a story is that of English science! It began with the work of the Anglo-Saxon monk Bede in the 7th century. Then there was Roger Bacon, one of the greatest pioneers of the Middle Ages; and Harvey, who discovered the circulation of the blood; and Newton, author of *Principia* (1687), probably the greatest single book in the history of science; and Newcomen, who first made a steam engine that worked, and thereby taught mankind how to make —engines! Few readers will know the significance of Mr. Street's Patent No. 1983 of the year 1794. In his specification Mr. Street set out his ideas for an 'explosion engine'. The explosion, he explained, "was to be caused by vaporizing spirits of turpentine on a heated metal surface, mixing the vapour with air in a cylinder, firing the mixture, and driving a piston by the explosion produced".[20] That was the first principle of the internal-combustion engine. One hundred years were to pass before Street's idea was taken up energetically, with the result that the first half of our century was to become over the civilized world and on its fringes what in justice could be called Street's Age—the age of vehicles and aeroplanes driven in accordance with ideas first propounded by that obscure Englishman, whose name can mean little or nothing to more than one in a million motorists.

These observations about the past record of English science have a direct bearing on contemporary England, and it is this. Never in the history of the country can there have been a period in which so many English men and women turned their minds towards science and engineering. The record of the past gives hope for the future, especially if considered with other circumstances. The indications are that, in adapting themselves to the changed conditions in the modern world, the English in this post-war period are proving themselves to be as flexible, as progressive and as ready for bold experiments as ever. In mass-production and quantity they cannot and do not try to compete with some other countries. But they keep abreast or ahead in ideas, and this also applies to the quality of many of their products. There is never any knowing when some obscure single-minded English scientist will come forward with a new idea to revolutionize the old, as Baird did with his television, which in a few years changed our whole conception of broadcasting. It is, indeed, the regret of some observers that the concentration on sheer utilitarianism, on technical advancement, on those things calculated to help material progress, has been so great that many of the old cultural and moral values have suffered accordingly. This is probably true; but it is equally true for the rest of the world.

Some of the best efforts of the post-war years sprang from a pooling of ideas on which the Conservatives, Liberals and Labourites had for some time been in general agreement but differed as to ways and means. Education was one of them. Before the war ended, a very comprehensive and enlightened Education Act (1944) was passed. Time was to show up many weaknesses or faults in it, which was only to be expected of such a measure. Since it was first passed, there have been amending Acts, and no doubt there will be more of them. But, in the main, national education had been reviewed, overhauled and in general adapted to the requirements of a new era. The youth of Britain is now reaping the benefits of this great measure, by which the State school system became highly decentralized, with 146 *local* education authorities in 61 administrative counties, 83 county boroughs and 1 joint board, and London. The change came gradually. The age for leaving school was raised to 15; special schools to meet special requirements are allowed for; and a schools' meal service provided for. A very English feature of the system, one which can provide either a check or an impetus, is that of Voluntary Agencies which, as a rule, greatly assist in educational development. A sum of over £300 million is allocated in the annual Budget to help in every branch of the education of young people, with provision for adult and technical education, scholarships, special allowances and a host of amenities that were the dreams of past generations of educationists, so that the English child of to-day can have free education up to the age of 15 and, if ability is shown, up to the stage of a university degree. Some 90 Public Boarding Schools and about 10,000 Private Schools remain independent of the State system, though many Public Schools allocate places to nominees of local authorities. This bald statement merely represents the framework of a vast improvement and wider dissemination in the country's educational facilities. Time will tell the results. A pressing problem of to-day is that of teachers, of which there is a shortage; one partly due to the greater financial attractions in other professions for men and women of the right type and with the necessary qualifications. Yet considering the magnitude of the problem, the system works remarkably well.

Of even greater magnitude, and one of the world's great social experiments, is Britain's National Insurance Scheme embodied in the National Insurance Act of 1946; again, this was based on ideas, old and new, contributed by all parties, with amending Acts since then. Subject to certain exceptions, every person living in Britain over 15 (and under pensionable age) becomes insured and continues so throughout life. Every person, whether employed, self-employed or non-employed—unless exempted, as for lack of income—pays a weekly contribution; if he or she is employed, the employer also pays a contribution. From the central fund benefits accrue to insured persons: the employed contributors benefit when unemployed; sickness, maternity, widowhood, a guardian's allowance, retirement pension and a death grant are included. There is Public Assistance to meet nearly all other cases. In 1950, there were 21 million insured employed persons, 1,400,000 self-employed and half a million non-employed. No attempt can be made to discuss this bold and far-reaching measure, which affects every person in the country from cradle to grave. It is *working*. Years must elapse before it can be fairly judged. Meanwhile, interested people come from many foreign countries to see this new aspect of Britain, the working of the Welfare State. What they do not always realize is that it is still in the evolutionary stage, and that many of its features are always likely to be subjects of controversy, or liable to be modified with a change of the party in power, or to become modified in accordance with experience. Yet there is one thing on which all parties are agreed: National Insurance—on some such basis and in some such framework as those now existing—has come to stay. It represents perhaps the greatest change that has taken place in the social administration of post-war

England. It works remarkably well for mothers and young children who, because of it and the amenities it provides, and because of the modern educational system, are *all* entitled to and receive benefits that were unknown to their ancestors. It is a guarantee for the young generation. Austerity and Welfare have done good work in this respect, it seems to be generally agreed, whatever other criticisms may be brought against them.

2

From Empire to Commonwealth

The title of 'Empress', the reader will remember, was conferred on Queen Victoria in 1876 by Act of Parliament, but only in reference to India. Of all other British possessions she was Queen. Nevertheless, from then onwards the general term 'British Empire' became common, and by the 20th century almost universal, although strictly speaking it was a misnomer and without a place in English law. After the First World War the term 'Commonwealth' began to appear, and all but 'Imperialist' statesmen now spoke of the 'British Commonwealth', which was more pleasing in the atmosphere of the time, and especially to the great self-governing Dominions, Canada and Australia. The Irish of the South—those living in the 26 counties-area which was partitioned from the 6 northern (Ulster) counties after the Anglo-Irish Treaty of 1921—had long been calling for a completely independent Irish Republic. Their Constitution of 1937 declared Ireland to be a "sovereign independent State" with the right to choose its own form of government. As all but a few outstanding problems between England and the Irish Free State had been settled—the English regarding Partition as a matter to be dealt with by the Irish—a Republic of Ireland Act was passed by Parliament in 1948, to come into force in April 1949, by which the English Government retained some control in Irish external affairs but otherwise left everything as the Irish desired. The Southern Irish opted that the Republic of Ireland should remain outside the Commonwealth, and the Northern Irish that their six counties should remain as Northern Ireland and a part of the United Kingdom; a remarkable tribute to the

Coronation Day, June 2, 1953
Photo: Fox Photos Ltd.

ingenuity and powers of compromise on all sides. The centuries-old Irish head and heartache to all intents and purposes now ceased to exist for the English. All the old rancours—apart from Partition—seemed to have disappeared.

India had long presented a vast political problem to England. But even that was solved, and also in a characteristic English way. The Indian Independence Act of 1947 provided that, by agreement, India would remain a full member of the Commonwealth, accepting the English monarch as "the symbol of the free association of its independent member nations and, as such, the Head of the Commonwealth". The Indian Constituent Assembly in November 1949 adopted the Constitution of the Republic of India, and the Republic was formally proclaimed in New Delhi on January 26th, 1950. Here was one more superb piece of compromise. Pakistan remained a separate Dominion which could become a Republic; the former Princely States of India came under a series of flexible and ingenious adjustments which provided for their special circumstances. It is all very complex, but we may sum it up for this purpose by saying that Britain's Indian 'Empire' ceased to exist as such. Instead, that vast territory became an autonomous—and friendly—area within the Commonwealth. Ireland and India for long represented two of England's most difficult political problems, and what remains of their links with London may, in the eyes of some, seem to be of slender strength in comparison with those of the past. But the former bonds depended on force, whereas now there is free partnership. This great readjustment was inevitable, for the days when force could be applied had passed. The political settlements with Ireland and India represented a complete change in outlook on the part of England's rulers. The old power and resources of the pre-1914 era no longer existed, and the new policy for England *had* to be: "Let us save all we can, for we cannot afford to lose any more than we have lost in those two wars." And so, the present is an epoch of political readjustments based on compromises in so far as those territories are concerned in which there are movements in favour of independence or home rule. The basis of readjustment is evolved from a combination of strategic reasons plus an evaluation by the Government in London of whether a given territory has

Yeoman Warders, The Tower of London
BTHA

reached a sufficiently 'advanced' stage in social and political development to justify a measure of self-government. This has taken place with the Gold Coast. It had been tried elsewhere, but the disquieting experience of British Guiana in 1953 weighed with the new and changing state of the world indicated that the end of all these problems was not even in sight. Britain's relations with the Commonwealth remain in a state of perpetual flux, but, in so far as major affairs are concerned, there is on the whole a steady evolutionary policy. Statesmen deal with major problems and civil servants worry out solutions for the minor but often far more difficult local details. The old idea of Empire based on Power has been replaced by that of a Commonwealth based on enlightened self-interest and friendship. To those unacquainted with English political realism and the English logic of politics, the new idea may seem of doubtful practical power-value in comparison with the old. Their arguments are negatived by one fact: that, in a time of world crises, when the Commonwealth is threatened, its various elements quickly form up together like soldiers ready for a call; and, as has been brilliantly demonstrated in both world wars, they work together spontaneously like a well-trained team. If somebody mentions Ireland's neutrality in the Second World War, the answer is provided by the number of Irishmen who voluntarily left Ireland to enrol in Britain's fighting forces. Both Kaiser Wilhelm II and Hitler believed in turn that this 'ramshackle Empire' was finished. They were proved to be mistaken, chiefly because they failed to allow for something which cannot be measured in terms of statistics or depicted in graphs: a common emotional factor which shows itself in action in moments of difficulty.

3

Coronation of Elizabeth II: a Landmark in History

Victoria came to the throne as a mere girl of 18 with a sincere, deeply religious feeling for the responsibilities which devolved upon her as monarch of a great people. She was strong-willed, conscientious and very conscious of the weaknesses of some of her predecessors who had lowered the prestige of the Crown; and she was determined to obliterate them from memory by her own exemplary behaviour. She was not an intellectual woman as Elizabeth I had been, but she had an abundance of common sense and an imperious way with her which exactly suited the people of 19th-century England. She came to the throne when England was enjoying the great peace and was very prosperous; her only enemies were a few scattered Chartists. She had no serious handicaps. Everything was in her favour. These simple facts, considered with her own imposing personality, go a long way towards explaining her outstanding success. In the 20th century, England has been equally fortunate in her monarchs. Not one of them but has been greatly liked by the people, who have become attached to an institution which suits them as becomingly as the crowns fit the monarchs. It remains only to add that in the very critical period from 1910 to 1939 King George V ('The Sailor King') and his unassuming son George VI, by their sincerity, quiet dignity and exemplary public behaviour endeared themselves to the people of the Commonwealth as no monarchs had ever done before. Ever present and invaluable during this period was the strong, wise personality of Queen Mary, George V's impressive wife, who died in 1953 at the age of 86 after a life of great service. When Elizabeth II at the age of 25 succeeded George VI, the prestige of the British monarchy never stood higher.

It seems to me that in the England of our time the monarchy is the most permanent element of feudalism to survive; and it is as a symbol that it survives. But there are many minor survivals of feudalism, and a major one is land law. The minor survivals are mostly represented in the hereditary aristocracy: the peers (941 of them) and the baronets and their cadets (about 12,000). Active political power has passed from this aristocracy, excepting that hereditary peers have a right to sit and vote in the House of Lords, which enables the Upper House to exercise a restraining influence on measures from the Commons of which the peers do not approve. For example, a new Criminal Justice Bill containing a clause for the abolition of capital punishment was submitted to the Lords in 1848, and they deleted this clause. But the percentage of people to whom rank and privilege come by heredity is very small and, as modern taxation makes bigger and bigger holes in private wealth, the position of many in this category tends to become difficult to sustain. For all that, there are public occasions when peers and peeresses, baronets and cadets, turn out in their full panoply, and provide a highly colourful element which is greatly enjoyed by ordinary people. Of these none is more impressive than the coronation of a monarch. A coronation provides a panorama of pageantry, a blending of the old (sometimes of the very remote) with the new such as no longer exists in any other country. The English are not pictorial artists in the sense that the Latins are; but when it comes to pageantry, they are unsurpassed. Of all English pageants, none equals a coronation, and the coronation of Elizabeth II on June 2nd, 1953, was a day to remember not only for one of the greatest pageants of the 20th century, but because it was a landmark in English history. Those who are interested in the full details of the pageantry must refer to the official form and order of the coronation ceremony and to the newspapers of coronation week. Here only those aspects of the event which made it of exceptional importance, a landmark, need be mentioned.

First of all, in this world and its uneasy, disturbed state, with revolution rumbling or happening in vast areas, old régimes falling or threatened, countries in the grip of hysteria or neuroses, or not knowing either how their destiny is shaping itself or how to shape it, here was England not merely going calmly on in her own old way but flauntingly exhibiting—in an almost medieval public pageant—a social phenomenon which, to those unacquainted with its tough nature, must have seemed in its very impressiveness a towering anachronism. That was not how English people saw it, for deep down in the heart of every English person there is a great pride in their way of life and their past, and an unbounded confidence in what is English. *Here was a parade of 'Englishness' in all its glory.* On the occasion of this coronation, hundreds of thousands of people were able to *see* on television the great pageant from beginning to end and exactly as it happened. Millions more saw it afterwards in the cinemas. They loved it; of that there is no doubt. An audience of which the vast number can never be computed heard a broadcast of the event with an intelligent commentary which brought it into their homes. Never had the Press provided so many details, such competent and comprehensive accounts of the event, down to the minutest details; how some lady-in-waiting wore her hair, or how little Prince Charles, in solemn moments in Westminster Abbey, behaved just as an ordinary boy of his age might be expected to behave. The Abbey ceremony was attended by the whole corpus of the nobility in ceremonial robes and bejewelled coronets: in all their magnificence and grandeur. A congregation of 8,000 carefully chosen people packed the Abbey to its uttermost recesses, while the higher dignitaries of the Church of England under His Grace the Archbishop of Canterbury—with Her Majesty the Queen as the central figure—played the principal parts in the ancient ceremonial. It was more like a great film than a play—as if it had been specially conceived in sequences rather than in acts or scenes. It moved in unvaried slowness. The form and order of the coronation service are of interest, not only to historians and antiquaries but to those who take account of literary presentation. The whole can certainly be called a work of art. Early in the service there is a moment of drama when the Archbishop, together with the Lord Chancellor and other important Lords, go to the east, west, north and south of the 'Theatre' (which is so officially described), and the Queen, standing up by Edward the Confessor's 1,000-year-old chair, turning at each point "to show herself unto the People" as the Archbishop says:

> "Sirs, I here present unto you Queen ELIZABETH, your undoubted Queen: Wherefore all you who are come this day to do your homage and service, Are you willing to do the same?"

The text reads:

The People signify their willingness and joy, by loud and repeated acclamations, all with one voice crying out:

GOD SAVE QUEEN ELIZABETH

Then the trumpets shall sound.

The Queen next takes the Oath, the most important part of the ceremony apart from the actual Crowning. She is exhorted to maintain (to the utmost of her power) the Laws of God and the true profession of the Gospel, to maintain to the utmost of her power "the Protestant Reformed Religion established by law", and to "maintain and preserve inviolably the settlement of the Church of England, and the doctrine, worship, discipline, and government thereof, as by law established in England", and to "preserve unto the Bishops and Clergy of England, and to the Churches committed to their charge, all such rights and privileges, as by law do or shall appertain to them or any of them". The Queen replies: "All this I promise to do." The next part of the service is entirely medieval: the Anointing, the Presenting of the Spurs and Sword and "the Oblation of the said Sword", the investing with the Armills, the Stole Royal, the Robe Royal, and the delivery of the Orb. All this takes us back centuries. The Queen then receives "the Ring of kingly dignity, and the seal of Catholic Faith", and receives also the Royal Sceptre, "the ensign of kingly power and justice". This is preparation for the climax, the Putting on of the Crown. The Archbishop takes it from the Dean of Westminster and the text says that he *"shall reverently put it upon the Queen's head. At the sight whereof the people, with loud and repeated shouts, shall cry:*

GOD SAVE THE QUEEN".

After the Crowning comes the Homage: *"all the Princes and Peers then present shall do their Fealty and Homage publicly and solemnly unto the Queen"*. In this, the Duke of Edinburgh ascended the steps of the Throne, and, having taken off his coronet, knelt down before Her Majesty, and placing his hands between the Queen's, pronounced the words of Homage, saying:

> I, Philip, Duke of Edinburgh, do become your liege man of life and limb, and of earthly worship; and faith and truth I will bear unto you, to live and die, against all manner of folks. So help me God.

The remainder of the service is entirely religious and ends

with the National Anthem. Afterwards there was the Queen's drive round London and what in a previous age would have been called a 'procession of Empire', but was now a procession whose elements represented almost every territory in the Commonwealth. There was even another Queen in it: Queen Salote of Tonga, a delightful lady whose good-humoured personality stole thunder and won the hearts of Londoners. Alas! —there was one element which could not be caught in the grip of the perfect official organization, that element which, on so many great occasions, evokes the curses of the best organizers in this country: the English weather! During the procession it rained 'cats and dogs'. Good Queen Salote did not shelter herself: in her open carriage during the downpour she kept smiling, waving her hand to the multitude, which was delighted. Sir Winston Churchill's coach found itself in a slight mix-up in which vehicles got two abreast. Fearing greater disorganization, he ordered his coachman to the roadside to let others pass. When he continued, he found he was following behind the Royal Coach, that part of the procession being the Queen's place of honour. He pulled out of the route and drove home to Downing Street.

The great day ended with fireworks and bonfires. A new monarch had been crowned and every one of us had learnt some history.

The coronation of Elizabeth II is a landmark not only because it was the first coronation *seen* by millions as well as by those present—thanks to television and to colour-photography in the cinema—but because in the year 1953 it represented a sort of English proclamation to the rest of the world that, whatever may be happening *there,* England fully intended to pursue her own English way. Foreign visitors returned home greatly puzzled by many things, not the least being that the English continued to remain *very* English! One has only to have experienced Coronation Day to realize how superficial all things are in England that are not English. In their treatment of the event, radio and cinema drove this home with such cogency that the mere Man in the Street felt a rising pride; possibly due to a perception that he simply must differ from other mortals in this mechanized and regimented world, if only because he is of a people who master the illogical in life. The illogicalities, incongruities and paradoxes of Coronation Day seemed quite natural to him. The fact that here was a ceremony, most of it medieval, mostly in medieval costume but in electric light and conditioned atmosphere, with television cameras turned on the centre point of drama, radio commentators broadcasting to the whole world in many languages their accounts of what was happening; yet none of this would strike him as anything but natural. The curious mysticism of it was absorbed with the realism. No astonishment was evoked by the fact that most of those people dressed up in wonderful costumes, some of which dated from Anglo-Saxon times, would drive off home in modern automobiles. It would not strike the average person that the Queen's title of 'Head of the Commonwealth' is not logical if one thinks of the Republic of India, or that it stretches political flexibility beyond the bounds of reason to have a monarchical title which will allow for almost any sub-régime that may appear, whether it be republic or realm. Or that an Earl Marshal who is a Roman Catholic should not only participate but even officiate in proceedings which involve a severe and unmistakable discrimination against the Church of Rome. Or that the solemn, traditional rite—the oldest of its kind to function in mid-20th century—should be sufficiently adaptable to meet the political and social requirements of the moment. Visitors from abroad were astonished that in 1953, and in such a world as this, it could be possible to witness such an extraordinary national manifestation as that coronation ceremony, with its medievalism, and that whole pageant of paradoxes and breath-taking illogicalities. To English people it was all as acceptable and as deeply appreciated as what Lewis Carroll has put into words for us in *Alice in Wonderland* and *Through the Looking-glass*.

4

Conclusion

If I were asked to name in order the outstanding characteristics in the nature of the English, I should put first their love of stability. Next, I should say their remarkable capacity for dealing with the confusions and illogicalities of life. For the third, I should suggest their curious genius for turning almost any kind of defeat into victory. They are also world masters of empiricism. Permanent and ever-present as a flavouring to these characteristics is the quality of humour, and mostly good-humour. Some excellent observers—English and foreign—regard their humour (and with it good-humour) as the outstanding characteristic of the English people, but I prefer to regard it as a curious general quality which characterizes them rather than as their outstanding characteristic: a quality which pervades rather than dominates their other characteristics and gives these a flavour which nobody ever succeeds in defining or explaining, but which is easily illustrated. It is altogether an 'imponderable' in their character. And it is found on all sides and in all circumstances, proving itself in adversity to be remarkably effective as a mainstay of sanity and level-headedness. To say of an English person that he or she is humourless indicates a very low mark of esteem. The term 'bad-humoured' is almost the equivalent of 'ill-natured'. 'Good-humoured', then, we may take as 'good-natured' and a little more. Nobody who knows them well can doubt that the English are good-humoured, and a people with a sense of humour that is their own and unique.

I leave it to others to list for themselves the less desirable qualities, and only add that the most hostile of foreign writers have never yet succeeded in presenting the misdeeds and failings of the English with half the power that is shown by these people in dealing with themselves. From the pages which have gone before the reader will form conclusions in regard to qualities to which I have not specifically drawn attention or even mentioned, and if the story told makes no attempt to define many qualities, it is, quite frankly, because they are better left to inference. It can reasonably be claimed that foreigners acknowledge the English to be a practical people, but find it difficult to believe that they can also be quixotic, idealistic and very sentimental. The announcement of the great achievement of (now Sir) Edmund Hillary and Sherpa Tenzing in climbing Mount Everest [21] came as a climax to Coronation Day. From the moment the news was received, it shared importance with the stirring event at home. Edmund

Hillary and John Hunt were immediately knighted by the Queen. They were national heroes of the kind England loves, the English ideal of what their manhood should be—modest, unassuming, cool-headed, brave and capable of taking great risks, and in a matter of sport quite unspoiled by the cash motive. It is impossible to find a wholly satisfactory way of 'analysing' the English people. They cannot be docketed and pigeon-holed with any sort of accuracy. It is safer to be content with a picture which is incomplete—because it can never be completed—rather than attempt the impossible in regard to the highly problematical.

The English are the most peacefully inclined people in the world to-day, and if one looks for a motive it can be found in enlightened self-interest. But it is as well to remember at the same time that they are survivalists who do not know the meaning of the word defeat. As these lines are written, the Englishman hopes that the world will leave him in peace, for he feels confident that, granted this condition, he can contribute something of great value to a troubled world and continue to achieve great things—as in the past.

PART II

SEEING ENGLAND

There is no countryside like the English countryside for those who have learned to love it: its firm yet gentle lines of hill and dale, its ordered confusion of features, its deer parks and downland, its castles and stately houses, its hamlets and old churches, its farms and ricks and great barns and ancient trees, its pools and ponds and shining threads of rivers, its flower-starred hedgerows, its orchards and woodland patches, its village greens and kindly inns. Other countrysides have their pleasant aspects, but none such variety, none that shine so steadfastly throughout the year.

H. G. WELLS.

CHAPTER I

INTRODUCTORY

I

Some General Observations

WHEN I had lived for ten or twelve years in England, I used to think that I knew the English fairly well. Now, having been here for nearly forty years, I often wonder whether I know anything whatever about them; that is, when something unexpected shows itself in their character or behaviour, which happens almost every day in the week. I have been able to confirm what many better men discovered: that in dealing with this country and its people it is not safe to take anything for granted. You must not ever assume that you are dealing with the 'average' English person—for even if such a person exists, he or she would be difficult to find. It is best to regard each one separately as a distinct individual, and individualist. Perhaps the most important thing I have learnt is this: that although it is feasible to draw up from observation and experience a list of pointers to character that are in most cases not far off the mark, there is in almost every English person *the unknown factor*: a surprise element which may rarely have an opportunity of showing itself but which on occasion—in an emergency and when there is some urgent need for it—can rise with uncanny speed and prove some very modest-looking person to be capable of soaring to unexpected heights; or, it may well be, of sinking to astonishing depths. The point I would make and emphasize is that the ordinary English person is seldom ordinary.

It may well be that this mysterious quality is responsible for the fact that no country on earth has produced such a list of notable eccentrics, of men and women who have done extraordinary things and often for no apparent reason at all except the pleasure enjoyed in doing them. You can pick up any English newspaper or periodical in the certainty of finding examples. I do so as I write and—here we are!—can immediately quote the following: "The remark was recently made by Lord Jowett that if potato-growing in Peru came up for discussion in the House of Lords, one of their lordships would be discovered to have spent his youth planting potatoes in Peru. This phrase embodies an interesting aspect of the British character, which is that it has always manifested (in all ranks of society) an extraordinary capacity to throw up individuals who make themselves experts in some particular branch of scientific or cultural activity, or who become supreme authorities on one foreign country or another, often in remote parts of the world. Britain produces its experts, its eccentrics, male and female, its collectors and its scholars, in every generation by the score. Vice-Consul Coverley, who on his own account collected and collated over a period of twenty years, for the benefit of the Natural History Museum in South Kensington, every scrap of information concerning wolves in the province of Traz-os-Montes (what foreigner would do such a thing?), was a minor example of the national versatility." [1]

We must always allow for the existence of this baffling and ever-present element. But there are many other almost equally interesting facets to English character which need never fail to provide material for comment and speculation. In Part I, I have endeavoured to draw a sketch of history with commentary which lays emphasis on those racial and other elements which in their own curious way must needs have been the soil and roots that produced what, for want of a better word, we call Englishness. The mixture of unruly, intuitive Celt with the stolid Germanic and self-confident Norman, together with a sense of values due to the nature and circumstances of life in an insular environment, may account for many things which otherwise seem inexplicable. Why is it, one may ask, that for centuries the English have been suspicious of almost every religious or political way of thinking which restricts freedom of thought? We can trace at least one reason for it to William the Conqueror, who seems to have planted the idea. William did not like anything that threatened his power or that of the Norman ascendancy, and in his time Rome and Roman Catholicism represented not only a supra-national spiritual power but one which demanded and was accorded great deference in matters that were purely secular. William asserted himself in regard to the latter, and expressed a distaste for the restricting dogma and ultramontane claims which impinged upon what he regarded as his own province. His attitude towards the then all-powerful Church was, with certain exceptions, that of the English people and their rulers afterwards, and especially since the reign of Henry VIII. Loyalty to dear old England takes precedence over loyalty to religion or political group! When the moment of test comes, England has the first call. In regard to such systems as Russian Communism, or indeed any rigid formula for life or thinking, the English have always preferred their own way, however illogical it may seem to others, being completely convinced that the empirical method suits them best. In this they seem to be quite unshakable.

There is often something about talking with English people which the stranger may not at first understand. Americans are usually frank and outspoken in conversation; the French regard it as an opportunity for sallies of intellectual exhibitionism, of wit and wisdom leading up at the end of each phase to a definite *quod erat demonstrandum* as if it were a theorem in Euclid; to the Irish it provides a God-sent occasion for verbal posturing, for producing a wonderful spate of words, and often for entertaining self-dramatization. But to your Englishman a conversation, especially with a stranger, is often merely an opportunity—providing always he is sufficiently interested—for finding out the exact nature of that other person, for weighing him up, 'getting his full measure', and, at the same time, of covering over his own nature so well that, when the conversation is finished, the chances are that the other fellow knows little or nothing about the pleasant, polite and apparently very naïve islander. The stranger is faced with a human reservoir from which he can draw very little. In this I naturally except the conversations of old friends, and refer particularly to that which takes place on a first meeting, or until the English person and the stranger have got to know each other (or at least until the English person knows the stranger!). There is no more amusing or more instructive game than observing this matter of conversation. In the long run the stranger will not find a better way of studying the English, among whom the apparently simple person, one at last discovers, is not nearly so simple as he or she seemed to be. The stranger quickly becomes familiar with and appreciates Welsh exuberance, Scottish intellectualism and the Irish gift for telling a tale. But it usually takes some time to realize that, when the Englishman talks, he very often talks behind a mask. He is reticent and economical with words, and to strangers he is rarely his full natural self. The moment he finds that he is letting himself go or giving way to some emotional feeling, he will consciously pull himself up. There is no such thing as the deliberately set 'poker-face': the Englishman has never any need to affect such a face, for Nature provides him with a serious, good-humoured, fixed countenance behind which his real thoughts are perfectly concealed. And with all this, he is usually very alert, seldom misses any point that really matters to him, and he has a natural gift for sorting grain from chaff and at the same time seeing what is behind the other person's words. To sum up: until you know him well (which you will never do unless he wants it) he is not an easy person to understand; and if he really does not wish you to understand him fully, he can draw the wool over your eyes as neatly and with as great art as Providence itself. I trust that in saying all this I have not conveyed the impression of a cold, calculating being who has always something to conceal, something to hold back. It is not that. It is merely that, until he knows you well and feels that he can trust you, the Englishman remains on his guard. But once he knows you and trusts you, you will find that in the great human values he can be the equal of the man of any other race or country. If he can be a very dangerous enemy, he can also be a very good and genuine friend. In using the term Englishman, I include also the Englishwoman; for her qualities tend to be similar.

Let nobody ever imagine that the English are a cold people incapable of frankly, openly and enthusiastically expressing their emotions. It is doubtful whether excitable France or extrovert Italy has ever known anything to equal, for example, the release of emotion shown by the English after (to take an instance) the signing of the Armistice at the end of the 1914–1918 War. The lid went right off the moment the population

BTHA

Windsor Castle

For 850 years the principal residence of English sovereigns

BTHA

Tom Tower, and Christ Church College, Oxford

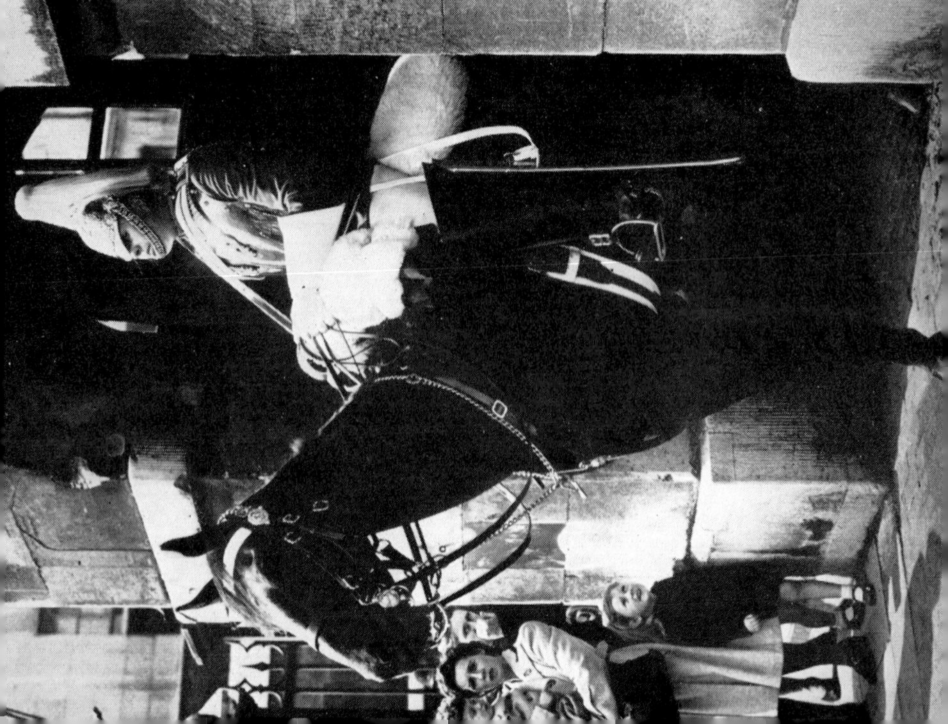

knew that the terrible war had ended. Millions of people dropped everything they were doing, and for days they went good-humouredly and relievedly mad. In Trafalgar Square, the sentimental centre of the Empire (with which can be counted Leicester Square and nearby Piccadilly), a dense crowd gathered and people remained there shouting, singing and letting themselves go for all they were worth. An attempt was made to leave a passage for vehicles, for automobiles, omnibuses and taxis. But when a vehicle appeared, its top was covered with girls and youths, who stood there just yelling themselves hoarse. Bowler hats worn by the staid, the official and the merely pretentious were seized by the more rumbustious and kicked like footballs all over the place. Men, and sometimes women too, got hilariously tipsy; on every side there were comic incidents or practical jokes which raised laughs but never a word of anger. Bald-headed men came in for it: in the restaurants they had their shiny pates kissed by the bibulously exuberant. They did not mind, and often embraced those who made fun of them. The police joined in the fun. They often lost their helmets; at least one officer lost his trousers and ran off—laughing! Considering the madness which was let loose, the number of arrests for being drunk or disorderly was negligible; and for serious disorder—nil. That Armistice occasion was certainly exceptional, an extreme case. But hardly a year passes that London does not witness the same sort of exuberance on a lesser scale: for example, after a football cup-final, when we see the winners' partisans letting themselves go in 'good old English style'. It is a mistake to think, as Froissart and others have written, that the English *always* take their pleasures sadly.

Nor are they incapable of the deeper emotions. To exemplify this, I need only mention the passing and funeral of the late King George V. History will tell whether he was a great king; but few English monarchs have been better liked by the population of England. George V was a simple, kindly man who devoted his whole life and thoughts to his job. His job was his duty, and so he regarded it. Furthermore, he knew his job thoroughly. He had been a professional sailor and acquired the hearty bluntness, the easy quality of give-and-take which sailors have. His broadcasts to Britain and the

The Horn Blower of Ripon, Yorkshire
BTHA
Life Guard, Whitehall, London
BTHA

Commonwealth no doubt contained items which ministers persuaded him to insert for this or that political purpose. But I understand that he wrote the scripts himself, for no politician, civil servant or court official could ever have achieved just that personal touch which was unmistakably his. They were written in excellent English, in the noble diction which springs from sincerity, integrity and deep feeling. I have heard distinguished critics assert that his broadcasts are as well written as anything in our time. After hearing one of George V's broadcasts the listener could only say: "That is a good man." When the King's end came, it did not come suddenly. As he lay dying the people were told by the British Broadcasting Corporation's most impressive announcer: "The King's life is moving peacefully towards its close." The nation was hushed, and when the final announcement was made, the man in the street felt not only sad but that he had lost a friend. Whoever decried or underestimated the political significance of the deep emotion which then swept over England would be a fool. It was genuine. It could not have been artificially created, and it was probably more deeply felt among the humbler elements of the population than among the rich or the sophisticated. And it was general, without a discordant note. Its significance for the future of the monarchy rests on the fact that it represented the popular goodwill. Monarchy at its best is to-day a strongly challenged institution the world over; some great nations have decided that it is outmoded. But the English monarchy is unlike all others, for, in terms of political reality, England is a unique sort of republic with an hereditary monarchy taking the place of an elected presidency. The English Constitution is far more flexible, more elastic than that of any existing republic; it is, for example, much easier under its working for an English king to be removed from the throne than for the President of the United States of America to be removed in accordance with the rigid terms of the American Constitution. Hence the English monarchy depends for its continued existence entirely on the goodwill which it creates and maintains. It was never stronger than at the death of George V. Whatever one's ideas about monarchy as an institution may be, there can be no gainsaying that, politically, the English monarchy is in a very strong position. One cannot think of contemporary England without taking it into account.

If I were asked to give my opinion as to the dominant characteristic of the English, I should give this answer: love of STABILITY. They are a stable people, or try hard to be, in almost everything; and although they rarely refer to it, they worship stability in most of its forms but especially in regard to matters of government and everyday social life. They would rather have it than money. Stability is the lake into which all English rivers flow. In certain things this is self-evident and does not require explanation, but there are far more in which it is not so apparent. Some of these I shall attempt to deal with.

If you are not English, and especially if you should happen to be Irish—foreigners believe that all the Irish hate the English, which is simply not true—you will hardly fail in your travels to meet people who speak of 'English Hypocrisy' as if it were something that can be taken for granted like English roast beef, or level-headedness or love of cricket. I have always been rather amused to hear this jibe, having discovered long ago that what the foreigner regards as hypocrisy in the Englishman is seldom true hypocrisy, but usually something quite different and often far more subtle. It may seem a little far-fetched when I say that it can even be a form of protective shell which helps the English people to make life what it is in this country, and acts as an aid to stability. I try to explain somewhat as follows. Hypocrisy means acting a part to deceive somebody, and it can include pretence, dissimulation or the simulation of virtue or goodness where it does not exist. Consider these carefully and you will find that they are attributes common to mankind in general; that few people of any race or creed are entirely free from them; and that they need not necessarily be based on evil motives. The English share in the weaknesses of their fellow-men, as most of them will admit. What usually is taken for hypocrisy in the English is more often than not a kind of aloofness springing from that feeling of superiority which a people long accustomed to being members of a great empire, of a 'ruling race', acquire from the cradle and, unless rudely awakened, take with them to the grave. The Romans had it, so also had the Normans, the

Spaniards, the French; the Americans are not losing time about acquiring it, and possibly the Russians also. It tends to make a people 'put on airs', to deceive themselves; and, naturally, it is resented by others. But 'putting on airs' is surely not hypocrisy! Furthermore, however much the English may have suffered before 1914 from this chicken-pox of all imperialisms, one does not now often encounter the malady. It has been fairly thoroughly eliminated from the mentality of the younger generation. There are other ways of the English that are called hypocrisy which, on scrutiny and analysis, also prove to be something else. For example, there is that sometimes infuriating attitude of utter indifference which the Englishman will strike when confronted with what the foreigner may regard as something extremely unpleasant which should deeply affect the islander. Again, this is not really hypocrisy. It is merely using a protective shell, and it comes back to the desire not to be ruffled or disturbed in any way—to our old friend love of social stability, for which anything will be by-passed or ignored. I shall quote just one example of what has been mistaken for hypocrisy but usually has something else behind it. A cultured West Indian Negro describes [2] how it works in practice: "In the United States of America, the Negro is plainly told where he is not wanted. He is segregated into certain quarters, has his own schools and universities, and eats in his own restaurants. A British Negro, for instance, landing in New York will go immediately to Harlem to find living quarters. But a coloured student coming to London may telephone an hotel, and being assured that the rooms are vacant will hurry round to the address. Imagine his feelings when a surprised clerk or landlady discovers that he is not white! Shamefacedly they will declare that it was all a mistake; that, after all, there are no vacant rooms. Or else, merely annoyed at having to waste time, they will bang the door against his nose. Few Negroes in England, I imagine, have not passed through the bitter experience of looking for apartments and being told constantly: 'We do not take coloured people.' . . ." The writer prefixes his statement with the comment: "Colour disaffection in England is of a peculiar type and largely hypocritical." He must forgive me when I say that it is not hypocrisy that is at work here but plain commercialism. The hoteliers and landladies in question are merely afraid that the presence of Negroes may drive away custom that is otherwise assured; their motives are entirely pecuniary. But enough of hypocrisy. There is too much of it everywhere, and every country has its own particular brands of this unpleasant attribute.

Among the great bulwarks of stability is religion, which for the majority is represented by the Church of England; that is, the Anglican Communion, in America called the Episcopal Church. In Part I there is a brief account of how the Anglican Church came to be established. This Church is a great national institution, but religion is something that is either not spoken of in England—it is regarded as every person's own and very private affair—or it appears publicly in the form of pageantry. The Coronation Service—broadcast and televised for the first time in history in 1953 on the coronation of Queen Elizabeth II—was certainly a religious ceremony; but to the public it was just a magnificent pageant. No doubt many people were impressed by the religious element in it; everybody enjoyed it as a pageant.

I doubt whether anybody has claimed for England that it is or ever was a 'religious' country; there has never been a 'Holy England' as there once was a 'Holy Ireland'. The English are not greatly inclined towards mysticism, though they are most certainly capable of deeply religious feeling and of feeling religious. There seems to survive in the English some strain of remote Celtic, Anglo-Saxon or possibly Scandinavian paganism from which springs the average man's desire to have More Gods than One, the desire to be mentally independent, and other curious phenomena including the Nonconformist conscience. For centuries Roman Catholics suffered from grave disabilities in this country. But is there anywhere in the world, other than England, a country in which Protestant divines (such as Sydney Smith, Canon of St. Paul's in London) actively campaigned for the abolition of Catholic disabilities? There can surely be no religious toleration anywhere to equal that existing in England. Incidentally, the Catholic disabilities have so far disappeared, and Catholics and Protestants get on so nicely together that the very English Cardinal Griffin, Catholic Archbishop of Westminster, could be present at the

Coronation of Queen Elizabeth and hear her take the solemn oath to do the utmost in her power to "maintain in the United Kingdom the Protestant Reformed Religion established by law" and the rest of that unequivocal passage, which is the measure of the exceptional protection accorded to the Church of England. It begins with the monarch, is supported by Lords, Commons and, it may reasonably be claimed, by the people in general. But this is political rather than religious. Again it comes back to the desire for political stability, for if there is one thing that the English have learnt by bitter experience, it is that nothing can cause greater disturbances than religion, especially when used for a political end. A man's religion is his own affair. Hence, in conversation it is never even discussed! The unwritten law of the English pub is: *No religion.* Religion, in other words, is kept severely in its place and, outside strictly religious communities, there is no such thing as even an attempt to allow it to permeate everyday life. Sunday is a day of worship for those who care to go to church; the number seems to have been declining since the First World War. The others behave like pagans and worship a variety of gods of their own choice, from gardening (Nature Worship) to Walking, from Sports to just having a good read of the delectable Sunday newspapers, and an afternoon snooze in an arm-chair in front of a cheerful fire in winter or in the open air in summer. The Sunday practice of nine-tenths of the population is just relaxation and recovery from the cares and grind of the other days. The phenomenon of crowded churches on Sundays, such as exists in the United States and elsewhere, is now rarely found in England. As a political cement, however, the State Church is as strong as ever. To change the metaphor, the Church of England acts as a gyroscope to keep the ship of State on an even keel.

Since I first thought of 'stability and love of stability' as the master-key to English character, I have considered in that light what some distinguished foreign commentators have said about our islanders. The more I study the vagaries of the English which those commentators have recorded, often very wittily, the more I find that they stem from that same desire to 'keep life on an even keel', to evade or by-pass troubles great and small, and even to avoid being ruffled by the petty annoyances of life, including the many trying and, we hope, ephemeral frustrations that have followed the Second World War. Our commentator [3] writes of the English as having a 'Ritualistic Conception of Life', and I find it relevant. He says: "Eating and drinking, love-making, and perhaps even the sexual act, clothes, the choice of reading and the organization of pleasure, the manner of spending a holiday and of killing time in a seaside boarding-house, conversation, taste, building, and the intercourse between human beings, and between human beings and animals, are regulated by ritual. . . ." And later he adds shrewdly: "The advantage of ritual is that it makes *all things function with perfect smoothness.*" Precisely. And why does the Englishman want to make all things function smoothly? Because, I answer, he likes stability in life! It is, I think, as simple as that—though many will say that there's more in English behaviour than the mere desire for stability. Of course there is. I am a believer in what the French historian Marc Bloch calls "the solidarity of the ages", and have found that, when the living seem puzzling, they can often be explained by a clarification of something that they have inherited from the dead, by something which they are conserving, perhaps for reasons they may not themselves know. In this sense, the English are a 'conservative' people, and I do not mean by this that they are all subscribers to the Conservative Party, but merely that when there is something which has worked fairly well in the past, and has pleased them, they much prefer it to something new. They will hold on to it, even when it may have become outmoded. And if a change simply must be made, it is achieved by a process of peaceful evolution and not by violent revolution. To maintain the stability of life, they will often retrace steps they have already taken. This curious conservatism or, as I prefer to call it, desire for stability, shows itself in all the political parties, none of which is in the least revolutionary. It has its symbols in everyday life, and some of them may surprise the foreigner. One of these is the bowler hat, which our American friends call the Derby. It went rather out of fashion during the Second World War, but there is a steady campaign to bring it back, and it seems to be again increasing in favour, though in a slightly different sense from that which formerly prevailed.

The old symbolism is fading. Until that war, the bowler hat was the male's everyday symbol of *respectability*, of respect for law and order, of English stability. It used to be worn by nearly all 'office' classes and by professional men, ranging from august members of the great London clubs down to minor civil servants, municipal officials, and in general the less spectacular membership of the upper and lower middle class, the 'white-collar' section of the population. Bowler hat and umbrella are still affected by those men who wish to impress others!

Nothing is more extraordinary than the English gift for what they themselves call—and with pride!—'muddling through'. It shows itself on the grand scale in wars. And the reason the English are so proud of it is because it enables them to pass off errors good-humouredly and to take credit without need for boasting, the Englishman's pet horror. On the rare occasions when it seems called for, boasting is achieved in silence by a look of modesty, a gentle smile of self-satisfaction or, in extreme cases, by a telling little gesture and a 'There you are!' attitude. There is something very human about showing pride in 'muddling through', for it is a perfect example of how the proud English person refuses to over-estimate ordinary values in a realization of man's weakness as God made him. It indicates a refusal to take personal credit for what may be—and quite rightly in his estimation—the working of Providence in his favour. Of course, those who have had the opportunity of witnessing and studying how this apparently nonchalant 'method' of muddling through works in times of great crisis are not always convinced that it is largely attributable to good luck. No specimens of *homo sapiens* have a more remarkable capacity for dealing with a real danger than the English when they have to face it. Then they act as if guided by a collective instinct like that of a good sports' team showing its best form. Logic is applied, sometimes an astonishingly brilliant logic, but it is cast aside when it seems that pure opportunism would be better. The logic of events is never accepted when it indicates that, by all the rules, the battle is as good as lost. The English, I have heard it said, are too stupid ever to know when they are beaten in battle. What an error of judgment this is! The English know better than anybody the curiously advantageous effect which a victory over them can have on an enemy; and that sooner or later he will show weakness, and by then their own wits will enable them to shoot ahead and outflank him in some way which they may not know in the moment of defeat, but which they are quite sure they will one day find. This comes down to depending on that form of will-power which is sometimes called obstinacy. They have a gift for keeping the other fellow guessing, for not showing their hands, and for rapid and original improvisation to meet difficult situations. All this is governed by cool-headedness and a courage that will face any odds. If a defeat is experienced, it is not regarded as defeat but as a round in a game, and in which there will be a 'return match'. That this is not a superficial interpretation of the English attitude towards warfare, for example, is proved by the words of that great soldier Field-Marshal Lord Wavell, who (when dealing with the old question: Is warfare an art or a science?) said that warfare might be both but was *most aptly comparable to a game*. In other words, the personal and collective qualities which the people bring into play in warfare are similar to those that almost every male and female has developed in games at school; when they grow up, the spirit that was engendered remains. If anyone should wish to have a perfect example of how this works out in practice, he must read the story of the Battle of Britain in the Second World War. That was a case in which not only the individual fighters of the Royal Air Force, but their ground forces, and especially the civil community behind them, showed an extraordinarily powerful collective instinct which enabled them to do the right things—very unexpectedly for the enemy!—and thus achieve victory when the odds were heavily against them. Apart from the heroic combats and brave aerial achievements, the Battle of Britain is worth study for the many lessons it teaches of the national psychology. Among other things it showed the sinewy nature of England as a society: the collectivity of persons, each of them a full and free individual, being ready to act and react powerfully and in similar ways depending on circumstances. When that society was threatened, the collectivity acted as one man. No special training was necessary. Games and the way of life had already provided it in the main essentials.

The reader will forgive me if I leap suddenly from so important an aspect of English character to one which some may think has no importance whatever: English snobbery. The snob is accurately described in the *Shorter Oxford Dictionary* as a person who has an exaggerated respect for social position or wealth, and a disposition to be ashamed of socially inferior connexions, to behave with servility to social superiors and judge merit by externals. They are not likeable attributes. Nevertheless, I do not always find the English snob unlikeable; he can be quite engaging and is often very amusing. Hypocrisy, I have read, is produced by social conformity as applied to character; snobbery by social conformity as applied to behaviour. I do not attach importance to these analyses, for there are so many kinds of snobs that they do not always apply; there are snobs which completely defy analysis. Most forms of English snobbery are, I am happy to say, without the slightest element of malice. I can record an authentic instance of Irish snobbery of a nature which simply could not happen in England. The elderly mother of a middle-class 'gentleman' noticed that their housemaid, a young girl from the hills, was pregnant. Inquiry elicited from the girl the statement that mama's beloved son was the male responsible. When he came home that evening, his mother tackled him and he acknowledged the fact. Whereupon the mother said: "You must marry the girl." He agreed, the couple were married, and moved off to a home of their own. When they had settled in, the gentleman told his new wife that she must continue to keep her housemaid's place as before: that she must not show herself otherwise than as a servant when anyone called on him; and she must eat her meals in the kitchen, while he ate his in the dining-room. And so it was. That is an abominable piece of snobbery with an element of malice in it, and I quote it merely as an example of what could *not* happen in England. For the Englishman would either marry the girl and abide by the social consequences in the realization, or at least hope, that his friends would understand and forgive him because of his chivalrous act; or he would refuse to marry and pay up; or, if a cad, just clear off. But there would never be any malice in his attitude. And so it is with all English snobbery, which is usually unconscious and nearly always harmless. We see examples of it all around us: in the Press, on the news-reels and on television, or hear it on the radio. And nobody is a bit the worse for it, or regards it other than as a common element in everyday life. The intellectual snobs laugh at other snobs; the other snobs laugh at them. Royalty and what remains of the old aristocracy provide impetus, and so we find such newspaper headlines as: "Peer's cousin in motor-car accident." The newspapers seldom miss a legitimate opportunity of making these far-fetched associations; and nobody notices anything incongruous about the using of the word 'royal' to describe a filly. Putting on an artificial 'Oxford' accent (which invariably gives itself away to the trained ear) is quite common and a favourite way of conveying the idea that the speaker is 'upper class' or at least a person of university education. And there is the snobbery of the Old School Tie. Those who have been to a 'first-class' Public School may wear its tie on certain occasions; but they rarely parade it. It is the bogus or third-class Old Public School Man who most often affects it. All but the most simple-minded will know perfectly well that he is wearing it to make an impression of good upbringing. Nobody minds, and there is even a certain amount of sympathy with so praiseworthy an attitude! The great aim of the snob is to convey the idea that he—or she, for there are as many females as males—is a person of some social status. The English respect social status, and as individuals rather fear it when it is above their own. Therefore, it is rare that this type of snob is challenged, especially if he or she should be quite a pleasant or, at least, a harmless citizen. A favourite form of snobbery is an affectation for certain animals and a dislike of others. Some snobs prefer dogs to cats, perhaps because they can imperiously command the dog to do this or that in the certainty of obedience, whereas self-respecting cats will give them a wide berth the moment they attempt any sort of bossiness. But there is cat-snobbery also. Then there is the horse-snob, the type of man who may never have been on a horse's back but knows all about horses and horsemanship. What he doesn't know about possible or certain winners and their points isn't worth knowing! Some of these forms of snobbery are easy of achievement. Others require as much time and effort to attain the desired perfection as would a liberal education. Manners, speech, walk, tone of voice, taste in clothes and personally adopted formal airs and graces all require study—and constant alertness in everyday use—if our snob is to be satisfied that he has achieved, at least in his own imagination, the ideal in social status at which he has aimed. The foreigner will meet many such men and women in England, and it may take him half a lifetime to be able to tell them from the real thing. English people usually have keen social noses which sense the harmlessly bogus as it approaches, and they know the real thing a mile off. Umbrage is never taken at the harmless snob. The true aristocrat, becoming rarer every day, is respected—"The English dearly love a lord"—and royalty has an elevation of its own in public esteem. The snob, if he behaves well, can even command the respect of many. For, strange though it may appear, in England even snobbery can play its little part in maintaining social stability. Hence, unless it is of the malicious sort, it is regarded with tolerance, and accepted by all classes as an element in the national pattern.

I feel that if I continue this attempt to convey some ideas of English attributes and characteristics, I may confuse the reader, lead him into a state of bewilderment rather than of enlightenment: a risk which must always be run by whoever attempts to write about a subject on which few of us can ever agree. A disconcerting feature of this country is that, although tolerant towards the stranger almost to the point of indifference, and probably the European country which makes fewest efforts to attract and fix the attention of other peoples, whatever their nationality or relationship may be, *it is the most difficult of all to explain.* It is always rather a mystery, even to the English themselves. For, as well as the recognizable quantities and qualities, there is an infinite number that are vague to the point of being indefinable. I see that in my notebook I have jotted down that the Englishman is disciplined, conservative, reserved, humorous, practical, businesslike, philosophical, political and—poetical. It would not be difficult to add to the list of good qualities, but it would be an injustice to omit mention of the fact that he is also very polite. A chronicle of bad qualities, I leave to others; they have often been over-written, and by the English themselves. But, lest the reader's head should begin to swim, I think it better to bring this very tentative survey to an end, and, in what follows, deal with an important though quite common aspect of English life that is likely to cause some bewilderment to the stranger.

2

The Language as Spoken To-day

It hardly seems necessary to say that, in a non-technical book such as this, it is impossible to give this highly complex subject the treatment which it deserves. No attempt can be made to discuss the various dialects, excepting Cockney, about which I must say a few words. What I shall say in general refers only to colloquial spoken English and not to the written language. And if, in this short treatment, I devote a considerable proportion of the space available to accent, it is because in English, more than in any other European language, accent (with pronunciation, tone of voice and manner of speech) is of *social* importance.

It is necessary to begin with the warning that the colloquial idiom which is the everyday speech of educated English people differs greatly from the colloquial spoken by those who have not had the same educational advantages. This fact involves considerable difficulties for the stranger whose mother-tongue is not English. It is, perhaps, as well for him to know from the outset that, in every person's conversation, his particular background, social status and general attitude to life is reflected. And that of no country is this truer than of England. By speech and accent the Englishman proclaims his class, his position on the social ladder.

Accent is the immediate touchstone for this among the English themselves. What is called 'Standard English', in which idiosyncrasies in accent and manner of speech are reduced to a minimum, is increasingly the goal of educated people. It is the most easily comprehensible kind of English and, thanks to the efforts of the British Broadcasting Corporation, it is beginning to achieve importance as a standardizing influence in clarifying the speech of the people; so much so that some of us think that if it continues to make progress it will take away much of the interest from life in replacing the old ways of speech. Those other ways come under two broad headings: the affected and the unaffected (which might also be called the unnatural and the natural). An affected accent is common, especially in cities, and usually proclaims that the person who uses it is either trying to conceal an imperfect education or a modest origin; it may be just one of the many harmless forms of snobbery, in this case one which conveys the impression of higher status. The affected accent can be sophisticated and effective for its purpose; so much so that there are schools of elocution which will, by their teaching and training (and of course for a fee), eliminate an unwanted local or dialect accent and impart in its place one which will pass muster among all but those who are possessed of the real thing, and often even among them. I often wonder whether there is any country but England in which this happens. The good schools of elocution do it very well; but there are also bad schools, and then the results can be comic or tragic, depending on the speaker's personality. You may ask, what about the majority, those who have no such training but who affect an 'upper-class' accent? Here the vagaries are astonishing, and they seem to be more common among women than among men, who tend to be content with straightforward 'imitation Oxford', if this can be achieved.

The genuine Oxford accent has a highly respectable ancestry and is everywhere accepted as the 'best', the highest in the social scale, the usual accent of a person of highest culture. It may be acquired at home from 'good-class' parents; or at a good Public School; or by residence at the University. One always speaks of 'Oxford accent' in England, never of 'Cambridge accent', though that which is natural to Cambridge University differs so little from its Oxford equivalent as to be indistinguishable from it—except possibly to experts in phonetics. Genuine Oxford speech is noted for its slight drawl, its peculiar pitch, precise enunciation and easy, unfaltering manner of delivery. The accent is regarded as an asset, an impressive *cachet*. It is so highly esteemed that when a poor man of modest origins makes money and 'gets on', he will rarely fail to send his children to the best schools; certainly to be educated, but often of far more importance in his mind, to be taught to speak in the manner of the upper class. He hopes to see those children end their education with a genuine, that is, 'natural' Oxford accent. Its achievement is an ambition, and not unreasonably so, for its great quality and indeed value in life is that it is distinctive, unmistakable, and genuine, by which I mean that it is patently natural to the speaker and is not mere affectation. This is something which strangers do not always grasp or allow for. It is one of the first things which the stranger—especially if he be American—does well to learn; I have known many who make the profound mistake of thinking that the English person who speaks with an Oxford drawl is either an affected creature or a bit of an ass; whereas, to put it modestly, at least he may represent a fine old culture.

I have stressed the importance of the genuine 'Oxford accent', in character with which usually goes an unassuming, casual or off-hand manner and tone of voice. Too often its importance is either under- or over-estimated: under-estimated by those who fail to realize that it is natural and represents, if nothing else, the tone of a first-class education; over-estimated, because, going to the other extreme, many foreigners and even English people, imagine that, when a person has this accent he or she is a member of the upper ten. Like all other accents, it is merely a matter of education and habit.

It is when we come to consider the imitations (the synthetic, the pseudo-, the super-, the blah-blah and other bogus variations of the genuine Oxford accent) that the fun begins. The genuine University product—male or female—is usually a retiring, unassuming and restrained person. The bogus is forward and irrepressible. It is quite easy to tell the difference. The 'super' Oxford accent is more often than not aggressive: as if the speaker wished to emphasize his superiority. Perhaps most pathetic of all is what has been called the 'Morris-Oxford' accent (after Lord Nuffield's inexpensive Oxford-made motor-cars manufactured when he was still plain Mr.

Morris). It is the great affectation of the good-natured and not over-gifted lower middle-class person; of the harmless nobody who wishes to be thought somebody. Akin to it, but far more vigorous, is the offside-Oxford manner of speech which I can only describe as 'blah-blah'. One often hears it from those who have been to one of the minor Public Schools, and have risen to some rank or status in an outpost of, say, one of the Colonial Administrations. It is an off-Oxford accent, greatly exaggerated, and, I should say, has been found useful in impressing 'natives'—so useful that it is made into a habit. Standard English is colourless in comparison and, in a company of blah-blah speakers, the Standard Englishman has difficulty in making his presence felt. One very often hears blah-blah in American films; it always provides as much fun for English as for American audiences, and so it is often put on deliberately. There is one feature common to these and to all other variations of the bogus Oxford accent: the fact that they are not the real thing is immediately perceptible to all people who have a right to call themselves upper or upper middle class, or who have had the advantage of education at one of the two old Universities; and it seldom really deceives anybody else. Ordinary people usually sense that it is not 100 per cent. the real thing. But they accept it good-humouredly as a part of the make-believe of everyday life. So much for the commonest accents one finds among upper- and middle-class people. I have not attempted to be exhaustive, but if I have shown in these brief comments that in England accent is socially important and can proclaim a speaker's status, this is what most concerns the stranger.

Now for the speech of ordinary people, of the working class in general. In every part of England there is an accent peculiar to the locality, and in many parts not only a local accent but a local dialect. For example, in Lancashire, Cumberland, Yorkshire, Somerset, Devonshire and Cornwall there are dialects. Ordinary people of the locality always have the local accent, and if there is a local dialect, they tend to speak it among themselves. These dialects are to me one of the liveliest and most expressive features of English life, and I have found that the little trouble it takes to learn a dialect is rewarding. Alas, a flat standardization is steadily replacing them. The

St. Paul's Cathedral, London
Wren's masterpiece, its dome unequalled for beauty and outline
BTHA

stranger will not understand these dialects unless he studies them as he would any language that is foreign to him. This need not worry him, for the 'local inhabitant' will always understand the stranger's English if it is clearly expressed, and the local will usually speak to a stranger in a way to be understood.

Of the dialects, accents and manners of speaking, there is one which outshines them all for vigour, raciness, expressiveness and sheer heartiness: Cockney—the speech of the London workers. I have seen with dismay that some excellent foreign writers have made the unpardonable mistake of stating that Cockney is "the language of the English working classes" in general. It is the language of *Londoners only*, and Londoners will tell you that only those born within the sound of Bow Bells are 'true Cockneys'—"I scorn", says a writer of the year 1600, "to let a Bow-bell Cockney put me down"—though in recent times a generous extension of the term includes people born in the metropolitan area. If you are not born a Londoner, you will never learn Cockney speech unless you are prepared to work hard, devote perhaps years of study to it, and have a gift for making an astonishing variety of sounds. Any expert in linguistics who has given this question attention will tell you that the phonetics, the pronunciation of the Cockney dialect of English, is extremely subtle and difficult. But it is not only pronunciation that makes Cockney difficult: it has several kinds of slang (including the rhyming variety: 'up the apples and pears' for 'up the stairs'), a vocabulary of its own ('mog' = an ordinary cat) and a great wealth of idioms. It is rich, warm-hearted, familiar, and the true Cockney manner of speech goes with treating everybody as an equal and as a friend. Plays are written in Cockney: *Down Our Street* by Henry George ran for weeks in the West End of London. Sometimes one comes upon wonderful combinations and uses of words. I jotted this down recently:

" 'Ello, ole cock, ow go? Ain't see yerfer monfs, I ain't! Blime if ye'r not lookin bet'ern I seen yer fer years. Seen ole Fred litely? Nah? I sor im wiv a very commeelfow bitta lars week, n'im werin' the funniest titfer ever wos. Crikey!

Pearly King and Queen of Hampstead, London
True representatives of the Cockney spirit
BTHA

Wotta peach! Fancy ole Fred, 'n ye woodn' fink but'r'd blinkin' well melt 'n 'iz mowf! . . . Wot'd 'iz drum 'n fife sigh!"

That was the greeting I once got from an old Cockney friend who, some years ago, used to be a municipal dustman. For those who are not Londoners, here is a translation:

> "Hallo, old cock, how goes it? Haven't seen you for months, I haven't. Blind me, if you're not looking better than I've seen you for years. Seen old Fred lately? No? I saw him with a very *comme il faut* lady last week and him wearing the funniest hat ('tit-for-tat') that ever was. Well now! What a peach! Fancy old Fred, and you wouldn't think that butter would blinkin' well (ever by any chance) melt in his mouth! . . . What would his wife say!"

I had to make my friend repeat the phrase "a very commeelfow bitta" a couple of times before I grasped that it was 'a very *comme il faut* bit of fluff' that was meant. The above is not a long speech. It takes fifteen seconds as spoken by a Cockney. Yet, it contains at least thirty peculiarities—differences from normal English. Two for every second!

The reader who is not English should realize from this very short example that Cockney is difficult. The specimen may even give him some idea of the Cockney's spirit and humorous way of looking at things; and of how he expresses himself. I cannot promise the stranger that he will always understand the Londoner—at least not until he has lived there for some time and made some attempt to master the commonest features of this rich dialect. But I do promise him that, should he make the effort and become familiar with it, he will reap a rich reward.

3

Seeing England: to Plan or Not to Plan?

His own temperament and the time available are two demons which the traveller ignores at his peril. My sympathies are always on the side of the person who has that serene wisdom which enables him or her to set out hopefully, and in the mood to be interested in whatever is to be seen or whoever may be met. To get full benefits from such travelling one must not be a slave to clock or calendar; or indeed to anything. England is a wonderful country for such idealists, who, alas, become fewer as life becomes more complex. Beset as we nearly all are by time and the circumstances of our age, we are driven willy-nilly to make some sort of plan: one depending, first, it seems, on the particular time-factor which is our master; and next, more happily, on the vagaries of our own temperament, which we can never afford to ignore. For those whose time is strictly limited, two courses are possible. One may travel quickly over a considerable area and be satisfied with a bird's-eye view, and a quick glance here and there at those things listed in every guide-book (and useful for citation to envious and less fortunate friends on return to the daily grind). Or, one may pick upon a 'Convenient Centre' in some area which attracts—Stratford-on-Avon, for example, in the 'Shakespeare Country'—settle there for a period of the holiday, and take a leisurely look at everything that attracts in the area. For both kinds of traveller, this list should be useful:

Convenient Centres

London — Canterbury — Brighton — Bournemouth — Exeter—Truro—Cheltenham (or Malvern)—Stratford-on-Avon—Shrewsbury—Chester—Blackpool—Windermere—Newcastle upon Tyne—Scarborough—Lincoln—Norwich—Leicester—Oxford—Reading.

If the reader will glance at the map facing p. 272, he will see that, up to Norwich, this list also represents a 'circular tour' of England. I can promise that, followed round to Norwich and thence back to London, it represents a good all-round route for a bird's-eye view which will comprise a multitude of places, sights and things of absorbing interest. The Leicester–Oxford–Reading route cuts across the centre of the country. So much for the traveller who likes the cinematographic way of seeing the country—the constantly changing scene and diverse contrasts of England should satisfy the most exacting of mortals. The same list also serves the purpose of that other kind of person, the one who likes to settle for a time in one place and, in a leisurely manner, allow the surroundings to work their magic upon him. Note well that all the 'Centres' mentioned are cities or biggish towns, and that their names are given here not necessarily because they are the best places for a holiday, but because they are useful geographical centres from which to visit other places. Around them are smaller towns, villages and areas which many visitors will find more attractive or even better centres than the bigger places. Accommodation to suit different purses can usually be found. The best of the smaller towns for the traveller's purpose can usually be discovered by judicious inquiries at the town hall in the 'Convenient Centre'. One can always write to the town clerk in any big town for information.

These are merely broad hints, first-aid, so to speak, for whoever may be a little vague about how best to set about things. For those who like to plan more carefully they will not be enough, and here the temperament of the individual must play its part. What follows is not intended for the sturdy individualist who always likes to go his own way in his own way. It is intended, rather, as general guidance for those people—English or others—who are either uncertain of their own minds or unaware of the vast possibilities which England offers them. It is really remarkable how few English people know their own country. But it is also encouraging to see that more and more of them each year are finding how interesting it can be to go to some place in England other than the fixed seaside resort which they know so well, and to launch out into exploration of this fascinating island. In a visit to certain places in the home country there is an element of adventure and excitement which can be just as rewarding and refreshing as the trip abroad. The truth is, it seems to me, that England is so full of attractions that the English tend to take them too much for granted and show too little of the enthusiasm or appreciation that comes from the overseas visitor. England is so full of attractions that, in order to make up one's mind about how best to begin, they must first be roughly sorted out. One may consider the approach in accordance with a first list * of possibilities under such headings as:

* See Appendix II, p. 321.

Abbeys
American Associations
Art, Art Galleries
Britain by Car or Caravan
Canals
Cathedrals
Castles
Country Houses
Cross-country Walks
Cycling
Dancing (Folk and Country)
Drama and Music (Festivals)
Farming
Fishing
Gardens (Great or Interesting)
Golf
Hiking
Hunting and Shooting
Industries
Industrial Areas
Inns
Lakes
Literary Associations
London, Aspects of
Museums
Norman Britain
Prehistoric Britain
Racing
Rivers
Roman Britain
Royal Palaces
Seaside Resorts
Shopping Possibilities
Sport
Theatre
Yachting

There is also the mainly geographical* approach; that is, by

* See Appendix I, p. 321, Notes 6 and 7.

concentration on a certain *area* and its attractions. Thus:

London and nearby
The South-east
The South-west
The West Midlands
The North-west
The North-east
East Anglia and East Midlands

There is still another approach which many have found attractive. It is based on the nature of the special features of a particular area which may be in one shire or extend into two or more shires. In the South-east there are, for example, the Downs, Ashdown Forest and the New Forest. In the South-west there are Salisbury Plain (with Stonehenge), Dartmoor (with the famous prison!). In the West Midlands there are the Cotswold Hills, the Shakespeare Country and the Potteries (Arnold Bennett's 'Five Towns' area). In the North-west there are the two great contrasts: industrial Lancashire and the Lake District and hill country of Cumberland. In the North-east there is another set of contrasts: the hill country of Northumberland and the 'black' mining areas of Durham; and in Yorkshire the delightful vales. In East Anglia and the Eastern Midlands there is the Fen Country (of Hereward the Wake), the Norfolk Broads (inland waterways for boating and yachting, which run into the sea at Great Yarmouth and Lowestoft). And there are, through the heart of England, the canals.

In fact, the more closely we look into this question of making up one's mind, the more attractions loom up before us and the more difficult it is to decide. Each traveller must decide for himself. But let us be content for the moment to keep the above suggestions in their place, and in the pages which follow may be found deciding factors. There is one other important question which must meanwhile be settled. It is this: whether the stranger should begin his visit with London, or whether his first approach to England should be by way of the provinces. To me, London seems a little overwhelming for a first approach. It is probably best left until the last. Otherwise first impressions of London are usually so powerful that the traveller may be bewildered for the rest of his visit, and miss those features of the English countryside which are so different, in such terrific contrast with the metropolitan area (not only one-fifth of England in population but the acme of city civilization) which is becoming a standardized form of agglomeration for capital cities everywhere. On the other hand, the English provincial cities and areas, and especially the little towns, villages and the countryside in general, have no parallels or equals anywhere. They deserve, I think, the privilege of providing the first impressions of England, for in them more than in the human agglomerations will be found the native poetry.

Is there any need for me to say that the leisurely traveller gets best value for his money? Rushing about may be a kind of sport, but how much does one see to appreciate, if, before we have had time to savour a panorama, we must rush off in search of the next? Some may find it advantageous to prepare for a holiday in England by reading a work written by a great English traveller. Defoe and Cobbett [5] each has attractions, and even to-day they cannot be beaten for their general pictures of the country and people. The intelligent traveller always finds the books of most interest about the district or subject in which he is most interested. A reliable guide-book,[6] giving the most important factual information and routes, is always a help. A good map [7] is essential. That is about all one requires. For the rest, it is not possible to get the full value of a visit without some general historical background such as I have attempted to provide in Part I.

Although I have suggested that London might be left as the last place to be visited, I shall for convenience of arrangement begin by dealing with it, after which will follow those geographical areas listed on p. 230.

CHAPTER II

LONDON AND LONDONERS

FIRST a few facts which we all must know. The population of Greater London in 1951 was 8,346,137, which makes it the largest city in the world; with New York a good second, Tokyo third and Moscow fourth. It is the capital of the British Commonwealth of Nations. One is apt to forget that there are two 'cities' within Greater London: first, the 'City of London'—the centre of finance and big business—usually referred to as 'The City', which represents London within its ancient boundaries, the part with the longest and fullest historical record; and second, the 'City of Westminster', the important area which includes the Houses of Parliament, Westminster Abbey, Whitehall (with the principal offices of Government), the Law Courts, Buckingham Palace and St. James's, the more select Clubs ('Clubland'), many theatres ('Theatreland') and cinemas, the fashionable (though declining) districts of Mayfair and Belgravia, and, in Oxford Street, Regent Street and Piccadilly, the exclusive shops, some of the big stores and a great variety of other shops. For purposes of its local government, the Metropolitan area is divided into 28 Metropolitan Boroughs, one of which is the City of Westminster. The 'City of London' is picturesquely and very competently governed by the Corporation of London, with a Lord Mayor and 25 Aldermen (dating from Saxon times) who are elected and assisted by the 'Common Council of London', of which the 206 (elected) members are known as Common Councilmen. Among the interesting survivals there are the ancient City Guilds, also called Livery Companies from the assumption of a distinctive dress or livery by their members in the 14th century. The Tower of London must not be missed.

In stating these few bald facts we have been drawn into history. Looking for the earliest authenticated date, I find that at the time of the revolt of the Iceni under Boadicea (A.D. 61), London was described by Tacitus as "a busy emporium for trade and traders". So it has remained ever since then, growing bigger and bigger every year, making itself into communities (some officially recognized, some of them not): unplanned, but all of astonishing variety. The result is that now London is a great urban federation: a conglomeration of cities, boroughs, towns, villages, parishes and little communities, many of which differ so strikingly from one another that, on moving from one to the other, the stranger feels that he is going from one country to another. Perhaps this is London's special charm: its infinite, infinite variety.

This variety comes from sheer lack of consistent planning. In the last 150 years London has just grown and grown haphazardly like one of those overpowering plant growths of the tropical jungle, spreading out tentacles and shoots anyhow, with blossoms and colourful or open parts here and there, some parts fresh and flourishing, others falling into decay and others rotting. There is no metropolis in the world which resembles it even approximately, or approaches it in the number of surprises it can offer even to old Londoners. The area referred to by the name London is so vast that it is advisable for even the most lackadaisical visitor to make some effort to establish his bearings at the outset. He simply must attempt to do so, or be content—as many people are, and enjoyably so—to be always getting lost or looking for the way. There is much to be said for getting lost in London—time permitting. The extraordinary thing is that, vast and impossible as Greater London may seem on a first approach, it is not really difficult to establish the essential bearings. The stranger should think of, say, the City of London with the City of Westminster as the real centre of things; the River Thames as the dividing line between North and South; and then think of Greater London (the Administrative County with its 28 Boroughs) and, finally, of Greater London and its suburban districts. The last represents an area of about 700 square miles, and includes interesting places for trips: Romford and Epping in the north-east, Esher and Uxbridge in the west and south-west, and north-west from Watford to Caterham and Orpington in the south. Within an hour's journey from the central area are many other interesting places: Maidenhead, Windsor, Guildford, Brighton, Gravesend, Southend, Chelmsford, Hertford, Welwyn, St. Albans and Beaconsfield.

The near suburban districts are in general uninteresting, all much of a muchness: rows of houses or housing estates that are dormitories for mostly middle-class workers who go to and from the centre of things as their daily routines demand.

In the main, what the stranger will find of most interest will be in that 'centre of things' on the north bank of the Thames; the Thames itself and dockland; and a strip along the south bank of the river beginning above Tower Bridge and extending westwards as far as Battersea Bridge. This area we may call Inner London. So, looking at his map, the first-time visitor must make himself familiar with the general configuration of that Inner London. It is there he will wish to go for most things, from amusements to shopping, even if he might prefer to live outside it, as I should. He need not, at all events to begin with, attempt to master the lay-out of Greater London, more than to know roughly where the various postal districts are; and Outer London—that is, Greater London's outlying districts—may be left to the map, which can always be consulted as needs or inclinations demand. Outer London may be a good field for desultory exploration on Sundays.

Inner London, then, is the first happy hunting-ground for the stranger; a fact which, though obvious, was more than ever impressed upon my mind during the last part of the Second World War. It was then nearly always filled with a concentration of American men and women from the Services. To them Piccadilly Circus was the great Mecca of Delights; at Piccadilly Circus the mere Londoner found himself in a realm of chewing-gum. I remember one day saying to a Cockney window-cleaner, standing there beside me with his ladder, waiting to cross the road: "Isn't it strange that they all come here when there are so many really interesting places in London they might go to?" He looked at me with a twinkle in his eye and replied: "This is the part of London that most reminds them of home." Piccadilly Circus is a useful landmark, a sort of centre of the centre of London. Leicester Square, just beside it, was the favourite haunt of English Servicemen in the First World War. In time of peace, Piccadilly Circus, with its statue of Eros and at certain hours the flower-girls around it, is the point on which students from Oxford and Cambridge concentrate their attention for a 'rag' when they come to Town in numbers for some great event such as the Boat Race. I cannot pretend to explain why it should be so famous in song and story, and can only say to the stranger who is disappointed with its modest outlines that, if he will walk for ten minutes southwards, he will come to Trafalgar Square, which the average Englishman prefers to regard as *his* centre of things. There he can look up at Admiral Lord Nelson standing defiantly on the top of his monument; he can see the fountains play, feed the almost tame pigeons and proudly contemplate the great metal lions on the plinth which, apart from its ornamental value, serves as a platform for speakers at mass-meetings. Who has not read of Lord Nelson, famous in our island history for his victory at the Battle of Trafalgar? But how many know of the Battle of Trafalgar Square which took place in 1887? It happened like this. A great meeting was called to demand the release of some Irish political prisoners. The Commissioner of Police prohibited the meeting, which was to be held in Trafalgar Square on Sunday, November 13th. When the time came for the meeting, the Commissioner had about 5,000 men on duty, most of them near the Square. Processions of demonstrators who made their way there were broken up, whereupon the demonstrators continued on their way as individuals. Mounted police tried to drive off the crowd which had gathered in Trafalgar Square, and soon they had to be assisted by 300 Grenadier Guards (infantry) and 300 Life Guards (cavalry). A stipendiary magistrate in a grey suit and top-hat rode between two officers at the head of the Life Guards holding in his hand a copy of the Riot Act, which he would read. Meanwhile two men were standing nearby waiting for an opportunity to get through to the plinth from which they were to speak: John Burns, a well-known politician, and Cunninghame Graham—'Don Roberto'—the Scottish nobleman and author. When they tried to force their way they were badly manhandled by the police, who finally arrested them. Free fights now arose on all sides. It took several hours to restore order. Thenceforth the event has been known in English agitational history as the 'Battle of Trafalgar Square'.[8] Those were the days! Such a thing as even a moderate riot does not happen in London in our time. Open-air meetings, yes: in Trafalgar Square, Hyde Park, Tower Hill—to mention only three of the many places where they are held. The most amusing are at the Marble Arch end of Hyde Park on Sunday afternoons.

One of London's saving graces as a dense agglomeration is that it is well provided with open spaces, squares and parks. I have seen it stated that the open spaces and parks of London occupy some 30,000 acres or 10 per cent. of the Metropolitan area. The London squares, it has been claimed, represent the warm, peculiar beauty of London; they are regarded by the authorities as worthy of protection for this reason alone. The law restrains owners of the land from building over the squares, many of which have been officially acquired in order that they can be kept as public open spaces. These open spaces and the many parks, none of which is far from busy or populous areas, are the lungs of London, and parks especially are mentioned now because of the amenities, delights and interests which they offer to the newly arrived stranger who may find himself at a loose end and wish to have a pleasant walk or a breath of fresh air. Incidentally, there is no better way of seeing the Londoner take his leisure than by going to one of the parks. (It is advisable to make inquiries before doing so as to the best season, day and hour for a particular park.) One might begin with a walk through St. James's Park and Green Park, which are conveniently situated on the south side of Piccadilly and The Mall: right in the centre of London. I suggest this walk because it takes in many things.

Turn from Whitehall into Downing Street, not a very impressive alley but containing the residences of the Prime Minister at No. 10 and the Chancellor of the Exchequer at No. 11. Unimpressive as it is now, only a century ago it was a mean, narrow little street. One pauses opposite, on the other side, to contemplate the residence of the Prime Minister of Great Britain. The stranger will be taken aback by the simplicity of that plain, unimposing building, which nobody would ever guess as the official home of the highest political office-holder in the British Commonwealth, still less as consistent with the dignity of the Head of the State. It is sentiment and the rich historical interest of that little house which preserves it from destruction. Without doubt it is the least showy house for such a purpose in the world; a standing example of English understatement in stone, a monument to the sentimental feelings of the English. One is therefore wise to contemplate it for a moment—for this reason only. No need to go inside—they might not allow you!—because, like the outside, it is plain, simply furnished, and striking only in its simplicity and unassuming dignity. The English would not wish it to be otherwise.

The south side of Downing Street is fronted by fine though not very big Government buildings, the Dominions Office, Home Office and Foreign Office, which are approached through an archway leading to a quadrangle which also has the entrance to the once important India Office. Facing west, from the end of Downing Street you will see St. James's Park, with the Horse Guards Parade to the right. Cross the road, and you are in the park. But first be sure to look into the quadrangle, and glance at the ornate architecture of the buildings with their many statues to set off the third-floor windows. It is rather gloomy.

The best time of year to see St. James's Park—if you wish to see its most constant users—is any time except in the dead of winter. In the spring, summer and early autumn months hundreds, often thousands, of Civil Servants, male and female, from the nearby Government offices flock into the park between noon and 3 p.m., taking their lunches with them, and sit on the seats as near to the ponds as they can get: to eat their sandwiches and look dreamily at the colourful water-fowl, especially the pelicans, the prime attraction when they are there. It is a good way of seeing at close quarters a fair cross-section of English Civil Servants, especially those of the rank and file, though in recent years seniors have been found sitting in the park during lunch-hour. There is something very restful about watching water-fowl, especially when you are surrounded by plants and flowers. It refreshes the tired brain of the overworked official. Who knows how many deep problems have been solved with the active assistance of the gay mallard, the busy water-hens or the royal pelicans? Royal, because St. James's Park is one of the 'royal' parks, like Hyde Park and Regent's Park, in contrast to most of the other parks which are cared for by the ubiquitous London County Council: Battersea Park (one of the biggest and proud to grow all the flowers Shakespeare mentions); Victoria Park, the East Enders' playground; and Finsbury Park in North London.

At the west end of the adjoining Green Park is Buckingham Palace, the London residence of the reigning monarch and royal family. It is so called because it was built for John Sheffield, Duke of Buckingham. George III acquired it for a song: £21,000. It was reconstructed in the Palladian style from designs by Nash, but William IV disliked it and it was hardly ever occupied until Queen Victoria came to the throne. Alterations, improvements and new buildings on the south side have made it what it is now. These improvements represent many times the original cost: the east front of the south wing, built in 1846, alone cost £150,000. Behind the Palace are its magnificent pleasure grounds of forty acres, with a lake; and the whole is surrounded by a high wall or railings. The sentries at the main entrance never fail as attractions for English people and strangers alike when the guard is being changed. The real work of keeping out the unwanted visitor is, however, done by an ordinary, humble policeman who, nevertheless, knows his business. Again, we come upon the unostentatious in everyday matters. The English people know that, when the occasion justifies it, the quiet, somnolent Palace can blossom into life and colour; one of the sights of London is the vast crowd of cheering people who assemble in front of the Palace on occasions when the monarch is expected to appear on the balcony and wave to them. That is all the people demand. On very great and exciting occasions such as a Coronation, the monarch may have to appear many times to appease the yearnings of the crowd; a finally satisfying touch is sometimes added by the appearance of the whole royal family. That is a rare event.

Continuing along Constitution Hill, the pilgrim crosses Piccadilly into Hyde Park, which runs into Kensington Gardens, the two together being over 600 acres. Thus we have a continuous series of parks running for a distance of nearly three miles from the Horse Guards to Kensington High Street, the shopping centre for the Royal Borough of Kensington, which the more select people of the middle class regard as providing attractive residential areas. When one thinks of the vast London agglomeration, one can hardly fail to be astonished on finding nearly three miles of delightful public parkland right in its centre. St. James's Park and Green Park are small with innumerable diversions, but in Hyde Park and Kensington Gardens we have room to step out. The Serpentine, an artificial waterway, connects the last two; and at one part on its bank is what Cockneys used to call 'Lansbury's Lido', after the Labour leader who fought hard so that they might have it for sun-bathing as well as for the permitted dips in the shallow water. It is amusing to go there on sunny Saturday afternoons or on Sundays to watch the youth of London disport itself. There are little boats which can be hired on the Serpentine, and I know of worse ways of spending an hour or so than in one of them. You have a good seat in this way for watching the passers-by, and there are few better places than Hyde Park and Kensington Gardens for indulging in the delightful pastime of just looking at passers-by. I used to live in Kensington and so made that discovery, for I enjoyed a game which consisted in assuming the mantle of Sherlock Holmes as I sat on a park seat, and attempting to make something of those who walked past: their age, occupation, nationality, history and present destination. What brought them there at precisely that moment? *Who* was that middle-aged man wearing a beret and sandals and an old overcoat, smoking an obviously home-made cigarette which drooped from the corner of his mouth? As he approached, I saw to my surprise that he was wearing the long outmoded pince-nez. He was tallish, stolid, and I thought about fifty years of age. A self-contained foreigner, no doubt. I decided to speak to him; and so I asked for a light. "With pleasure," he said, handing me a box of matches. I took one and lit my pipe carefully, remarking that it was a lovely day for the park. Immediately his bright grey eyes sparkled. "It certainly is, gov'nor. I never get tired of walking in the parks. Come 'ere every time I get a chance. Work and live not far away. Am just on the way to Marble Arch, to listen to the spouters: that's the place for fun, and you don't have to pay for it, either!" I asked him if he were a Londoner. "Yes, gov'nor, a Londoner born and bred, though not 100 per cent., mind you, for I wasn't born within hearing of Bow Bells, I was born on the south side—

Southwark. I reckon you're not a Londoner?" and he looked at me quizzically. I confessed that I was not born in London, and I think that I saw his face cloud with gentle sadness, as if to say: "Well, you can't help it, but you've missed something all the same." I asked him to be seated for a minute, and he did so. We chatted for a while, and I elicited from him that he was a professional rat-catcher, and, as I expressed more than ordinary interest, he proceeded to give me a lecture on the fine art of rat-catching in London. He told me that London rats are more cunning, far more educated in the tricks of escapism, than country rats, which are mostly simpletons and fair game for any fool. But in London: "Blimey, mate, if you don't keep your wits about you, the devils will beat you every time—even when you use the most up-to-date scientific methods." And with that he was off like a flash towards Marble Arch, leaving me bewildered. On the main point I had made a mistake: I took him—on his appearance—to be a Continental of some sort, probably a Latin. That is what continually happens in this great city: one is so often completely deceived by appearances. You cannot ever be sure of knowing a Londoner just by his looks, for London has always been cosmopolitan; and biology does not recognize national frontiers.

I have no intention of attempting to compete with standard guide-books and, if I have taken the reader by the hand through those central parks, that was merely to indicate to the almost inevitably overwhelmed visitor a pleasant and even instructive way of escaping periodically from the hurly-burly of the West End. We shall visit Soho, which is central and worth knowing. But if I were to attempt to do the same for each of London's interesting parts, volumes would be required; and the result would be imperfect and unsatisfactory unless a team of experts collaborated. Fortunately there is an abundance of informative literature with maps which serves admirably to help the stranger, not only in finding his way about, but in listing those things which visitors, especially those from overseas, will wish to see. The Tourist Information Centre (66 Whitcomb Street, Leicester Square, W.C.2) or the Travel Association (6 Arlington Street, St. James's, S.W.1) invite inquiries and can supply all the information and free

Aerial View of Westminster Bridge and the House of Commons
Centre of the British Commonwealth
BTHA

Royal Festival Hall, Exterior, London BTHA

Simplicity the keynote

Royal Festival Hall, Interior, London

Perfectly planned and unequalled for its acoustic qualities BTHA

literature likely to be required; not only about London, but about the United Kingdom of Great Britain and Ireland. There is no need for me to cover the ground again. To the person interested in buildings and architecture and who requires still greater general details about London (with a scholarly, up-to-date presentation of the facts), I can confidently recommend *The Face of London*, by Harold P. Clunn.[9] It is the kind of book one reads with great pleasure and advantage after a visit. I am convinced that it is undesirable before a visit to read more about a place than will stimulate a general interest and perhaps provoke curiosity about certain things, and I feel that, the less one's head is cluttered up with miscellaneous facts beforehand, the better and more satisfying is the impression received during a visit. This is a personal matter, which every traveller must decide for him or herself.

Not far from Piccadilly, between Shaftesbury Avenue and Oxford Street, is the district called Soho. It is a perfect example of what has happened in many other parts of London: the formation of a distinctive, homogeneous community, in this case mainly foreign. Farther west, in Mayfair and around Piccadilly are the more select and more expensive restaurants. In Soho will be found restaurants to meet almost any pocket and any taste. There is a considerable element of chance about visiting a restaurant in Soho, the chief reason being that owners and chefs often change. What may be a poor restaurant to-day may be an excellent one to-morrow, and vice versa. One should therefore obtain the latest information before venturing. With that warning the visitor has, I am assured, some 400 restaurants and cafés from which to choose in this small district. The variety of restaurants and food available is impressive. Italians and their cooking dominate Soho, but there are also French, German, Spanish, Greek, Cypriot, Jewish, Russian, Danish and Chinese restaurants, and I may have missed a type or two. A feature of Soho is that, to do best in it, you must have what amounts to 'inside information' as to the best place to go to at a given moment. There is no really reliable information about the vagaries of change—not that it would be of much practical use to anybody—but I have worked it out for myself in this way. A new restaurant opens and, shall we say, starts well. It offers good food at acceptable prices.

Word quickly goes round, customers recommend it to their friends, and 'pop goes the weasel!' The place is soon packed at meal-times, the restaurateur develops swelled head, and all this in due course far too often has a devastating effect on everything. The original admirable service becomes casual, the comforting *Consommé au Fumet de Perdreau* or *Crème Ambassadeur* either lose their fine flavour or are replaced by a tepid *Consommé à la Portugaise* or a weak and inferior *Minestrone;* and so on down the menu until the whole becomes quite uninteresting and one is glad to get out of the place. You may make up your mind not to go again but, hey presto!—next time you pass you see that there is a new proprietor, and the same old gambit starts *da capo.* Meanwhile the former owner may have acquired a bigger restaurant with better amenities, and, if you can find it, you will enjoy what he really *can* do when he wishes and is in that initial phase of 'working up' his business. I have said enough to show that one must keep up to date in regard to Soho; its world of restaurants, with the exception of a few steady old landmarks, changes kaleidoscopically. Some of those old places are famous and still attract distinguished people, from film stars down (or up) to Cabinet Ministers and even royalty. In them you can always be sure to get a good meal, though it will not be cheap. There are none of the risks of pot-luck. And in Soho, if you know where to go, there are few dishes in the culinary repertory which cannot be obtained. Restaurants specialize in certain dishes: in the snail season (April to October) a famous restaurant imports these slow-moving comestible molluscs from Burgundy; and in that restaurant with a sign outside presenting an expectant snail, the gourmet can have a dish of them as imaginatively prepared as in France. One must keep in mind wars, tumults, upheavals and political 'curtains', or the quest for some special foreign dish may prove futile. Do not, for example, expect to find Birds' Nest Soup when there are difficulties about importing the nests from China. And do not go to Soho for English fare, which is best obtained in the grill-rooms of the superior City restaurants, or, less expensively, in the dining-rooms of good pubs, or even in pull-ups for taxi-drivers.

One of the attractions of Soho is that no buses run through

The district of Soho in the West End of London was once a fashionable residential centre. Since 1685 it has been predominantly a foreign quarter, now famous for its restaurants, its little drinking clubs, and the many shops in which foreign comestibles can be bought. The map includes Charing Cross Road, notable for its secondhand bookshops; Oxford Street and Regent Street, for shops; Shaftesbury Avenue, for theatres. This area is one of the liveliest and most interesting in London.

its mostly narrow streets; the tempo of life is unrushed. One must walk or move by taxi. People of all nationalities stroll or loll about, chatting and behaving as if they were at home in their own sunshine. Soho has a reputation for law-breaking, and some serious crimes have occurred there, occasionally *crimes passionnel* of Continental type, and usually in one of the innumerable 'joints', speakeasies or shebeens generically described as 'clubs'. At this point the visitor may usefully learn something of contemporary England's laws relating to the sale of alcohol. If you know the lie of the land—and the local customs—you can get a drink in London at any time of the day or night without breaking the law. But note this: to do so requires some detailed knowledge and practical experience, hence all I can offer here must be in the way of general observations. In general, public licensed premises throughout England are open for the sale of drink only during certain hours: usually between 11 a.m. and 3 p.m. and between 5 p.m. and 11 p.m. on weekdays; and between noon and 2 p.m. and from 7 p.m. to 10 p.m. on Sundays. In many of the café-restaurants it is possible to drink up to midnight if a 'meal' is consumed: a sandwich comes within the legal description! Otherwise licensed premises are closed, and the thirsty must look elsewhere: in their hotel, at a friend's house —or at a club, though the more serious clubs follow the usual licensing hours. No offence is intended when I describe the Soho clubs I have in mind as the 'less serious' clubs, for I am conscious of the fact that to some people drinking is a serious business. It is when the ordinary pubs and normal drinking-places are closed that these drinking clubs open. One is introduced by a friend, one pays a modest subscription, and membership is thereby acquired. You can drink to please yourself during the hours for which that particular club has been specially licensed. You may wish to drink at other hours: then you must join another club, one with other hours. Hearty drinkers often enjoy membership of a variety of clubs, and thereby assure themselves of the wherewithal to keep up their morale by day and by night. In recent years these drinking clubs have sprung up in most London districts. The nature of the district usually sets the tone of the club; for example, in Mayfair there are the 'ritzy' and chromium-plated establishments, with congenial men or smartish women of the world as bartenders and hostesses, and proprietors or managers of the ex-officer type. One pays accordingly. The atmosphere is free. In Soho the variety of clubs is extraordinary. There are dozens and dozens, perhaps hundreds of them, and they range from the highly respectable and thoroughly well-conducted to the altogether doubtful and, alas, sometimes utterly disreputable, which get far more publicity than the better and safer places. The newspaper description of 'Soho club' conjures up visions in the reader's mind of everything that is lurid and vicious whereas, more often than not, there is little in it but the merely sordid—though even this can at times be quite lively. It may be taken as a general working rule of life for the stranger that, the easier it is to acquire membership of a Soho club, the more likely it is to be a bit doubtful, but I must in fairness say that there are many exceptions to the rule. One should, above all things, avoid those clubs which employ touts who accost strangers in the street out of normal licensing hours and try to entice them into a 'joint'. Prices and quality of drink can provide their own warnings. I do not wish to dwell too heavily on the evils of these bad places, and have no intention of making that detailed exposure—under pretence of 'moral indignation' or as if I were partly responsible for the immortal souls of my readers—which, when examined in terms of practice, merely provides a guide to the evils: a literary technique which has been developed into a highly profitable art form by some widely esteemed writers. I cannot emphasize too strongly that there are dozens of modest little clubs in the district of Soho that are honestly and decently run, and in which will be found at all hours many good people who work at odd hours and need such places, where one can have a quiet drink and meet friends for a chat or to discuss business. For years I enjoyed membership of such a club—The Byron—which was kept by an old Spanish friend named Pedro. The Byron's membership list included a fine representative of the Order of Merit, a few Foreign Office officials and several distinguished Civil Servants, at least one author known wherever English is read, not to mention editors, journalists, artists, musicians, ordinary seamen, ships' firemen, waiters, cooks, commercial travellers, all set off by a few kindly and discreet ladies of the oldest profession. They were the 'regulars', but in addition there were members who called at intervals and, during the war, many of them came from the four quarters of the globe. There was no place that I could find in those days which provided a more entertaining or more friendly atmosphere; and there was never 'trouble' of any sort. It was all due to the remarkable personality of Pedro, a man with the inestimable gift of friendship. Pedro is gone from us, but we old Byronites will not forget him. To me there will never be anybody quite like him, though I have no doubt that he must have some worthy successors.

I can almost feel some readers thinking, as they read what I have written about Soho, "This is all very nice, but Soho is a *foreign* community; it is not typical London." But it *is* typical London, if such a word as typical is permissible at all in regard to London. In the metropolis every district differs from the next until you get well out into the suburbs, where sameness is the rule rather than the exception. Almost every part of London has its special community or communities, one might almost say its differing villages and village life within the metropolitan area. Londoners tend to be gregarious in groupings, and at the same time sturdily independent and individualist; this is just one of the innumerable paradoxes one finds. The City is the quarter of big business, of the great banks with the Bank of England ('the Old Lady of Threadneedle Street') dominating major transactions. Moving west from it one comes to Fleet Street, the 'Street of Ink', the centre of newspaperdom, journalism and, traditionally, of endless talk that often acquires an alcoholic tinge. Off it are Chancery Lane and the Temple, with the Law Courts almost opposite and Lincoln's Inn nearby: the lawyers' quarter. Next, still moving west, is Covent Garden, London's market for fruit, vegetables and flowers: a rich Cockney quarter. Walk a little to the east of the City and you are in an area where Jewish people are active in trade, especially the 'rag trade', which means the making and marketing of clothes, mostly women's garments. Take a bus from there to the East India Dock Road, and you are among stevedores, sailors and the people who live on and off ships. Cross the Thames and make for the Elephant and Castle, where you will find yourself in a true Cockney area, certainly one of the most interesting for the visitor who wishes to see real Cockneys in their element. Why is it called Elephant and Castle? There is always some history behind these out-of-the-ordinary names, and I have read that in this case the English term 'Elephant and Castle' is the Londoners' version of the Spanish *El Infante de Castilla,* a great house which once existed nearby and was the London residence of an expatriate Spanish dignitary of that rank. At 'the Elephant', as Londoners call it, six important thoroughfares converge, and it has long been the most congested centre of traffic in South London. All is changing thereabouts because of a new scheme which will include a fine traffic roundabout that is to be surrounded by eight- and ten-storied buildings. The new Elephant Circus will become, it is foreseen, one of London's most important centres, the greatest on the south bank of the Thames, and a sort of headquarters for Cockneydom. It will have a new Underground Station with wide platforms, fast escalators and every amenity to deal with the multitude that will use it. More than six thousand houses were destroyed in this neighbourhood or damaged beyond repair by German bombs during the Second World War. New housing estates take their place. London's scars of the bombing have not yet all been covered, but the work goes on, rather too slowly for the liking of many who are waiting for a new home. Post-war conditions, which have included a great shortage of certain essential building materials, are largely responsible for the delays. We must remind ourselves that one house in seven—that is the general average for the whole of England—was destroyed by enemy action. If the stranger finds England backward in some things—the rebuilding of bombed buildings, for example—let him not forget what has to be made up of the destruction and loss, amounting to billions in terms of monetary wealth, and vast quantities of raw materials which have to come from abroad.

Those which I have named are communities in the centre of things. Go out a little, say to Camden Town, and you will find a busy place with a distinctive flavour of its own. Many Negroes, many Irish and some Indians have taken to this part in recent years. There is a good shopping centre and an excellent open-air market. Take a bus to Hampstead, and here you will find a more exclusive 'village life'. Bloomsbury—near the British Museum—used to be the headquarters of the *literati* and *illuminati,* of the writers and poets, of the 'unacknowledged legislators of the world'. Many of them, as well as painters, sculptors and musicians, are now in Hampstead, Swiss Cottage and St. John's Wood; and in the pubs of each of these three can be found not only gregarious groups representing that other contradiction in terms, respectable Bohemia, but real natives of those parts, people born and bred there, who love their own particular village and would never change it for any other. Hampstead, and especially the Swiss Cottage part of it, became a favourite residential area for the more prosperous refugees from Germany and Central Europe in Hitler's day; most of them have remained there. It is a pleasant district, high up, and from the Spaniard's Road on the top of Hampstead Heath on a clear day you will get the best possible panoramic view of the metropolis, if lucky through a telescope provided by a thoughtful benefactor who comes there in clear weather and, for a few coppers, will allow you to look and will even indicate the most notable points on the vast landscape of brick and stone. Londoners are not always sufficiently interested to look through that telescope on the Spaniard's Road, taking it for granted that they know their London—how many of them know it well?—but I have a warm spot in my heart for it. In the days when I was still unfamiliar with this great city—it was while on leave from France during the 1914–1918 War—the telescope, or *a* telescope, was there. For a penny you could have a look, which was usually accompanied by a brief commentary from its guardian. I used often to think that, if I lived to be as old as Methuselah, I could never hope to get better value for a copper than that telescopic survey of London from Spaniard's Road, accompanied as it was by its much-to-the-point description in good Cockney speech: vivid, informative and well flavoured by wit and humour. Apart possibly from a trip in a helicopter—and that can now be arranged—it is the best way to see and marvel at the immensity of London's panorama. On a really clear day—one of those days so abnormally clear that you feel the English weather is playing a trick—this view of London is unforgettable.

Having mentioned tricks of the weather, the famous (I would prefer the word infamous) London fogs come to mind, and in any case simply must be mentioned in passing. In some circumstances I used to enjoy what was called the 'London particular' or 'pea-souper'—that is, a fog so thick that you could hardly see your hand held up in front of your eyes. You could certainly not see a yard ahead. Well muffled up—and it is risky for health to be out in winter fog otherwise than well muffled up—and provided with walking-sticks to feel the way like the blind, a few of us used to go out together and enjoy the great game of finding our way from one comforting tavern to the next. It may sound simple enough, this amusement, especially on the assumption that it would take place on closely familiar ground. Yet, familiar as we were with the routes, we often found ourselves utterly lost. During the last war I once found myself not more than a few hundred yards from home, and it took me well over half an hour to find my house. There is a special brand of humour which Londoners have developed for dealing with such problems. Yet, allowing for all the inconveniences—surface traffic all but stopped, buses either stopped altogether or the drivers being guided by conductors on foot, with or without a torch; taxi drivers unwilling to undertake any but short trips—the general good humour is extraordinary. It becomes a case of collective collaboration in which everybody helps everybody. Politeness rules the fog. One hears cussing, but it represents merely heart-relieving expletives. On one occasion I was on the top of a bus during a fog and my patience was becoming exhausted by the slow progress. I said to my neighbour: "This is terribly slow—I don't ever remember a bus as slow as this." He was an elderly man whose nose was buried in a newspaper. Without looking at me he said: "Just take a dekko at the road on your left." I did so, and to my horror saw that we were creeping along not more than a foot from a yawning chasm, one that was certainly marked off from the traffic line by a make-shift piece of rope held in place by tripods, but a chasm just the same. A yard or so in front of the bus walked the conductor holding a white handkerchief in his right hand, a little electric torch in his left. He walked slowly along by the rope directing his light well on the edge of that chasm, and, if you please, the man was gaily singing the old song:

Oh, what a beautiful morning,
Oh, what a bee-u-ti-ful day!

Those of us who saw enough of our perilous situation through the fog to realize the grim humour were grateful. We forgot the danger, a real danger; a foot or so miscalculated by the driver and . . .! We got safely to the end of our journey without mishap; and that, on the whole, is what usually happens.

The fog season usually begins in November and seldom continues beyond February. Sometimes a season passes with little or no fog, and then London is exceptionally lucky. It is in November and December that we expect the worst, and one year (1952) we had in December a few days of really appalling 'smog'—a mixture of smoke and fog. I should perhaps explain that London suffers from these attacks of 'smog' for a combination of reasons, the first of which is that the greater part of it lies in a valley through which runs the Thames, and it sometimes happens that there is not even the prevalent south-west wind to clear the air. Next, and most sinister reason, London's civilization is based on coal: coal to create power in the factories, coal—in open grates—to warm the interior of millions of private dwellings. Thus, in winter there is a vast outpouring of coal-smoke in all directions; and when there is no wind it inevitably hangs about. Malevolent Nature often steps in just at such a moment, when the atmosphere is permeated with smoke, and currents of upper air come downwards replacing the surface air, bringing with them the particles and impurities which might otherwise have been dispersed. In the December 1952 'smog', the greatest coal-wasting city in the world paid dearly for its *laisser-faire*. Elderly people, those susceptible to bronchial troubles or asthma, and many others, suffered severely from the five-day fog, which tortured them, made them ill and killed many of the weaker ones. For years the London fog-nuisance has been studied by experts; it is at last realized that 'Something Must Be Done About It'. And a beginning has, in fact, been made

'Smokeless Zones' are being established; in private houses grates are being installed to burn smokeless fuel. That appalling December fog had killed several thousand people and caused damage costing £10 million. And this fact may be responsible for the first real effort to deal with what has become a problem of public health. Those romantics—I was once one of their number—who in the past wallowed in the old London fogs, may not have their strange joys much longer. Speaking for myself, I am grateful that fogs do not come very often, and that the really bad ones are comparatively rare. I shall be glad when they are well under control.

Wander about London, imbibe the atmosphere and the life around you, and do not ever allow yourself to become overwhelmed or bewildered with too much 'information'. Console yourself with the possibly disconcerting fact that, if you were to live here in London for the space of several lifetimes, you could never get to the end of mere information relating to it—unless you are a specialist of some sort. Anyhow, there is something much more important—and that is the spirit of London. And what a spirit! No person in his senses would claim, for instance, that bombing is a pleasant experience, but in London during the 'blitz' there was a wonderfully infectious spirit, and never in spite of the tragedy has a huge population so well and so good-humouredly self-disciplined itself. People then often asserted rights in the face of authority. For example, in the early days of the blitz some pundit put out an order that the platforms and passages of the Underground railway must not be used as air-raid shelters; and the gates were closed when the warning sirens sounded. The order was sensibly ignored by the public; and then sensibly withdrawn. No panic, no hysteria anywhere. It is always the same, whatever the emergency may be. There is more excitement in London about a cup-final than about a war.

With a few words of warning to those strangers who may be glad of them, I shall leave the reader to his own way of seeing and enjoying London. Just because the English are quiet and, until they know you well, appear inclined to be uncommunicative and, you may think, just coldly polite, do not therefore run away with the idea that they are people of less intelligence than yourself. They have more depth of focus and, I think, as much worldly wisdom as any other people, though they often seem to be doing their best to conceal all this. They are usually anything but as simple as they seem. If there is some thing about their life and its conventions which you do not understand, be patient; one day you may discover the reason, because there is always a reason for what must be recognized as the old, highly complex and varied pattern in the English way of life. Be cautious about everything *personal.* You can say almost anything in England without giving offence, so long as it does not touch on the personal and it is quite clear in what you say that you do not intend it to be personal. The Englishman does not take kindly to being quizzed about things which he regards as nobody else's business: his personal politics, his religion, his salary, his own way of living. Once he knows *you,* he may not mind talking about these things. But you must give him time, for his methods of evaluation are his own. He hates being rushed by other people, and usually insists on making his own tempo; though, when he feels that it is required, he can move as quickly as the next person—and of whatever nationality or race. He dislikes anything which savours of violent change, and in conversation remains unmoved when spoken to in expletives. He does not wear his ideals on his sleeve; but he has ideals, often very lofty and even romantic or, some may think, sentimental ideals—which he keeps severely to himself. So, tread lightly on what may be his dreams. . . .

I could continue, but there is no need so long as there are people whom you may meet who, in everyday interchanges will impart those little flavourings which cannot be imparted in mere words. Even in finding the way about, you can hardly fail to observe some of the main qualities of those around you. Finally, there is no need to be timid or backward about asking the way. As the world knows, the police are wonderful, but not more wonderful than the ordinary citizen, who seldom fails to be obliging to the stranger.

CHAPTER III

SOUTH-EAST: THE GATEWAY TO ENGLAND

THE south-eastern counties of Kent, Sussex, Hampshire and Surrey have been called the gateway to Great Britain, for reasons which should be apparent from the map, and from Part I of this book. It was here in Kent that Hengest and Horsa landed with their Jutes in the 5th century; it was here that the Romans landed, first in 55 B.C., and again in A.D. 43; and it was in Pevensey Bay that William the Conqueror landed in 1066. Farther back in history Celts came here, among them the Belgæ to Hampshire, and many others, who landed somewhere near our Southampton, to make their way inland to the north and west to Salisbury plain. This corner of England, the part nearest to continental Europe, is not only scenically beautiful, it is saturated in history and, as it is near to London, it may be a good idea for the first-time visitor to see it before any other, especially if he should be considering a more extensive tour. I have already (p. 230) provided a rough plan for such a tour. One could do worse than begin it with the south-east, making Canterbury, Brighton and Bournemouth (possibly also Southampton) Convenient Centres from which to visit interesting places in the country around them.

This south-eastern area, like all areas to be visited, should be considered for purposes of approach in accordance with its chief attractions. These are scenery, historical associations, seaside resorts, and amenities for holiday-makers. From Herne Bay round the coast to Bournemouth and including the Isle of Wight, there are not only popular and famous seaside resorts such as Margate and Ramsgate, Hastings, Eastbourne, Brighton, Worthing and Bognor Regis, but innumerable smaller ones, many of which strive—in the face of the ubiquitous automobile and the now frequent motor-coach trips from all over England—to preserve some of their old exclusiveness, but not always with success. Dover and Folkestone are busy ports chiefly associated with Continental travel: the former is also a delightful old town with a very long history;

the latter is an increasingly popular and attractive holiday resort.

Canterbury, our first Convenient Centre, does not require recommendation. The name is enough. History books first record it as Durovernum, an important Roman town and post on the military roads connecting the coast with London and the North; and later as the Saxon Cantwarburh, the 'Town of the Men of Kent'. Ethelbert, King of Kent, made it his capital in A.D. 560, and it was here that St. Augustine came with his Christian missionaries in 597. Their church became the first cathedral in England. Canterbury is and always has been the See of the Anglican Primate of All England. The present (and 99th) Archbishop is Dr. Geoffrey Francis Fisher, P.C., who crowned Queen Elizabeth II. Roman Catholic association with Canterbury ended and Protestant domination began in the 16th century. The main interest of the cathedral is its antiquity. In its present form—which represents many changes and enlargements on the original building—it is very beautiful. It has an impressiveness of its own because of its vast historical associations. It was on the steps of the altar of Canterbury Cathedral that Archbishop Thomas Becket was murdered in 1170. Behind the high altar in Trinity Chapel was erected his shrine, destroyed in 1538. Pilgrimages used to be made to the famous shrine, and have been described in Chaucer's immortal *Canterbury Tales*. There is a fine effigy tomb of the Black Prince—of Poitiers' fame (1356)—between the south piers. This old city was first represented in Parliament in 1283. It was made an important centre of silk weaving in the 17th century by the large community of Walloons which had settled there. In fact, there is no period of English history from the time of the Romans onwards in which Canterbury is not mentioned. But we can go back even farther. From Winchester to Canterbury is the Pilgrim's Way, usually associated with Christian pilgrimages. I have in Part I mentioned that it was trodden long before the coming of Christianity to England; in fact, during the time of the pagan Celts. Apart from the religious associations, the city is a most pleasant and interesting old place. One can trace the old city walls of the Middle Ages, and there is a public walk called Dane John, which runs along the top of a high artificial mound from which there is a good view of the cathedral. There is also the early 18th-century Guildhall; a statue of Christopher Marlowe (*d.* 1593), who was born here; and a pillar to mark the spot where Protestants were burned at the stake in the reign of Mary.

From this dignified old city of Canterbury one can quickly reach Margate which, with Blackpool, may be regarded as in the topmost rank of England's *very* popular seaside resorts. In Margate, whether you wish it or not, history is driven from your head by the bewildering and colourful array of attractions for the fancy-free holiday-makers who go there on their special pilgrimage year after year. Margate has an allure of its own. The air is bracing, as it is almost everywhere facing east in England. The town is conveniently situated for London, and it is from London that the majority of its summer visitors come. The holiday area along this piece of coast has made itself into connected parts for the different kinds of visitor: Margate for the lively; Broadstairs for the quiet; Ramsgate, akin to Margate; and Kingsgate—rather select. Margate in the summer months is for the hale-and-hearties who, as long as I can remember, always seem to expect and are provided with the same sort of attractions: a fine sandy beach, bathing from the beach and in pools, games (tennis, golf and others), theatres, cinemas, and—Dreamland, a vigorous, noisy and minor Coney Island, providing facilities for dancing and many side-shows with all sorts of special draws—palmists, 'gypsy' fortune-tellers, crystal-gazers—and much besides.

Now for something which may arouse wonder. As you walk from the railway-station along the street overlooking the sea (in every part of these seasides there are shops, restaurants, little places of amusement with pin-tables and suchlike), you will find many shops displaying dozens of coloured picture-postcards with characteristic English comic drawings and captions in the simple, coarse humour which seems to have become almost entirely associated with picture-postcards sold at all popular seaside resorts in this country since Victorian times. The characters represent drunks or at least holidaying gentlemen 'on the spree'; buxom ladies with callipygian charms; mashers and lady-killers who, one deduces, as often as not are married men set temporarily free and now gushing to approach the fine ladies, who are equally free and welcoming; bathing scenes in which the generously proportioned hindquarters of the ladies dominate the seascape. There are pictures of comical mishaps, often of an embarrassing nature; and on many of the cards there is an obscene or ill-behaved or embarrassing dog. In these comic cards father, dressed in his ludicrous summer best, has the time of his life; and mother, if she has no children, is permitted to sit back grandly and put on superior airs. If she has children, these are depicted as squalling, mischievous brats for ever ready to do something to spoil the holiday. George Orwell was fascinated by these comic cards. He made a study of them, and even drew sociological conclusions from them. To me, much of the humour in them is strongly Germanic, and without the least flavour of the Gallic. The interesting thing about them is that one rarely finds the cards or this kind of humour anywhere in England outside the popular seaside resorts. Last year in one of the more select seasides I discovered a shop where the cards displayed outside had numbers so that, if you wished to buy one from the salesman inside, all you had to do was give him the number or numbers on those you wanted. As some cards are risky and verging on the obscene, this is a concession to hypocrisy which also facilitates business; a wonderful compromise! What an altogether curious phenomenon is this matter of seaside comics! I have my own ideas of how it could be analysed, but prefer to keep them out of these unpsychiatric pages.

Of that group of resorts—Margate, Broadstairs and Ramsgate—I have always found Margate of most interest. You may think it worth while to run out along the north coast of Kent to nearby Herne Bay or, better still, in the oyster months to Whitstable, which from time immemorial has been famous for its oysters, delicious 'natives' which have soothed the palates of Celt, Roman, Saxon, Dane and Norman; and continue today as highly priced delicacies for the new rich and as fond memories for the new poor.

When you decide to move on from Canterbury to the next Convenient Centre—Brighton—you should try to take in on your way the ancient Cinque Ports. These were originally Sandwich, Dover, Hythe, Romney and Hastings. Rye and Winchelsea were added later, but these two are no longer

High Bridge, Somerset
BTHA

Royal Pavilion, Brighton
BTHA

Falstaff Hotel

ports, the sea having receded. Cinque Ports is the name of an ancient jurisdiction, which still exists but with many modifications and greatly diminished authority. It is a curious remnant of an institution whose origin sprang from the need for co-ordinating defences around this inviting coast. Until the time of Henry VII the Cinque Ports had to furnish the Crown with most of the men and ships required by the Government. The oldest Charter relating to it is dated 1277, but it refers to previous documents of Edward the Confessor's time and of William the Conqueror. In return for services, the Cinque Ports enjoyed extensive privileges that have now mostly vanished. The old office of Lord Warden of the Cinque Ports still exists; he acts as governor of Dover Castle, having also a maritime jurisdiction as Admiral of the Cinque Ports. This is a highly esteemed office, and is bestowed only upon highly esteemed national personages. When King George V was Prince of Wales, he was Lord Warden (1903–1907) and, since 1941, Winston Leonard Spencer Churchill has enjoyed the honour of holding this most ancient office, of which I have been told he is very proud. Within the grounds of Dover Castle is the oldest standing building in England: the *Pharos* or lighthouse used by the Romans to guide their ships into the harbour. Shakespeare Cliff, the great precipice mentioned in *King Lear,* stands to the west of the town. In time of peace Dover is one of the busiest of the ports for traffic with the Continent. In time of war it is a fortress: in 1914–1918 it was a well-fortified naval base, headquarters of the famous 'Dover Patrol'. In the Second World War it was consistently bombed and shelled, and suffered much damage. Throughout the ages this has been an important landing-place, beginning in the record as the Roman Dubris (or Dubræ), the starting-point of Watling Street and the great road system. It was later one of the 'Forts of the Saxon Shore'—the line of defences made by the Romans to withstand the early maraudings of the Germanics. From Norman times onwards it grew in importance. To-day its chief feature of interest is the Castle, which so beautifully adorns the summit of the East Cliff. In summer many of the Channel swimmers make Dover their headquarters, and thereby add to its excitements. There is enough

The Falstaff, Canterbury, Kent
For centuries the faithful have entered the city through the West Gate and passed the Falstaff Hotel *BTHA*

The Leather Bottle Inn at Cobham, Kent
A favourite haunt of Dickens *BTHA*

of interest here to occupy the visitor for much more than a day.

Rye is simply delightful. It is much favoured by artists and writers: by the former because it provides endless scope for the picturesque and Olde English; by the latter because it is a quiet, old-world place in which to live. The narrow, winding streets, with their old and on the whole well-preserved houses, are enchanting. As you stroll along them, now and then on turning a corner you have a fine view of the salt marshes in the direction of Winchelsea, its companion Ancient Town. Rye has now little or no commercial or industrial importance. As a working port, it no longer counts. In other words, it is entirely a place of residence and a resort for visitors. The golf-links are famous. It is an excellent place for those who wish to avoid the boisterous attractions of the more popular resorts.

A few miles westwards along the coast are Hastings, St. Leonards and Bexhill-on-Sea. Hastings is the popular end of these three towns, St. Leonards is a little less boisterously alive, and Bexhill considers that it strikes the right tone for those who like the right tone. Hastings and St. Leonards are joined together, and one may almost think of them as one continuous town; Bexhill is five miles farther along the coast. Of most interest from the historical and other points of view is Hastings, one of the Cinque Ports and famous for the battle which in 1066 decided the whole future of England. Inland a few miles is Battle with the site of Senlac, the hill where William fought the Saxons and afterwards founded Battle Abbey, the spot on which King Harold set up his royal standard, and there he was killed. It is open to visitors and well worth a visit. In the church, dating from the 13th century and completed in the 15th, will be found a memorial to Edmund Cartwright, a Nottinghamshire man who died at Hastings in 1823. Cartwright was an Anglican clergyman, a Doctor of Divinity, who might have been forgotten but for his remarkable achievements in mechanical invention. More by accident than anything else—or so it seems—his mind began to think of using power-machinery for weaving, and he invented a clumsy kind of power-loom which, nevertheless, showed by tests that it had the right ideas behind it. He took out a patent for it in 1785, and, continuing his experiments, so far improved it that by 1787 he achieved the power-loom, parent of nearly all the modern types of weaving machines in the world. This remarkable man of God then founded a factory for spinning and weaving, which provided him with much practical experience but was not a financial success: one little factory could not compete with the many hand-workers all over England. He tried again with a mill at Manchester, this time with a number of machines, but misfortune dogged him and the mill was maliciously burned down in 1791. Next he invented a wool-combing machine. But Cartwright had not the gifts required for making money, and this also failed to produce adequate financial rewards. Nevertheless, he always had the sense to patent his inventions and improvements, and only this saved him from complete bankruptcy. It was generally recognized that his new machines had conferred very great benefits on rising industrial England, and in the end Parliament voted him the sum of £10,000. He bought a small farm and continued working at his inventions, which included a rope-making machine, an engine that worked with alcohol, and some agricultural implements. Cartwright comes into the category of English eccentrics. Here was a clergyman who, from a certain moment onwards to his death, devoted his life to mechanical invention—and succeeded so well that his ideas brought about a revolution in the manufacture of textiles, not only in England but in time everywhere. In addition to this, in the church at Battle there is a handsome tomb, that of a gentleman named Sir Anthony Browne, Master of the Horse in Henry VIII's reign. This Browne must have been a king's favourite: on the Dissolution (1539) Henry bestowed on him the richly endowed Battle Abbey. Browne added a great Banqueting Hall, of which only the two turrets remain to be seen. And so, in these two names—Cartwright and Browne—the first with its modest memorial, the second with its imposing tomb, we have the symbols of two important aspects of the national history: in that of Cartwright, the clergyman-inventor, one of the most helpful advances in industrial progress; in that of Browne, of a bygone age in which a king's favourite could be given a rich endowment, a fortune merely because he was a favourite. But for a petition to Parliament, the great benefactor of humanity Cartwright would probably have died in poverty. It is all part of the history to be read in that church, of which the incumbent has the title 'Dean of Battle'.

In Queen's Avenue in nearby St. Leonards there is a tablet to commemorate the experiments of Baird (1888–1946), the pioneer in television. He died at Bexhill, but lived long enough to know that his pioneering work had not been in vain. There is not much of exceptional interest to see at pleasant Bexhill which, like Hastings and St. Leonards, enjoys a genial winter climate, good bathing amenities, and has a variety of preparatory schools. And so we may return to take a look over the interesting old fishing-port in the lower town at Hastings. Years ago, I lived in St. Leonards, and used to enjoy the walk along the esplanade to Hastings old town, where the fishermen set out their catches on trestle tables in the open, their nets spread out to dry outside tall, tarred storing-sheds, their boats drawn up on the shingle beach. I have often marvelled at those catches which, it seemed to me, nearly always contained specimens of fishes and molluscs with which I was quite unacquainted and whose names, when I heard them, conveyed nothing to me. Hastings is a good place for sea-fishermen. Simple tackle and bait will provide excellent sport, especially if you take a little boat and row out to sea as far as safety allows. On one great day I filled the bottom of my boat with the fish I caught. But fishing stories must be ruled out. . . . Try Hastings for yourself.

Next, on the way to Brighton, is prosperous Eastbourne, with a sea-front about three miles long. Again, an attractive seaside resort with a genial winter climate and all the amenities, though fewer of those seaside comic postcards—as befits its dignity—than in the more rumbustious resorts. What I like best about it is that it is just at the foot of the eastern end of the South Downs, the Sussex hills which sweep to the sea and are delightful for walks. On the surface of the hills is turf on which sheep thrive to produce the famous South Down mutton. Below the turf is chalk. It is worth while to make a trip to Wilmington—or it can be taken in on the way to Brighton—to see what is called the Long Man of Wilmington, a white figure on the face of the Downs to the right of some ruins of a 14th-century Benedictine priory. The whiteness is produced by cutting the turf surface and leaving exposed the chalk underneath. This extraordinary figure is 240 feet in height. It represents a man holding a staff in each hand, and what interested me is the fact that it has never yet been convincingly explained. It has been attributed to the monks who lived in the priory; but why, apart from amusement, should they cut out this vast figure, which does not represent any symbol that we can reasonably associate with those monks or with Christianity? Another theory is that it represents Baldr (Balder), the son of Odin and Frigga of Scandinavian mythology. But this also does not work, because, in the story of this Baldr there is nothing about a person or figure holding a staff in each hand. It has also been associated with Baldur, of whom Sir James Frazer has written in the *Golden Bough.* There may be something in this, because this Baldur symbolizes spring, which is a pleasant idea of general and immediate significance. I myself think that the figure is probably a survival from the Celts, one which may have largely disappeared and was recut by some people at a much later date, possibly by the monks. My reasons are based on the main fact that the figure could represent Beltené or Beltane, the old Celtic god who gives life to men and takes it away—he holds Life in one hand and Death in the other—and Beltene (*Bel* or *Bile,* the god's name; *teine,* fire) also symbolized spring. Beltene, Bel's fire, or the Feast of Fire, was the Spring Festival held on May 1st by the Irish Celts (Goidels) to celebrate the beginning of the Celto-Iberian invasion of Ireland by the sons of Mile. In Welsh (Brythonic) mythology we have an equivalent god, Beli. And the 'ancient Britons', as we have seen, were Brythonic Celts. Here the associations are at least plausible. I should not like to claim that this is the last word in explanation of the Long Man of Wilmington, for which all useful evidence, apart from the figure itself, is lacking. What strikes me as odd is that nobody seems to take the trouble to investigate the Long Man in the full light of modern knowledge; and it is only because of this that I offer my own thoughts on the subject. Incidentally, this is not the only figure cut out of the turf on a chalk face. About five miles west of Wantage in Berkshire there is White Horse Hill, so called because it has the sketchy figure of a horse cut in the turf, and there are good reasons to believe that it is the work of those same 'ancient Britons' whom we should more correctly call Brythonic Celts. The horse may symbolize the Sun; or in this case it may be just a figure of fancy. The important point is this: the evidence pointing to the Celtic origin of this particular figure is more reliable than that relating to the Long Man. And does it not indicate that the Celts must have been given to cutting out figures in the turf on England's chalky hills? If that is accepted, we may be one step forward towards a solution of the Long Man problem.

And so we move on to Brighton, London's principal seaside playground, which has been called—and not without reason—the queen of seaside resorts, a title challenged only by Scarborough. Three factors combine to make Brighton attractive: a considerable part of this large coast town is built in the elegant Regency style; it maintains a carefree, cheerful atmosphere all the year round; the climate is genial in winter, and the air is always invigorating. First, a word about the climate to-day. The world has heard so much about the 'unpleasantness' of the English climate in winter that it is good to be able to put on record here and now that few countries can boast of a finer autumn and early winter than was enjoyed by England in the year 1953. It was delightfully mild, and continued so until the end of December. The weather was then so amazingly kind that already the English countryside was dressed in the colours of spring. We saw around us Nature as she usually appears in May or June, which, it must be admitted, is most unusual for this time of year. But it shows this: that it is wise for a prospective visitor, especially in winter months, to work on the principle of taking a chance with the English weather. Those who did so in 1953 cannot have failed to reap a rich and unique reward. I was on the south coast on December 5th and the sights I saw were those of summer: children paddling, men and women bathing—and sun-bathing! In Brighton the thermometer registered 86° in the sun. Bathing belles on the beach and crowds sunning themselves! Next day the newspapers reported that the same sort of weather was enjoyed over most of England. "The mildest December for years," commented a meteorologist. It even affected trade, for people refrained from buying new overcoats in the hope that their old ones would see them through the winter. I put this on record for the benefit of those who may have unjust ideas about the English climate.

The Borough of Brighton comprises a considerable area: it stretches inland towards the South Downs for nearly four miles, and the sea-front from Hove to Rottingdean is over seven miles long. It is a seaside resort with a high percentage of permanent residents, many of whom travel daily to and from their work in London, taking advantage of the frequent service of fast and comfortable electric trains which cover the distance (fifty-one miles) in about an hour. Needless to say, Brighton has every amenity that the visitor may require. Domesday Book mentions it as a fishing village under the name of Brighthelmston, and a fishing village it remained until 1651, in which year Charles II, just before his escape to France, spent a night here. But its prosperity and popularity date from about the middle of the 18th century, when a famous Dr. Richard Russell recommended its sea-bathing and invigorating air to his patients, some of whom were distinguished people. Dr. Samuel Johnson, Mrs. Thrale and Miss Burney visited the town in 1770, but in 1784 the future destiny of Brighton was finally settled by the Prince of Wales (afterwards George IV), who not only came to live here but built the Royal Pavilion, restored in 1936, and now a concert and dance-hall. The princely romance with Mrs. Fitzherbert and its cheerful Brighton associations gave a great fillip to the rising importance of the town. Now Brighton is 'London by the Sea', maintaining similar strata of social classes, though the tendency in recent years has been to attract the well-to-do business-men and officials of the Welfare State. It is also a favourite place for daily trippers who, in the summer months, come in their thousands.

Brighton is so extensive that I shall not attempt to describe the town more than to say that it has an air, partly of grandeur surviving from those great days of royalty, distinguished visitors—and distinguished building—and partly, in recent years, of general popularity. Respectability and even gentility seem to mix well with vulgarity here. One finds examples of almost everything that is to be found in London—from the hearties of the East End to the slick boys and girls of Mayfair in their smart sports' cars. In marked contrast are the many elderly retired officials from far-flung posts of Empire. In Brighton you will find an interesting cross-section of society, a useful microcosm for study. Incidentally, in the Art Gallery there is a good collection of modern British painting, some excellent water-colours and interesting examples of Old Masters. In the Booth Museum the naturalist will find about 250 species of British birds presented in surroundings reproducing their particular habitats.

When fully satisfied with Brighton and the sea, you may turn inland, and from Haywards Heath visit the site on which the famous Piltdown cranium and suspect jawbone were discovered, and then, a little farther to the north-east, see Ashdown Forest. All of this is delightful, restful countryside, well worthy of a visit in the summer months. Or, pursuing the coastline, pass through Worthing, Littlehampton (with the Duke of Norfolk's Arundel Castle inland) until you come to Bognor Regis, which acquired its royal description after King George V, on the recommendation of his physicians, had convalesced there. Could there be a better recommendation for the air of a resort than this? You will find Bognor rather a contrast to Brighton. The atmosphere is a little quieter, perhaps a little more consistently genteel, than that of Brighton; it is altogether a more restful place, with a sandy beach for bathing and sunning. Nevertheless, I am anxious to get you on to Portsmouth, which is not only a great naval base but the place from which you embark for the Isle of Wight, a little island that is highly favoured by Nature, both in its geographical position and its configuration, apart from its innumerable attractions, amenities and points of interest. I am a partisan of the Isle of Wight, and if I extol its delights unduly, it is because I found it not only generally attractive and interesting but singularly suited to my inquisitive temperament.

You cross from Portsmouth in a ferry-boat, landing at the island port of Ryde. The water you cross is the Solent, with a part called Spithead (from over one mile to four miles wide) where the ships of the British Navy on great occasions show themselves in full display. The island is of an irregular lozenge shape, about twenty-three miles long from east to west and just less than fourteen from north to south, and it is divided into two 'hundreds' or 'liberties' by the River Medina (from whom the Marquess of Milford Haven has the title of Earl of Medina). Our history of the Isle of Wight begins in A.D. 43, when the Romans (who named it Vectis) conquered it. Long before that date it was inhabited by Celts, and I have been told that the skull of a sabre-tooth tiger has been found on the island—which puts it far back in prehistory. Ryde is a lively little port, convenient for Cowes, headquarters of the Royal Yacht Squadron and other clubs, a famous place for yachtsmen, and notable for its 'week' of yacht races.

When the ferry-boat which first took me to the Isle of Wight set out from Portsmouth—with as much excitement and hullabaloo as if it were the *Queen Mary* sailing for New York —I found myself in the expectant mood of the traveller who is leaving for some new kind of adventure in foreign parts. And then, when I settled in after a few days—but not before —I realized with some surprise that I was still very much in England! I made Shanklin my headquarters and, thanks to an admirable bus service, was able to visit all the principal towns very quickly. Newport, the capital, is inland. They are mostly pleasant seaside resorts with the usual attractions and amenities, but each with its own individuality. In 1953 there was a little railway that still preserved its 19th-century characteristics and aroma, with old-fashioned carriages and a locomotive which was certainly a distinct advance on Stephenson's 'Rocket'. As I sat in my compartment, I thought of the breathless excitement I used to feel as a child when travelling. I had precisely the same experience in 1953: the feeling of being projected back in time. It vanished immediately on my arrival in Shanklin, a nicely placed resort, built on high ground overlooking the sandy beach and pier. This is one of the chief attractions of Shanklin: its mostly high position, the cliffs above the beach, the gardens and the esplanade along the cliffs and facing the sea, where on the hottest days one can sit or, with luck, find a place on the grass to lounge, or stretch out and enjoy both the sun and the pleasant sea breeze. It is good for even the most energetic to punctuate moving about and sight-seeing with spells of absolute laziness and, although

I have enjoyed relaxing and lazing in many parts of England and the world, I have found few better places for such indulgence than the Isle of Wight. There is no part of the island where you cannot, even in the towns, quickly find a pleasant spot in which to sit back and do precisely nothing. In winter the island climate is mild. In summer it has as much sunshine as any part of England, and usually more. Throughout the summer of 1953 during hot spells I watched the newspapers for the sunshine records of the principal English seaside resorts, and the rough notes I kept indicate that Sandown, the Isle of Wight seaside resort chosen for the purpose, came out best. You can walk along the cliff from Shanklin to Sandown and, because of the height and the sea breeze, it is comfortable walking no matter how hot the day. Sandown is a sun-trap, with fine sands and excellent bathing, a golf-course and a swimming-pool. These two are popular resorts. North of Shanklin is Bembridge, a delightful coast walk of about five miles, some of it along the geologically interesting Whitecliff Bay. There are some attractive little places for yachtsmen around Bembridge, and every time I have been there I noticed that the yachtsmen do actually put to sea whenever the weather is in the least favourable, and are not like those stage yachtsmen who play the part so emphatically on terra firma in other places I could mention. This island, with the Solent, Spithead, its coast towns and other places, from the superb Cowes down to the many modest little havens around the coast, is a yachtsman's paradise.

The Isle of Wight, taking it all-round, is particularly attractive for those people who do not like rushing about from one place to another in quest of synthetic pleasures. Here one finds natural, healthy pleasures. It is ideal for those who wish either to relax altogether, or prefer to break the relaxation by taking a bus to some place and strolling from there into the neighbouring countryside or to some quiet, picturesque spot by the sea. You need a map of the bus routes, and that is about all. If you wish to be thorough, a more elaborate map is advisable. And it is so pleasant on looking at the map to feel that this is an *island*, away from the thick traffic of the mainland and compact in itself with everything to delight the eye and benefit health. You need not necessarily take advantage of any conveyance, for the island is so small that if energetic you can go from one end to the other on foot. A hiker's paradise. I went one day strolling from Shanklin to Ventnor, the latter built as a series of narrowish terraces overlooking the sea and one above the other, altogether inviting. I went by way of Luccombe Common and enjoyed a bathe at The Chine, after which I felt hungry, and, not having brought sandwiches or other food, began what I thought must be the usual frustrations in the quest for somewhere at least to stoke up, even if I could not obtain a 'restaurant meal' such as can be found in the towns anywhere. By the roadside I discovered a gay, attractive house with tables set out in a garden blooming with flowers, and there was a little notice to the effect that teas, coffee, minerals and 'light lunches' were served. I went in and sat down in the sunshine. The lady of the house came and offered me the choice of cold ham, tongue, with potatoes and salad; or, she said, she could make me a French omelet with that morning's eggs, and I could have a salad to follow; also fresh raspberries and cream, and Stilton cheese, bread and butter, with a coffee to conclude the meal. No chef in the best of luxury hotels ever made a better omelet. The salad was freshly picked, the potatoes were laughing, I could help myself to oil and vinegar. The raspberries were delicious, the cream fresh. The Stilton was perfect, the bread new, and the butter firm and cold, straight from the refrigerator or ice-box. And finally, the coffee was delicious. I could not have had a better, simple lunch anywhere, and it made me reflect on the great tragedy of England, which is that most of its hoteliers, restaurateurs, boarding-house keepers and caterers generally simply do not know how to cook or serve food in a way that can be called civilized. To them eating is merely a matter of filling a gaping void, and such things as the palate and the senses of the eaters do not enter into the question. Yet here, rather off the beaten track, I had found a lady with a real sense of food. She did not overcharge and she was polite. I decided to talk to her about it, and, having complimented her on the excellence of the meal, asked her where or how she had learnt to make so beautiful an omelet. Her answer was interesting. She said: "I knew my limitations as a cook, and decided from the outset that I would learn, at least to begin with, to cook a few simple dishes *supremely* well. That took time, and I had many failures. But I found that even the most apparently indifferent or lumpish people seldom fail to appreciate good food, especially when it is well served. The result is that I have a regular clientele of well-satisfied people who come out here regularly, and above all to enjoy my omelets and fresh salads. You must come and have tea and sample my home-made cakes. I'm sure that you'd like them." I did, and with great gratitude hereby record the place and the lady's highly intelligent and, in this country, somewhat unusual approach to a problem that is chiefly one of education. In this matter of catering, England must wake up. We cannot all afford to lunch and dine only in *de luxe* establishments; and, as other countries have shown, it is possible for the humblest caterer to provide good and civilized food. In fairness I must also say that things are improving, though they would improve far more rapidly if only the English victims of catering showed some of the energy in protesting against bad cooking and service which would be the fate of a restaurateur on the more realistic mainland of Europe. The English, to my mind, are just too polite to protest. Or too apathetic. Or protest is considered to be 'bad form', and is always more embarrassing for the innocent sufferer than for the real villain of the piece. I look forward to the day when firm and reasonable protests will have made themselves felt.

You may find that Carisbrooke Castle, near the village of Carisbrooke, is one of the most interesting castles in the whole of England. The site was that of a Roman fort, and the castle was founded in the early days of the Normans as one of the fortresses required to keep the Saxon population in order. It has many historical associations, and it is of considerable architectural interest. Of great sentimental interest is Osborne House, east of Cowes and accessible by bus from Newport. It is an imposing building with two towers, built in 1846 in Palladian style. Queen Victoria made it her seaside home, her doctors having recommended the fine air of this part; later it became her permanent residence. It was here that she died in 1901. You can visit the State Apartments, full of remarkable pictures and still more remarkable works of art, some of them of considerable intrinsic value, especially in the Durbar

Room, which is filled with superb gifts made to the Empress by Indian Princes. In the really lovely and beautifully kept grounds are some of the finest trees to be seen in England. And there is the curious Swiss Cottage, where the Queen used to enjoy tea and conversation with her friends and ladies of her household. You can also see the Queen's great bathing-machine: an astonishing engine built on the grand scale with huge wheels and a wooden canopy over the door, from which she emerged into the sea when the machine was let down there on lines and by a select party of retainers who held the ropes controlling its descent, and hauled it up after Her Majesty had enjoyed her discreet immersion. Victorianism is epitomized in this strange bathing-machine, which is now a show-piece of Osborne.

You must go right round this island, which is often described as the Garden Isle, and with good reason. In the summer, flowers and blooms everywhere, and in winter a genial climate. I should like to dwell longer on its attractions, but space forbids. Besides, you may wish to visit the port of Southampton, where you can see the biggest liners in the world. Then you may go on to Bournemouth, the most westerly of the resorts in this south-east corner of England. Bournemouth is select, dignified and a favourite place of retirement for the well-to-do. From it you can easily visit the New Forest, not a forest in the ordinary sense but an uncultivated region that became a royal preserve for deer-hunting in 1079 when William the Conqueror made it his own. It still has some red and fallow and roe deer, and there are the New Forest ponies, descendants from an indigenous breed. The most pleasant parts of the forest can be enjoyed only by pedestrians, and if you should wish to camp out, this is an ideal spot. But be careful to obtain a permit. The police will tell you where to get it. More than two-thirds of the New Forest is a Crown preserve. The Crown is jealous of its preserves, and always takes care that they are not abused.

CHAPTER IV

SOUTH-WEST AND THE WEST COUNTRY

For convenience, we shall continue to follow the suggestions for a tour with 'Convenient Centres in accordance with areas', and the general ideas outlined in pages 226 to 231. In the area now to be considered, whoever wishes to select a place for a holiday is embarrassed by the wealth of choice in the counties of Dorset, Wiltshire, Somerset, Devon and Cornwall. Those who like the seaside have many popular, and dozens of smaller, resorts from which to choose on both the southern and northern coasts of this area. This also gives one the additional advantage of a choice of air: on the south coast it is warmer in summer and more genial in winter than on the north-east, but this is more suitable for those who prefer a more bracing air or a more rugged line of coast. Again I would emphasize the remarkable variety which this country offers. Each of these five counties has its own distinct individuality: Cornwall and some western parts of Devon form a Celtic enclave in which the people have preserved many of their essentially Celtic characteristics. Here the Cornish language, a branch of Brythonic, was spoken until comparatively modern times. It is still spoken by a small number of enthusiasts who are proud of their old tongue. They alway refer to themselves as Cornish and to the English who live east of a line of demarcation as 'foreigners', and with reason regard themselves as forming an ethnic group that is different from that of the English. The Angles, Saxons and Jutes did not attempt to settle in Wales, and for long also avoided Cornwall. The result is that in Cornwall you are not always dealing with Celto-Germanic-Scandinavian-Norman people.

Let us begin with Dorsetshire, and work round through Devon, Cornwall and Somerset and on to Wiltshire. Dorsetshire was a part of the old kingdom of Wessex, which originated in A.D. 495 when Cedric and his followers first settled in Hampshire. Later, about the beginning of the 8th century, Saxon conquest and colonization spread farther west beyond the Kennet and Frome valleys until they covered the whole area now called Dorsetshire. Still later (A.D. 787) Scandinavian invaders landed in Portland, and then began a period of strife between Saxons and Northmen which lasted until the 11th century. At the time of the Norman Conquest, Dorset was part of Harold's earldom, and it put up a strong resistance to William, who took his revenge by ruthless suppression, in which Shaftesbury, Wareham and Dorchester were all but devastated and Bridport completely ruined. No Englishman was permitted to hold estates of importance. The King retained forty-six manors, and by the time of Domesday Survey the bulk of the land was in the possession of religious houses, the abbeys of Shaftesbury, Milton and Cerne being the most wealthy. The power and wealth of the area became Church monopolies; the Dorset forests favourite hunting-grounds of the Norman kings. For our immediate purpose that piece of history need not be continued, especially as it represents more or less what happened in many other parts of England. But this must be noted: Dorsetshire, from its original population of 'ancient Britons' (some of the Belgæ), became an essentially Saxon area with Scandinavian interminglings here and there, especially near the coast; and a fair sprinkling of Normans who became lords of manors.

Thus, the man or woman of Dorset tends to be sturdily Saxon in remote origin, but often with a flavouring of imaginative Celt or adventurous Scandinavian, or of both with the addition of Norman in the upper strata of society. If for a moment we consider the adjoining county of Devonshire, we find a similar pattern of history until we come to King Harold, to whom Devon was actively hostile. William the Conqueror was no less generous to those who did something for his cause —and he regarded hostility to Harold as being on his side— than he was ruthless to those who resisted the Conquest. Thus, the easy acquisition of Devon explains why in this part the new King allowed large numbers of Englishmen to retain their lands after the Conquest. True, his Norman barons held many and some of the best fiefs. All this resulted in a subsequent pattern different from that of Dorset. Now take Cornwall, whose pattern is another contrast. This was the last area of ancient British territory in the south of England to submit to the Germanic invaders, to whom it was not very attractive; and resistance was stubborn. In the year 815 King Ecgberht concentrated all his efforts on the subjugation of those recalcitrant Celts of what was then called West Wales. In spite of the superiority of his forces and resources over those of the Cornish people, eight years of fighting were required before they could be persuaded to acknowledge Saxon supremacy. The next generation of Cornishmen, who were joined by Scandinavians, rose in revolt against their conquerors, but were again defeated; very probably in A.D. 836, though the exact date is in doubt, as is the name of the exact place of the decisive battle, which may have been Hingston Down (Hengestundun). To mark a clear line in the conquest, Athelstan banished the West Welsh (that is, Cornish) people from Exeter, making the Tamar the boundary of their territory. The Saxon conquest was thorough: by the time of Edward the Confessor, men with English names held most of the land. Then, later, the Normans took most of it from them, but allowed ecclesiastical properties to remain in the hands of the Church. For a period of about four centuries after the Norman Conquest, Cornwall's history was that of a subdued people against whom the odds were too heavily weighted to justify further rebellion. After that it merges into English history. But to this day the true Cornishman—with his Celtic tendency to remember the past—differentiates himself from the Englishman. The old resentments have all but vanished.

One could deal with each English county in this way, and each would have its own pattern. To do so is not possible here; nor is it necessary. But the lessons of these three counties are useful to remember by the traveller who finds himself baffled by differences and the contrasting variety from one county—sometimes from one town—to the next. The brief statement given above presents the roots from which have grown some of the most important characteristics of Dorset, Devon, Cornwall and their present population.

About thirty miles inland from the coast in Dorset is Shaftesbury (locally called 'Shaston' and well described by Thomas Hardy in *Jude the Obscure*), which is strikingly situated on a cliff overlooking the very beautiful Blackmoor Vale. It is a quaint old place, and must be one of the oldest

PLACES OF INTEREST
BORDERS INDICATED ---
0 10 20 30 40
statute miles
S.Horne Shepherd
SCOTLAND
NORTH
SEA
WALES
ENGLISH CHANNEL
ALNWICK
NEWCASTLE
WALLSEND
CARLISLE
DURHAM
LAKE DISTRICT
Lake Windermere
ISLE OF MAN
YORKSHIRE MOORS
SCARBOROUGH
RIPON
HARROGATE
YORK
PEAK DISTRICT
BLACKPOOL
DONCASTER
ANGLESEY
LIVERPOOL
CHESTER
BUXTON
CHESTERFIELD
LINCOLN
THE WASH
THE POTTERIES
NOTTINGHAM
OSWESTRY
SHREWSBURY
THE BROADS
NORWICH
WOLVERHAMPTON
LEICESTER
BIRMINGHAM
COVENTRY
ROYAL FOREST OF DEAN
ISLE OF ELY
THETFORD
SHAKESPEARE COUNTRY
WARWICK
LEAMINGTON
STRATFORD ON AVON
GREAT MALVERN
CAMBRIDGE
BEDFORD
HEREFORD
WYE VALLEY
TEWKESBURY
CHELTENHAM
GLOUCESTER
WHIPSNADE
BISHOP'S STORTFORD
STROUD
COTSWOLDS
OXFORD
St. ALBANS
THAMES VALLEY
RUNNYMEADE
EPPING FOREST
UFFINGTON
ASHDOWN FOREST
WINDSOR
READING
LONDON
AVEBURY
BRISTOL
BATH
HAMPTON COURT
CANTERBURY
MAIDSTONE
CHANNEL
WELLS
GLASTONBURY
STONEHENGE
WINCHESTER
SHAFTSBURY
DOVER
FOLKESTONE
NEW FOREST
RYE
HASTINGS
SOUTHAMPTON
BOGNOR REGIS
BRIGHTON
BEXHILL
EASTBOURNE
BOURNEMOUTH
COUNTRY
EXETER
DORCHESTER
STRAIT OF DOVER
ISLE OF WIGHT
LISKEARD
PLYMOUTH
TORQUAY
PAIGNTON
BRIXHAM
TOTNES
SALCOMBE

The Enfield Chase Hunt Meet at Temple Bar, near Cheshunt

Temple Bar formerly stood in the Strand, at the entrance to the City of London

Test Match at Lord's Cricket Ground, London *Photos: Sport and General*

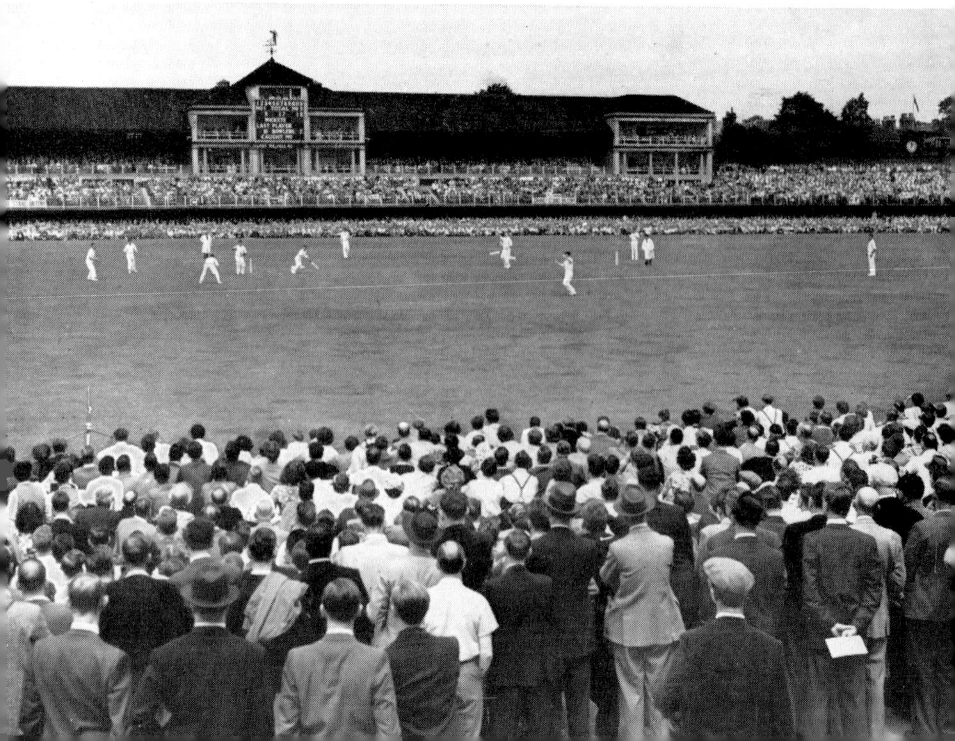

towns in England; the abbey was founded by Alfred the Great in the year 880. In 1861 the empty tomb of Edward the Martyr (*c.* 987) was found near the altar of the few surviving remains, and in 1931 some excitement was caused by the discovery nearby of a casket containing what were believed to be his bones. It is a town in which the visitor feels himself in an atmosphere of the past, and it provides a wonderful contrast to such busy modern towns as Dorchester (which nevertheless has a Roman amphitheatre), Weymouth and Lyme Regis. Thomas Hardy is commemorated by a statue in Dorchester. He lived and died there at 'Max Gate', a house built by himself. Dorchester ('Casterbridge') is the Mecca of his worshippers. Near Weymouth, a seaside resort and port for the Channel Islands, is the Isle of Portland, which is joined to the mainland by the shingle Chesil Bank, and notable for the famous stone quarried there; it has been used in the building of some of the finest edifices in England. There is also Swanage, a popular seaside resort, and Poole (note the *e*, for there are two other Pools, one in Devon, one in Cornwall; and there is Pool-in-Wharfedale in Yorkshire). I mention these few Dorset towns as worthy of attention, and would add that it is a most pleasing, restrained county, which depends for its attraction not on sights but on atmosphere. It has a green and varied countryside, one of gentle rural domesticity.

Devon, from the traveller's point of view, has to be considered in accordance with three main aspects: the south coast —with its warm and variegated seaside places; the north coast —mostly rugged and bracing, with fewer seaside resorts; and inland—with its pleasant towns and fine countryside for farming—typical rural England. The southern coastline is the beginning of what may be called the 'English Riviera', which extends down to the heel of Cornwall. One of the principal delights of Devonshire—and Cornwall—is that inland from the sea there is nearly always lovely countryside, and when one gets tired of the crowded resort or the quiet little spot on the coast, it is always possible to turn inland feeling sure of being rewarded by gentle rural landscape, interesting large towns or most pleasant villages. Sidmouth is an attractive watering-place with many advantages for those who like a little extra warmth: a circle of hills protects it from cold north winds, and thus, in a summer when other places along this coast and elsewhere may be cool, Sidmouth can be warm and even sultry. There are good walks from Sidmouth, and interesting bus trips. Attracted by the name, I once walked from Sidmouth through fields along the coast to a little town called Beer. I found that it was a sleepy little fishing-port built almost in one street near the sea and, after a refreshing bathe, I had some bread and cheese and excellent beer, all of which makes me remember it fondly. South of Sidmouth the popular resorts come one after another: Dawlish, Teignmouth, impressive Torquay, Paignton and Brixham. These are excellent places for a holiday, and in most summers get all the sunshine there is. In a hot summer they have an almost tropical atmosphere, and it is not unusual to see palm-trees and other tropical plants, especially at Torquay, which has been called a coquettish town. The great advantage of Torquay—apart from its amenities for every kind of visitor—is its equable climate. It is so situated that the temperature is never oppressively high even in the hottest summer; and it seldom goes down to freezing-point in a bad winter. This is the place for warm-blooded men and women. There is everything one might want in the way of amusements; and in the town and around it, many things of interest to those who prefer to amuse themselves away from the madding crowds. Torquay used to be rather a grand place, never quite so grand as Brighton once was, but grand nevertheless. And it was grand not because of any royal influence, but because the great English middle class, who apparently wished to have a seaside made after their own heart, imparted to it a rather superior tone, which still survives in the select parts. For it tends to become more catholic and popular as workers' pay-packets improve. South of Torquay is Dartmouth on the River Dart, mentioned in the Prologue to the *Canterbury Tales* as 'Dertemouthe', now a picturesque, landlocked seaport in whose estuary American troops embarked for the landing in Normandy in 1944. Devon's Pool is not far away, the birthplace of Sir John Hawkins. During the Second World War these Devon ports were American bases, or served as towns for bases nearby and inland. Farther south is Kingsbridge, which I have often in the past used as a Convenient Centre and for several good reasons. It is situated at the inner end of a lake-like inlet from the sea coast, which is easily available. Kingsbridge is a busy agricultural centre as well as being an attractive town, and it is convenient for a number of smaller places on the coast, many of which are off the beaten track and very peaceful. There is, for example, Salcombe, a short bus ride from Kingsbridge (no railway goes to Salcombe) and situated to overlook a beautiful, sheltered little cove (in which you can row, sail or bathe) and still preserving an atmosphere of its own. From Salcombe you can go to Thurlestone, where there is a good sandy beach for bathing, two hotels, a golf-course and some boarding-houses—apart from which you feel isolated and almost as if you are at the end of the earth.

It was not far from Thurlestone that I made friends with a farm labourer and his wife, after which I used to go every summer to their cottage to relax. Although I had before then known many Devonshire people, especially seafarers, it was only now that I was able to make a close acquaintance with folk whom I shall always feel are, with the sailors, the salt of England: I mean the landworkers. In what I am now about to say, I am providing both English people from urban areas and the stranger from overseas with the best of hints, not only for what some may think is the best possible kind of holiday and at a modest cost, but the best possible way of getting to know fine people. The little cottage was spotlessly clean, my room was comfortable, the offices were practical, hygienic and amenable. My friend's wife in her youth had been cook in a big house, and could put up excellent English fare as well as anybody. Good farm produce was available from all around us. The sea and excellent places for bathing were within a quarter of an hour's walk, the buses to Kingsbridge (and thence to the whole of Devon) ten minutes or so away. From the cottage I could walk to Thurlestone, and thence westwards along the cliff through fields to Bantham, a little yachting-place with a fine sandy beach and a back-of-the-world atmosphere; or in the other direction to Hope Cove, a snug little village for bathing, boating and fishing. Or one could turn inland and wander along country roads or lanes, or across fields until an inviting inn was reached. All these are pleasing factors, but it is of my host and hostess that I wish to speak, for those other things can be found elsewhere in England if you search for them. Devonshire people are notable for their *immediate* friendliness. It is not a friendliness that is worn on the sleeve, but a simple, genuine and entirely natural friendliness. With that goes a sturdy independence and an intelligent appreciation of things generally. Although gentle and usually easy-going, Devon people are not fools and will not stand for any kind of nonsense—think of those Elizabethan sailors!—though they will go right out of their way to help the stranger or the person in a difficulty. So it was with my friends, as they quickly became. After a gruelling day on the farm, the husband would come home, have his evening meal, and then we would sit outside in the garden, chatting. Occasionally we would be joined by his wife, and perhaps by a visitor. It was in those chats that little by little I learnt about every square yard of an area covering miles around us: who used to live in such a house and the family history; what such and such a place used to be like and how it had changed. I was told all—back to the beginning of the century, and even a little farther. In the telling, the personality of my friends unfolded—the wife filled in what the husband omitted—and one saw the poetic depth of their nature. What good humour and what a wonderfully tolerant attitude to life! Once in a while we would amble off to the nearby village of Marlborough for a drink and, as a good man of Devon, my friend preferred cider to beer; or, indeed, to almost any other beverage. Here I may perhaps usefully say something about Devonshire cider, which, at its best, is a remarkably fine drink. Those who are weaned and grow up on it need no warning about its dangers: they know that, when not abused, it is salubrious, comforting and even has admirable medicinal qualities, especially for those who are susceptible to gouty or rheumaticky complaints. They also know exactly how much of it to drink without doing themselves harm. Not so the stranger . . . but I must not go too fast. First of all, cider is not a taxable liquor in England, and its alcoholic content—not subject to constant and careful measurement, because not taxable—varies from as little as 2 per cent. to as much as 8 per cent. It is produced from the fermentation of the expressed juice of specially grown 'cider' apples. There are various kinds of cider, the very rough (darkish in Devon), the sweet (usually light and clear in colour), which are sold on draught; and the bottled still or sparkling varieties, rarely consumed locally and usually made for sale in towns and cities, and even for export abroad. I now speak of the ordinary draught cider which one can obtain anywhere in Devon, and those who believe in that wise old adage which enjoins us to drink 'the wine of the country' we happen to be in will not go wrong in following it—at first always with discretion. Devonshire cider is usually sold in mugs which hold a little less than a pint.

Now, the main point to remember—assuming that you are a stranger—is this: it is advisable to ask somebody before starting to drink—the landlord, a friendly-looking drinker, anybody likely to know—whether this particular cider that you are about to consume is strong, mild or weak. For do not forget that cider varies, and, unless warned, you can easily be enticed by a pleasant flavour into believing that it is quite harmless, whereas it may be as strong as old ale and stronger than table wine. For myself, I greatly enjoy a mug or two of light sweet cider; there is nothing better on a hot day. Rough cider is too 'rough' in flavour and too strong for my taste, but local drinkers usually prefer it. By way of final warning, I can tell of an episode I am not likely to forget. There was a shortage of beer in the last years of the Second World War when I was staying at the cottage in Devon. That did not greatly worry local people; they drank their local cider. But very often the American troops stationed in the neighbourhood suffered distress from the lack of alcohol and (I suspect, somewhat to their disgust) were driven back on cider, which they contemptuously regarded as a soft drink! Friendly patrons of the pub advised them to 'take it easy' until they got used to it. But those hearties just laughed, possibly regarding the civilian adviser as needlessly timid; and they just went ahead. At about the third mug the fun began—then the cider started to have effect. Another mug or two and the balloon went up. The usual effects of strong alcohol were felt: in this case of an alcoholic beverage to which those strong, healthy men were quite unaccustomed. We all felt sorry for them, and for their poor heads next day. And as, one by one they rolled off, the locals smiled and called for another mug saying: "Don't it just show 'ee!"

My friend would often reminisce and philosophize about cider, telling me that farm-workers used to have little barrels (he later showed me his; it held about a pint and a half) which they took with them to their work, but that the young generation know nothing of this. He thought that modern cider is better and purer than that of his youth. He had known of men who drank themselves to death on cider, but insisted that this is rare; because, he said, cider is one of those rare drinks which carries its own safety-point and, when that point has been reached—depending on the drinker's capacity and head—there is no inclination to drink any more. "How very convenient!" the conservative drinker will say. The illustrious may comment: "How awful!" There it is.

I need not continue with this pleasant cottage experience, which I enjoyed for many years; in fact until my old friend left us for ever and the cottage changed hands. The experience is something I can pass on in complete confidence to those who may be like myself and prefer this kind of friendly intimacy, the simple life, the wisdom of people who live close to the earth, and the health which comes from their company, to anything that can be found in a town.

I took a bus one day to Totnes, and thence through a sweet countryside to Buckfast Abbey, which not only has a great history but a new cruciform church with a square central tower and an interior in the modern style, all of it a superb example of good taste and dignity, and with the impressiveness of eternity. The original abbey was founded before the Norman Conquest, refounded in 1136, and colonized by Benedictines from France in 1882. Nothing is left of the original abbey but the old Saxon crypt and foundations that remain from the Cistercian church which came after it, and which dictated the shape of the new building. The new church has been built entirely by the monks themselves; every bit of it is the result of their own labour. They began their work in 1907, and the main part of it was finished in 1938. The mosaic pavement of the interior must be one of the most beautiful in England; the chandelier also is lovely. It is the general success of the modern style as here achieved which struck me:

it is carried right throughout; it was here for the first time that I saw the Stations of the Cross in this style. Buckfast Abbey is a busy community of monks, and a community of what struck me as very busy monks. Every man had a task, and without taskmasters or any driving force other than his own spiritual inspiration; each man worked as if his objectives in this world and the next were sure and assured. I took away with me some of the delicious honey from the bees kept by the monks; and a bottle of their tonic wine, which did me no harm. When I arrived back in Totnes there was time for a quick look around before catching a bus for home.

I have been searching for a word to describe the innumerable towns and villages in England which, even allowing for the wonderful variety on all sides in this country, strike the first-time visitor as being different from anything they have yet seen. The word which comes nearest to it is, I think, 'unconformity'. In their inner life and disciplines, few peoples can be more rigidly conformist to the traditions of their race than the English. But in their outward manifestations—as the reader will have realized—their individualism runs fancy free, and this is often strikingly illustrated by the seemingly unorganized lay-out and configuration of a city, a town or a village. To the tidy-minded planner all this is anathema, chaos, possibly sheer ignorance or even plain stupidity. But how very pleasant the results can be! Totnes struck me as a perfect example of 'unconformity', so much so that my first quick impression was that this could not be England. It was more like a Continental town, perhaps in the Netherlands or Denmark, I thought. One is not surprised to learn that this is one of the oldest little boroughs in England. The town consists manly of one long street which runs down a hillside. There are interesting old houses with quaint fronts and, I was told, still more interesting interiors; there are un-English piazzas, and the keep of a Norman castle at the upper end of the town. The church is four hundred years old and has a fine red tower; nearby is the colonnaded Guildhall. In the lower town near the Dart Bridge is a monument inscribed to the memory of Wills, a 19th-century explorer who was one of the first to cross Australia. I had in my pocket a letter of introduction to Sean O'Casey, the famous Irish dramatist, who lives in this delightful old town. But I found that I had become so interested as I wandered about that time had defeated me and I had to rush to catch the last bus.

On the south coast of Devon there remain Plymouth and Devonport, the former a great general port and fortress, the latter a great naval dockyard. The centre of Plymouth was mostly razed to the ground by German bombers in 1941, and is now mostly rebuilt. This town was first fortified in the 14th century, and since then its name recurs again and again in English history. It was in Plymouth Sound that the British Fleet waited for the Spanish Armada in 1588. The port was the starting-point of England's great captains—Hawkins, Drake, Gilbert, Humphrey—on their historic expeditions, and of that remarkable man, Captain James Cook, who not only discovered Australia, New Zealand and many islands for England, but made the first accurate charts of the Antarctic and Pacific Oceans. At Plymouth, on the causeway of what is known as the Barbican, stands the Mayflower Stone. It marks the exact spot from which the Pilgrim Fathers sailed to America in 1620. I once saw a group of Americans contemplating the Stone. One of them had removed his hat and stood reverently with his head bowed, and I thought that he must be saying a silent prayer.

The interior of Devonshire is agricultural, and it breeds some fine cattle: Devons, South Devons, Guernseys, Jerseys and others, and some very excellent pigs called Wessex Saddlebacks. Exeter, the capital, is worth a visit, and one must see the cathedral, successor to the Norman edifice finished in 1206, which took the place of the conventual church founded by Athelstan about 932. Exeter cathedral is not large. I find it very beautiful; perhaps because it is a little unusual both in regard to the contrast of its Norman towers and its many flying buttresses, and because of its situation. It is approached from above and, to look down on a cathedral, is an experience. This is altogether a fine edifice in the decorated geometrical style, with an impressive uniformity and purity of style in the interior. The Guildhall (1464), the Rougemont Grounds with the remains of a castle dating from William the Conqueror, and the Old City Wall; all are worth a visit.

It is pleasant for motoring or bus rides throughout the

whole of Devonshire; the stops at its clean, attractive towns are always rewarding. I can briefly summarize the north coast by saying that it is usually rugged, and ruggedly picturesque in contrast to most of the south coast, where the picturesqueness is usually soft and gentle. The northern seaside resorts do not differ greatly from those of the south coast, but the more invigorating air attracts visitors, who prefer it to the softer, warmer atmosphere of the south.

In Cornwall we are in another England, which the true Cornishman may say is not England at all but Cornwall. There are no very big seaside resorts in this country, but there is an astonishing variety of small ones. Down in Land's End, the heel and toe of England, say west of a line drawn from Falmouth to Redruth, the area, especially round the coastline, is a paradise for artists, not only for landscape and seascape but for the local Cornish types of men and women. You feel that you are not in England. The Celtic names of places and people help to remind us of the difference between Saxon and Celt. Penzance, which means 'sacred headland', is the ideal Convenient Centre for the whole district of Land's End. From it one can visit all the little towns and coves round the coast. My favourite place is Mousehole, a really picturesque and delightful little fishing village, where lobsters are plentiful when the sea is not too bad, and life is slow enough for anyone. From Penzance one can go by steamer (five times weekly in summer, three in winter) to the Scilly Isles, which I have several times determined to visit but never succeeded in getting there. Cornwall is an important territory in the Arthurian legends. The Scilly Isles, we are told, represent what visibly remains of Lyonesse—the Land of the Arthurian legends—the rest of which now lies on the bed of the ocean between the Isles and Cornwall at a depth of some forty fathoms. And, since the legends have been mentioned, if you are really interested you should go to 'wild Tintagel' which, anyhow, is worth a visit if you wish to see some of the most interesting rugged scenery of the north Cornish coast. The village is at some distance from the sea. Go down there and you find yourself in an eerie little cove surrounded by sinister cliffs of slate, with Tintagel Head connected with the mainland by a rocky neck. One regards it as an island. On it, and on the mainland opposite, are the ruins of a castle, and for reasons which are mainly poetical, some early chroniclers (who are followed by some later writers) accept this as the birth-place of King Arthur, the son of Uther Pendragon and Ygrayne. This, poetically, is as it should be; we have learnt enough to discard or denigrate old legends at our peril. In the village of Tintagel there is a hall dedicated to the Knights of King Arthur. You are invited to visit it; and there you will see many strange Arthurian mementoes and colourful reconstructions of historical romances that have baffled and bewildered generations of investigators. The legends are still dark enough to allow the imagination to play around them until, alas, the dull truth is one day discovered.

King Arthur and his romantic legends follow us into Devon and on into Somerset, where at Glastonbury Christianity was established at an early date. In the ruins of Glastonbury Abbey are the graves of Arthur and his wife Guinevere; and the legend has it that to Glastonbury was brought the holy chalice of the Last Supper by no less a person than Joseph of Arimathea. I fear that it will require a better man than myself to separate gold from sand in this realm of legend and romance, and must apologize for what I hope is a pardonable inability. At a distance of five miles from Glastonbury is Wells, which has one of the smallest but certainly one of the most beautiful cathedrals in England. The history of the original church dates from 704; the present cathedral was begun in about 1186. There were substantial restorations about the middle of the 19th century. This beautiful little gem of a cathedral, with its long history, its associations with Puritan vandalism and Monmouth's rebels, and its potent impact in this quiet market-town at the foot of the Mendip Hills, prompts me to reflect on what such small provincial cities—Wells has only about 5,000 inhabitants—would be without their cathedrals? Big cities acquire personality merely by their agglomerations of people and apart altogether from their great edifices. London would still be London without its great architectural landmarks. But such small places as Wells, without their cathedrals, which are always their finest buildings, would be unimpressive towns more or less typical and representative of their county. True, Somerset is a very

English county, mainly an agricultural area with lovely countryside, rolling fields, farmhouses, cattle (British Friesians and South Devons), and in general a gentle, rural way of life. It is at the opposite pole from industrialism and 'Industrial England'. Of course, in Weston-super-Mare there is a good seaside resort, but it does not differ in essentials from most other English seaside resorts. Undoubtedly of greatest interest as a Somerset town and for its associations is Bath, a natural spa where the Romans established elaborate baths towards the middle of the first century of the Christian era. What remains of those baths are considered to be the most important Roman survivals in England. Bath of the 18th century has a whole history of its own, a colourful, romantic and gay history, with Royalty flitting through it, and peopled by gay characters with Beau Nash at the top of a long list. Then, in the Regency period it was endowed with some fine architecture. The town is perfectly situated in a hollow surrounded by wooded downlands on whose steep sides the buildings rise in tiers, terraces, squares and streets; with the architecture, this is what makes Bath unique not only in England but in Europe. Its mineral springs are the only natural hot springs in Britain; they yield, I am assured, over half a million gallons a day, and at 120° Fahrenheit. You can bathe in these radioactive waters or drink them; and—again I am assured—they cure all sorts of troubles from complicated tropical disorders down to ordinary indigestion. There is a Grand Pump Room, and excellent Bathing Establishments owned by the Corporation. The Roman Baths, rediscovered in 1755, are near the Pump Room. You need a guide-book to Bath, and special literature—or expert advice—to inform you of the values of the natural springs and the proper use of the waters. Yet even assuming that you do not wish to improve your health, Bath is one of the most interesting and rewarding towns in England. It has an air of its own, and a tradition so firmly established that the mere mention of its name makes English people feel proud.

From Bath you can quickly reach Bradford-on-Avon in Wiltshire, the next county. English people talk of this part of England—that is, Devon, Somerset and, vaguely, Dorset and Wiltshire—as the 'West Country' and of the natives as 'West Countrymen'. I do not know that any clear line has been drawn on the map to mark off the 'West Country' from the rest of England, but I can assure the stranger that the term 'West Countryman' is one which is invariably heard with respect everywhere. West Countrymen and women are good people, as good as any in the land. They are mostly land-workers or, right round the coast, fishermen: always close to Nature on the land or on the sea. The fact of living close to Nature seldom has ill effects on human beings, and usually endows them with the better qualities. Trouble usually begins when the artificial creations of man become so great that they and their ancillaries tend to dominate him; and when they do dominate him, the results are seldom to his advantage in the long run. England is geographically so small a country that rural areas—and the sea—are never remote from industrial areas. The confined and restricted industrial worker very easily escapes back to Nature when the opportunity comes his way. In these rural parts, especially in the West Country, and more particularly in Somerset and Wiltshire, man remains unspoiled by the machine. The Wiltshire countryside is in every way a delight; like that of adjoining Warwickshire, this is the green and pleasant land of which the poet has written. Wiltshire has its sights: Stonehenge and Avebury, of vast prehistoric interest (see Chapters I and II of Part I); Salisbury, with a magnificent cathedral; outside it Sarum, an ancient British camp, a Roman fort, a Saxon settlement and a Norman town—an epitome of history; Marlborough, a fine modern town with the famous public school of the same name; and little Bradford-on-Avon, which has the distinction of possessing a tiny 7th-century Saxon church. The traveller by car or bus hardly needs a Convenient Centre in this lovely county. If he is interested in remote history, he will use Salisbury. But I rather fear that simple contemplation of the beauties of the green and pleasant land will drive other thoughts out of his head.

CHAPTER V

WEST MIDLANDS: THE HEART OF ENGLAND

THE group of counties which makes the area known as the West Midlands comprises Gloucester, Berkshire, Oxford, Worcester, Warwick and Stafford: geographically the centre of England. If one thinks of Shakespeare—some would add Birmingham for other reasons—it is not difficult to regard this area as the heart of the country. Stratford-on-Avon is approximately in the centre of the area, and for this reason alone would be a Convenient Centre for the visitor. It is Shakespeare's birthplace which alone justifies the choice, apart from the important fact that it is in its own right a very pleasant town in which to stay.

Two industrial giants and one colossus—Coventry and Wolverhampton, and Birmingham—bestride the part between Stratford and Stafford. Birmingham means metal-working industries of every kind; it is the metropolis of a highly important manufacturing district with no less than 1,500 industries and characterized by a multiplicity of trades with their 'small master'—about 8,000 of them—here and there overshadowed by the vast factories of great industries. They make everything in metal from razor-blades to enormous machines in Birmingham. They also manufacture small-arms, chemicals, glass and jewellery. In the great days of English colonial expansion, this city made vast quantities of cheap jewellery and inferior consumer goods that became known as 'Brummagem'. That day has passed in so far as inferior export goods are concerned. It is politically a mixed city, a fortress of Nonconformity and the principal centre of English Unitarianism; and it is justly proud of well-organized institutions, which include a university, its social planning and municipal enterprise. One first has the impression that it is a great, sprawling and unplanned area; but unplanned it is not. It does sprawl: over heights and in hollows, the main part in Warwick but with suburbs which stretch into Staffordshire and Worcestershire. Finally, it comes next after London in

English cities. Well may one regard it as important. Those who are interested in English industrialism will not be disappointed if they choose Birmingham as a district for close inspection and study. They will be well repaid. Those who are not interested in industrialism may give it a miss, unless they are interested in art, especially English art, in which case they must see the admirable collection in the Corporation Art Gallery and Museum. Students of Shakespeare may learn to their surprise that the biggest and most varied collection of books on the poet—25,000 volumes—will be found in Birmingham Central Library.

Wolverhampton is noted for its ironworks and hardware; otherwise it is a typical English industrial city. Coventry I find more interesting, not least because of the new cathedral which is to replace the very fine one destroyed in that terrible bombing of 1940—the episode which gave the language a new verb: 'to coventrate'; that is, to devastate by aerial bombing. The cathedral makes Coventry a city, but its lively cosmopolitanism would justify the title. For it has attracted workers from all parts of England, even from Scotland and Ireland, and a considerable number of Czechs and Poles who went there during the war years have remained. It is essentially a modern city with up-to-dateness as its keynote. All but the outer walls, the octagon tower and the fine tall spire of the cathedral were destroyed by German airmen in 1940, and Coventry has decided to replace it with a new and striking edifice, which will rise on the ruins of the old. The new cathedral will symbolize and typify the essential religious unity of English Nonconformity and the Church of England. It is a little early to speak of the architectural ideas to be embodied in the new building or of the elaborate decorations that are planned. But here again the lively modern spirit of the city is making itself felt. Both the ecclesiastical and secular approach to the problems of the new cathedral have been almost revolutionary and, if the plans are fulfilled, this city will present to the world what the architect calls a "Shrine to the Glory of God"—in the spirit of this 20th century.

Stratford-upon-Avon is a pleasantly situated old market-town, mainly on the right bank of the river. Because Shakespeare was born here in 1564, it receives the homage of the world; every year about 100,000 travellers come here to see Shakespeare's house and Anne Hathaway's cottage. The house in which the poet was born consists of two tenements forming a detached building, which was purchased by public subscription to be a national monument, and is vested in trustees. The west house, tradition says, is the actual birthplace. The east house is a museum and library. In the 19th century the double building was lovingly repaired and restored as near as possible to its original state, and in this much of the Elizabethan timber and stonework survives. I shall not attempt to scale the Himalayas of scholarship and research which have contributed a whole literature devoted exclusively to the innumerable problems and never-ending but rarely conclusive solutions relating to the birth, life and death of Shakespeare. All this is the province of specialists. I am content with a few simple facts, such as the period of the poet's life, his significance in the age in which he lived, and his *Works*. Stratford has been immortalized by the poet's vast contribution to the English genius, and when I think of Shakespeare, while admitting that he belongs to humanity at large, I invariably think of him as typically and essentially English. When I visited Stratford, and especially the country around it for the first time, I began to realize the significance of the fact that the poet was born right in the very centre, in the heart of rural England, and that this, and his parentage and upbringing (even the little we know of it), explain nearly everything apart from the inexplicable, which we must be content to accept as the superb endowment of grandiose Nature. I have often read in learned treatises that in Shakespeare's *Works* it is almost impossible to find anything which will provide even a slight clue to his nature and personality, and I find this rather absurd. His works are, to my mind, a just reflection of the English mind: full of paradoxes, often vague and misty, pointing not sharply in one direction like the hand of a compass which settles into a fixed position; but more like the markings on the face of a good compass, which indicate not only the four cardinal points but the innumerable little subdivisions in between. He has a sense of everything that is to be found in English character. His characters are, like English people, open to more than one interpretation. They are not mere types but essentially English individuals; when they are tragic, their tragedy—except when, as in Lear, it is near-madness—is restrained and reflective; and when they are comic, their comedy again and again has in it something of the grotesque, like that of the 'typical' ordinary Cockney. Because he lived during his formative years in Stratford and can hardly have missed the enjoyments of the countryside, and made London—the teeming metropolis—his workshop, he covers the two great arenas of life: country and town. Yet, wherever his scenes may be set, there is nearly always a return somewhere to the spirit of the English countryside, which is most perfectly caught in the faery atmosphere of *A Midsummer Night's Dream*. His women?—English women: noble, good, indifferent and bad. I need not pursue this line of thought, for I can almost hear somebody comment: "There he goes—speculating on the unanswerable!" And one concedes the justness of such a comment.

What is sometimes called 'Shakespeare Country' may be reasonably extended—because of similarities in its nature—from the immediate surroundings of Stratford to the part between Cheltenham and the River Severn and the border of Wiltshire: the Cotswold area, with the district of the Cotswolds. The old word 'wold' in the plural means rising uplands, and it is used in specific designation of certain hilly tracts in England: the Yorkshire Wolds, for example, and the Cotswolds. Cirencester is a good Convenient Centre for the Cotswolds. This is, again, rural England to perfection, with the additional attraction of hills and wooded uplands. In this area there are some of the loveliest villages in the whole of England, little towns that are works of art with buildings in the gracious domestic architecture of the Tudor period, their roofs of local honey-coloured stone, and in perfect settings. It is almost impossible to find an ugly building; an ugly village does not exist and, if it did, would stand out as a glaring anachronism. There are not very many areas left in England of which this can be said and without hesitation. As civilization advances, it too often has a vicious habit of destroying what has mellowed; what we have in the Cotswolds is what remains of an old culture, which includes an older and a now mellowed civilization. Agriculture, sheep and the products of wool were and are its economic background.

I could make a longish list of Cotswold villages which cannot fail to bring joy to the heart of the most exacting visitor. I select only a few and with the warning that they are merely representative and not 'show' villages or towns created to attract tourist traffic, for they are all old and perfectly natural growths. Here they are: Chipping Campden and Broadway, which are mentioned first for the benefit of those whose time is short. But—and each with its own particular beauties—there are Burford, Bourton-on-the-Water, Moreton-in-the-Marsh, Painswick with its old yew-trees, Bibury with its enchanting Arlington Row and a superb view from Birdlip Hill, and Chipping Norton nestling on the side of a hill overlooking a valley which has provided tweeds for Queen Elizabeth II. The hills of this area are ideal pastures for sheep, which flourish here and grow wool of the first class. There are sheep which come from the Hampshire Downs, and there are local Cotswold sheep that are specially noted for their long wool; one kind of local sheep has been named the Cotswold lion. At the foot of the Cotswolds is Witney, a town famous for its blankets, and unspoiled by this gentle manufacturing. And there is Stroud which manufactures cloth and has a golf-course, and is not so unspoiled.

The western part of Berkshire has a similar countryside, but it becomes more and more sophisticated as you move eastwards, until you come to busy Reading, a flourishing industrial centre with a university which specializes in agricultural science. The sophistication continues to increase until it is crowned by Windsor Castle and Eton, the former one of the great sights of England, the latter the home of Eton College, whose fame need not be emphasized. You are graciously permitted to visit parts of Windsor Castle at certain times. It is in every sense a great and imposing royal castle situated in a commanding position, and has been a residence of sovereigns of England since Norman times. During the Anglo-Saxon heptarchy, Windsor was a stronghold; the great moated circular mound survived from that period, and became mote and bailey in the original Norman building. If there is any other secular (that is, non-ecclesiastical) building in England with longer and more immediately popular associations, I cannot think of its name.

In this area at the time of the Norman Conquest there was a forest owned by Westminster Abbey, to which Edward the Confessor had given it. William I gave the Abbey another piece of land for this forest, which he used as a hunting preserve. From then onwards it became England's principal royal residence. The Conqueror strengthened the fortifications by replacing the wooden enclosure with a stone circuit-wall. Next, Henry III built the first round tower (*c.* 1272), and Edward III reconstructed it on a more massive scale (*c.* 1344) to provide a worthy meeting-place for his new order of Knights of the Garter. In one of Froissart's chronicles a legend is quoted to the effect that King Arthur used to sit on the summit of the mound when holding council with his Knights of the Round Table, a matter which attracted Edward and was adopted by him for the Knights of his new order. Every age from then onwards made its contribution, and so Windsor Castle, like Westminster Abbey, has become a repository of national history. From a distance and possibly more so on close view, the Castle looks an imposing fortress. On still closer inspection innumerable items of great beauty impress themselves on the visitor, and of them the Chapel of St. George, patron saint of England, must take a high, perhaps first place. It is certainly one of the finest examples of perpendicular architecture in the country, comparable only with the royal chapel of King's College, Cambridge, and that of Henry VII at Westminster. St. George's Chapel was begun by Edward IV in 1473 and completed about fifty years later. It is to-day still the chapel of the Knights of the Garter, and in it hang the historic insignia of the Knights—swords, helmets, banners—and on the dark oak stalls there is a very striking series of enamelled brass plates commemorating Knights of this, the oldest of English orders. A vault below the chapel has become the mausoleum of members of the royal family; in 1952 George VI was entombed there. South of the Castle is the Royal Mews beside the Home Park, in which is Frogmore with the Royal Mausoleum and royal gardens. A magnificent avenue, the Long Walk, dating from Charles II and William III, leads into Great Park, a distance of three miles.

At its southern boundary is a very beautiful artificial lake called Virginia Water. Windsor Forest used to extend well over southern Berkshire and into Surrey. Its original size cannot be accurately traced, but we know that so late as 1790 it covered some 60,000 acres. Roman tombs, a Roman camp and various other Roman items have been found at Windsor, which thus establishes itself well back in history. The Castle has been the centre of some interesting political episodes; its dungeons have held important political prisoners. In the Civil War of the 17th century it was used as a garrison for the Parliamentary forces; in it in 1648 Charles spent his last Christmas as a prisoner of Cromwell. There it remains, an eloquent proclamation of a faith—in stone, and in terms unmistakably English.

It is fitting that Windsor Castle should benevolently and approvingly overlook Eton College, the largest of England's great public schools and the most famous. The "King's College of Our Lady of Eton beside Windsor" was founded by Henry VI in 1440–1441, endowed from revenues of the alien priories suppressed by Henry V, and followed the models of William Wykeham's foundations of Winchester and New College at Oxford. The original foundation was modest in scope and intended mainly for poor scholars. It consisted of a provost, 10 priests, 4 clerks, 6 choristers, a schoolmaster, 25 poor and indigent scholars, and the same number of 'bedesmen', which is another word for those supported entirely by alms. The original school buildings were begun in 1441, and finished about fifty years later. Some parts of them still remain, but the College has grown enormously, and now has not only a new lower chapel, but new schools, an observatory, a laboratory and the best modern amenities of all kinds. There are still scholarships to assist the sons of poor people, but, on the whole, Eton is now quite definitely intended for the sons of those who are fairly well-to-do. The number of pupils exceeds 1,000. The education provided is first class, though he would be a rash man who said that it is better than that of some of the other great public schools. But Eton differs from those others in many ways, and of not least importance is the extraordinary *social* value of the *cachet* 'Educated at Eton'. In this country, to have had this schooling is one of the best starts in life a young man can have: it opens many a door to him which might otherwise remain closed. There are in England people—but they are usually ignorant of the fact that Eton provides a really excellent education for those willing to take advantage of it, and the majority of Etonians do—who are inclined to resent what they regard as the anachronistic 'snob-value' that is given to the *cachet*. Those people are in a minority; the majority are wholeheartedly pro-Eton, and there are not many English fathers or mothers who would not send their boy to this great school if they could possibly do so. The qualities which the school develops have often been extolled. I should say that the most important of them, from the English point of view, is a self-confidence that very easily becomes a sense of power, or at least a sense of superiority over other mortals, and with that goes a self-discipline to ensure that neither the power nor the superiority—whether real or imaginary—is ever abused. Furthermore, if the Old Etonian should become a political leader—and many do—he is extremely unlikely to become a dictator; for he has had instilled into him the fact that in England power has to be shared—and distributed: one of the secrets of success in the English system of government. It is this remarkable quality which so often enables the Old Etonian to sail through difficulties with his head above them but never in the clouds, and his feet well on the ground. The quality is approved and admired—and consciously—to the point that the 'Eton Boating Song' is widely and proudly sung by those to whom Eton is as remote as a Tibetan monastery. I have heard (and seen) people from the humblest stations of life sing this delightful song with a sentimentalism so great that, although smiling, the tears were not far from their eyes. What amazing factors for unity the English create for themselves! Unless the stranger has at least an inkling of these often very mysterious things, he will miss much of the spirit of the people. Yet, even if a little mystified by them, he should have a close look at the quaint old buildings of Eton College.

"A combination of town, gown and spanner" is an apt phrase used to describe the city of Oxford, its University and the biggest automobile assembly factory in Europe. The colleges (twenty-eight of them) are in really beautiful buildings, some of them very old; their gardens are a dream. As a sight, Magdalen College alone should suffice for the unfortunate visitor who is in a hurry. It seems almost indecent to rush a visit to these lovely old buildings and tenderly kept gardens. Magdalen has an impressively proportioned tower and a graceful bridge which spans the River Cherwell. Since the Second World War and the advantages offered by post-war legislation, the Colleges are populated by a generation of young men and women of whom a great number could not have afforded to go there in the old days. Oxford works its magic on them. They leave it possessed of a combination of the endowments of a great tradition and the spirit of the new age. If the atmosphere of the Colleges is quiet and even soothing, there is nothing very sleepy about the education that is imparted. In those old buildings and the education that goes on within them can be conceived the working of the present and past, with an alert eye to the future.

Worcestershire and Staffordshire remain of the West Midlands, and in the former there is an interesting medley of Malverns: Great Malvern, Little Malvern; North, South, East and West Malvern. The whole—usually called simply Malvern—is a health resort with medicinal springs and an inland climate as good as any in England. The Malvern Festival of Drama, dedicated mainly to the works of the Irishman Bernard Shaw, has been England's most fitting tribute to the dramatist. Worcester (pron. Wu'ster) is a charming cathedral city delightfully situated on the banks of the River Severn. It is good to pass through it, for here are some of the last of those 'quaint old houses' that you will not see for some time if you are intent upon a tour northwards. On reaching Wolverhampton in Staffordshire the traveller is near to some very beautiful country; the city itself is industrial, well planned and modern. He will probably find the town of Stafford more interesting; not only is it a very pleasant old place, but it has some interesting associations. Izaak Walton, author of *The Compleat Angler,* was born here; you can see his bust in handsome St. Mary's Church. George Borrow was an ostler—no doubt a restless and certainly a temporary one—at the Swan Hotel in 1825. Farther north is Stoke-on-Trent, the centre of the Potteries area that became world famous by virtue of the magnificent achievements in the art of pottery of Josiah Wedgwood (*d.* 1795). His potteries are worked by his descendants; they continue to maintain the very high standards established by the founder. You can go by bus from Stoke to Arnold Bennett's Five Towns: Hanley, Burslem, Tunstall, Fenton and Longton. Bennett was born in Stoke, where a tablet has been erected to his memory. His ashes are buried in Burslem cemetery. He would have liked that.

CHAPTER VI

NORTH-WEST AND NORTH-EAST

THE idea that the north of England is less interesting than the south has somehow found its way into the minds of many people. It is one of those half-truths that are more damaging than a good plain lie. London, which in population alone is a fifth of England, and by virtue of its wonderful position and being and having been a place of importance from Celtic times onward, has justly acquired enormous prestige. The interesting and variegated history of the Thames Valley and of the south-eastern counties, when added to that of the metropolis, is largely responsible for the easily refutable thesis (often propounded by the ignorant) that all the rest of England, and especially the north, is far less interesting. One may concede their points to London and the south-east, and at the same time assert that, in many ways, the North is equal to any other part of the country, but—and this is important—it has many features and charms that are entirely its own.

The group of counties now to be considered lies north of a line drawn from, say, Liverpool to Grimsby. The western section comprises Lancashire, Westmorland and Cumberland; the eastern—Northumberland, Durham and Yorkshire. The physical map shows the mountainous nature of the north-west, with the great line of the Pennines running southwards from the Scottish border to divide the northern area. In north-east Yorkshire are the Cleveland Hills, with the Yorkshire Wolds to their south and the great Vale of York between them and the Pennines. Thus, we have an area of far greater physical variety than any other in the country. Its inhabitants have used it to extraordinary advantage, and I will go so far as to say that it yields as many surprises, delights and features of interest as any other part of England, and often of a completely different nature. In no other part of England will the visitor find greater variety in the towns. The people are quite different from southerners in their speech, manners and attitude to life. Many factors contribute to this: the Celts, it will be remembered, took refuge in hills and mountains in the face of the Anglo-Saxon advance; the Germanic invaders were mostly Angles from north of the Elbe and Schleswig; and later the eastern part of this northern area was conquered and occupied by the Scandinavians. There were only isolated settlements of Normans, few of them, small, and only in cities or towns. To sum this up in very general terms, the population of northern England has a mixed ancestry of Celts, Angles and Scandinavians, with little Norman blood. The importance of the considerable Celtic elements that at first remained in the uplands, and in the course of centuries mixed with the settlers, is usually under-estimated. While it is unsafe to generalize too dogmatically when ethnic factors come into the picture, there need be little hesitation in claiming for most northerners that they have qualities akin to those of the sturdy and stolid Angles, the adventurous Scandinavians, with Celtic influence in many parts and, in some, very strong. Furthermore, there are here and there 'pockets' which are ethnically almost 'pure'; that is, dominantly either Celtic or Angle or Scandinavian. It is well to bear all this in mind. Not only does it help to explain the often puzzling contrasts in types of people met, but also goes a good way towards explaining what sometimes amounts to a different way of life from that of the southern English.

Liverpool on the Mersey is not only the chief port of Lancashire: it is the second port of England after London, and the fourth city in the United Kingdom. Its docks, graving-docks and basins cover a water area of over six hundred acres, and there are nearly forty miles of quays. (On the other side of the Mersey is Birkenhead, connected with Liverpool by the Mersey Tunnel, and served by an excellent service of big ferry-boats.) The city is a very pleasant one with the live, alert atmosphere usually found in busy ports. There are some striking buildings. Approaching the city from the sea, the outstanding feature in the agglomeration of buildings is the magnificent modern cathedral designed by Sir Giles Gilbert Scott when he was only twenty-one years of age! The foundation was laid in 1904 by King Edward VII. The total area covered by this magnificent edifice is 100,000 square feet, which I see is 23,000 square feet more than that covered by

London's St. Paul's, the masterpiece of Sir Christopher Wren, which comes next in size. Work on Liverpool's cathedral still continues.

It is dockland that provides Liverpool's greatest attraction, for here there is one of the finest dock systems, if not the finest, in the world. An overhead railway runs from end to end and, from a carriage window, one has a good view, not only of the docks but of their immediate neighbourhoods. For those whose time is limited, this is the best way of getting a fairly close cinematographic conspectus of a shipping fairyland from which no kind of vessel is missing. The flags of all nations are there; one sees sailors of every nation and race. I have never ceased to be fascinated by this astonishing panorama, by its moment to moment variety and constant surprises. I used to sail from Liverpool in those remote, halcyon days before the First World War, and knew that dockland like the palm of my hand. I visited it again in 1953, and noticed many material additions and improvements but no fundamental changes in the general panorama. Machines were better, facilities for loading and unloading were greater, and in most respects everything was more streamlined. But the same kind of work went on, and the men had not changed at all. They are a powerful race, those Liverpool dock workers and stevedores. You should see them at it when a great ship has to 'turn round' and sail again very soon after its arrival from a foreign port. There are thousands of Irish in Liverpool. They come there, attracted by wages much higher than any they could earn at home—and by the provisions of the Welfare State. You cannot fail to notice that Liverpudlians have an accent of their own, one that is not quite 'broad Lancashire' but, it seems to me, a Lancashire accent that has acquired a slightly Irish lilt. The spirit of the city is not nearly so cosmopolitan as might be expected. In spite of the constantly changing and considerable population of seafarers from the four corners of the earth, it remains very English—and strongly Lancashire.

From Liverpool you can visit the Isle of Man, an attractive little independent kingdom in the Irish sea, with a history dating back to the sea-god of Celtic mythology, Manannán Mac Lir, from whom it got its name. There is history in the pleasant little island, which in modern times has become famous for motorcycle-racing and facilities offered for a great variety of sports and amusements. To the south and east of Lancashire lie some very important industrial and coal districts: Preston, Wigan, Burnley, Bury, Bolton and Blackburn. And five miles from the last-named is Hoghton Tower, famous for a curious incident. It was here that James I knighted a loin of beef—"Arise, Sir Loin!"—and thus gave us the delightful word 'sirloin'. And then there is Manchester, connected with Liverpool by the Ship Canal, which can give passage to the biggest freighters. It is a great city, with innumerable industries, a vast general commerce and a progressive spirit; one so advanced that I have heard the claim, "What Manchester says to-day, London will say to-morrow". Along the Lancashire coast there is a choice of seaside resorts: Southport, Fleetwood (with steamers for Ireland and the Isle of Man), Lytham and others, with Blackpool as their queen and having all the attractions that a great seaside resort can offer. Here in the summer months come thousands of Lancashire lads and lasses for their annual holiday, usually a fortnight. How they spend and enjoy themselves! Once at Blackpool I became slightly involved in an incident which reminded me of the O. Henry story in which a young man and a girl each saved up for a holiday. They met in a select boarding-house at a resort, where each posed as wealthy and of a much higher social status than that conferred by their humble jobs and pay-packets when at home. It was a case of love, marriage and later disillusionment: not an uncommon experience, I have been told. In the north is Lancaster, the county town. It was the birthplace of Catherine Parr, one of King Henry VIII's Queens, a lady who kept her head in more ways than one.

Cross to Kendal in Westmorland and you are at the gateway to the Lake District, an area about thirty-five miles square in which there are very beautifully situated lakes, the only lakes in the whole of England. This is holiday country, pure holiday country for those who enjoy quiet or even dreamy surroundings with rich woodlands, hills, lovely walks and rugged mountains which provide good scope for climbers. Many hikers and campers come here in summer, and whoever wishes to stay here even for a short period would be wise to obtain a guide-book to the District or at least a good map. There is wildness and grandeur in the scenery, and this is wonderful territory for the botanist, the ornithologist, the geologist, for nature students or nature lovers in general. It is advisable to be provided with a good raincoat, for the climate is what the Irish call 'soft': often rainy or misty. The biggest lake is Windermere, which is also the most accessible of the lakes, and with scenery less rugged and more sylvan than that of the others. You must go into the next county—Cumberland—which rightly claims a great share of the glories of the area now under consideration. The whole area is easy to explore, for which purpose there are many good centres: Morecambe, Heysham, Kendal, Grange-over-Sands, Penrith, Keswick, Windermere, Ambleside, Appleby, Ulverston. Keswick is sometimes called the 'Hub' of the District: it is near to Derwentwater, called by many the Queen of the Lakes. It is always difficult in such circumstances to decide what is best, but I would favour Ullswater as the most beautiful lake.

The hilly and mountainous nature of the country gives the Lake District a history that is not overloaded with the political. Compensation for this may be found in the many literary associations: Shelley lived for a time in Keswick, which was also the home of Coleridge and of Southey. Wordsworth made Grasmere his home, and so also did Thomas de Quincey, the English opium-eater. The area around Borrowdale has some of the wildest and most rugged scenery to be found in England. If you should happen to be in Grasmere in the summer, you may see the famous sheep-dog trials that are held in the vicinity. The Englishman as shepherd trains his collie dogs to behave so perfectly and to achieve such marvels that the onlooker at these trials is lost in admiration. To the north and on the edge of the Scottish border is Carlisle, Cumberland's county town, notable for the smallest cathedral in England and, in modern times, for an interesting experiment in liquor-control. Just across the border is Gretna Green. Runaway couples used to be able to get married there by a smith whose fee was said to depend on the proximity and resources of pursuing parents. The romance has departed. You can still marry at Gretna, but only in accordance with the sober law of Scotland. Hadrian's Wall runs a little to the north of Carlisle, a good place from which to visit it when time will not permit a more extensive inspection.

The northern part of Northumberland is rugged or austere, and often both. Over the border in Scotland this English county has in the little town of Coldstream what used to be for runaway couples the equivalent of Gretna Green. A natural border is formed by the Cheviot Hills. If you should wander along here—it is good hiking country—you will sense a land where Scots and English fought to the death for centuries—until the good common sense of both peoples wrought its miracle, thereby enabling the Scots to invade England armed only with their intellect and toughness, both of which they have placed at the disposal of the English to great mutual advantage. The English do not now invade Scotland except as holiday-makers or for business, but the Scots continue to invade England, and make a wonderful contribution in a great variety of fields. One salutes Scotland and moves south-eastward to Alnwick, where the Percys, Dukes of Northumberland, have made their principal seat in Alnwick Castle. In this former fortress there is a gatehouse which enshrines an earlier Norman doorway; the original well and the dungeon still remain. Throughout the centuries the Castle grew, until it was largely reconstructed in 1854. The whole is one of the most impressive examples in England of a fortified castle. Farther south is Wallsend on the Tyne, the beginning of the great Roman Wall which ends at Bowness on the Solway. If I repeat the mention of Hadrian's Wall, it is because the walk along it is one of the finest and most interesting walks in England. Newcastle itself cannot be ignored: a cathedral city with a long history, and now a great industrial and commercial centre chiefly associated with coal. And there is Tynemouth with its golden sands, a lively and popular seaside resort for Tynesiders, who are collectively often called 'Geordies', a word once limited in meaning to pitmen. Tynesiders provide one more example of the great variety of types in England: many of them resemble the stocky, dark type of Celts, and their quick uptake in conversation is characteristic of the Celt. They are tough workers and make good footballers.

With the advent of atomic power, coal-mining on its present

scale—it is one of the main sources of England's wealth and of power for machines—is doomed. The county of Durham has within its borders the richest coalfields in Britain. Since the nationalization of the industry, the conditions of the miners have improved enormously, wages have increased, and in the mining areas there is much more money being spent than in the bad old days. There has been little or no unemployment among the Durham miners since 1939. Hence, the visitor interested in social conditions will now find contented people and happy communities: a contrast to the past. The city of Durham must not be missed. It has one of England's greatest architectural works of art: a noble cathedral, massive, and as breath-taking as any cathedral on the Continent of Europe, or indeed in the world. On the door there is a 12th-century 'closing-ring' or knocker, a survival from the 12th century and the days when, by clinging to it, fugitives from justice could claim the right of sanctuary. The cathedral dates from the Saxons, but no trace survives of the Saxon building. The present edifice dates from Norman times; the history and technical details of how it achieved its present magnificent form and interior would fill a book. Improvements, renovation and restoration continue almost without interruption. Not only the cathedral is interesting. There are monastic buildings, and a Norman Charter House, which was restored in the 19th century. Durham Cathedral is one of the great sights of England. The western side of County Durham has an unspoiled countryside, and the scenery is as beautiful as any in Yorkshire.

The county of Yorkshire is the largest and most versatile in England. It has an area of 6,000 square miles, more than double the size of Lincolnshire which comes next to it. The county is divided into three 'Ridings' (North, West and East), which are administrative areas. The greater part of the county is a plain of which the western part runs into the Pennines, and this part consists of hills and high moorland of great beauty, often bleak and wild. This district is famous for its valleys, usually called 'dales', those most likely to attract the visitor being: Teesdale, Swaledale, Wensleydale, Nidderdale, Wharfedale and Airedale. Many of them have enchanting streams, and even waterfalls, as at High Force in Teesdale and

Aysgarth in Wensleydale. The River Derwent marks off the northern moors from the Yorkshire Wolds of the East Riding. These wolds are rather like the moors in general appearance. The area covered by them is considerable: they abut on the coast, run westwards and turn south to overlook the central plain. The coast is diverse in character: low-lying south of Teesmouth, with cliffs in the area of the Cleveland Hills. At Boulby there is the highest elevation of sea-cliffs in England. South of Scarborough the coast sinks to rise again slightly round Filey Bay, with a striking promontory at Flamborough Head. Then comes a long, unbroken coastline down to Spurn Point, marking the mouth of the River Humber. From what has been said—and the brief statement is intended merely to give a general idea of configuration—the possibilities of this fine county for the holiday-maker can roughly be deduced. The variety of attractions is remarkable: fine seaside resorts, lovely upland areas for walking; valleys (vales, one must call them here) of infinite charm and variety; there is every kind of scenery and all the colours. Most of Yorkshire is paradise for the lover of nature and open air. The industrial area of the county is contained within a line drawn from Keighley, running north of Leeds, and turning down to Goole on the Humber. In that enclave are Leeds, Doncaster (mining), Rotherham, Sheffield, Huddersfield, Halifax and Bradford—names associated with innumerable products of industry which are known all over the world. Whoever is interested in this industry will find here scope for a lifetime of study.

The city of York was a highly important military centre in Roman Britain, and to-day the past is always with us as we walk through its streets, some of which are so narrow—The Shambles, for instance—that a person standing on one side can almost touch one on the other. The outstanding features are the Minster, a cathedral edifice that beggars description so far that it can only be called faultless. Its history goes back to the year 627 when Paulinus, first Bishop of York, baptized Edwin King of Northumberland in a little wooden chapel on the site of the Minster. The present building was completed in a period of about 250 years which ended in the 15th century. Visitors from all over the world go to see York Minster, and take away with them an ineffaceable memory. The City Walls, with a path along the top from which the traveller obtains fine and varied views of the Minster, almost encircle the city. Of much interest is the Hall of the Merchant Adventurers' Company, dating from the 14th century; and Cliffords Tower, the Treasurer's House (with 17th-century furniture) and the historic King's Manor. No visitor can fail to be enchanted with York's old streets and side-streets with their odd names and medieval atmosphere.

Ripon also has a cathedral with a history dating back to the Saxons, one built in a multiplicity of styles, some of which are unusual, perhaps unique. There is in Ripon a curious survival from the Middle Ages: every night at nine o'clock curfew is sounded on a horn blown by a man in medieval dress who stands in front of the mayor's house. To-day, of course, nobody is expected to go indoors. It is just one of those survivals which bring pleasure to hearts: completely non-utilitarian, perhaps a mere piece of sentiment, but more comforting to the ear than the modern curfew which told us to take shelter during the war. South of Ripon is Harrogate, a well-appointed spa in a healthy situation. One of the many merits of Harrogate is that it is an excellent Convenient Centre for excursions to the Yorkshire moors. Scarborough is also a spa by tradition, but it is of much greater importance as a seaside resort with modern amenities such as the marine drive, and old features such as the quaint fishing-harbour. Scarborough used to be a rather select resort, and in some respects it still is; but encroachments by vigorous pleasure-seekers on the restrained and polite requirements of the old type of visitor continue apace. For all that, I should say that it will take a long time before this town becomes vulgarized. The Sitwell family had their home here at Wood End; and Scarborough gave the world Charles Laughton, the actor. On the River Humber is Hull, England's third port. Its industries are milling, the extraction of vegetable oils and fishing. The port dates from about 1293, when it was chosen and laid out as a port by Edward I.

There are so many places worth visiting in this fine county that the line must be drawn somewhere. I hope I have conveyed something of its general nature. I must, however, say a few words about Yorkshire people, with the warning that I cannot give any but a biased opinion of them. They are everything that one expects of sturdy, independent English men and women; matter-of-fact, direct and straight to the point, friendly but generally off-hand until they know you. They are of quick intelligence, tending to take the long view of things. They are as honest as the sun, as hospitable and generous-minded as any people on earth; careful to save, but lavish in spending when the occasion demands. Furthermore, they are good people with whom to do business, for the Yorkshireman is competent and his word is his bond. I have never found better companions in adversity, if conditions at the front in the First World War can be given that description; I met all kinds of Yorkshiremen in those trying circumstances, and they never failed to be grand human beings.

CHAPTER VII

EAST MIDLANDS AND EAST ANGLIA

THE group of counties in this area embraces Derby, Nottingham, Leicester, Rutland, Northampton, Bedford, Buckingham, Hertford, Cambridge (with the Isle of Ely), Huntingdon, Lincoln, and East Anglia proper, which comprises Norfolk, Suffolk and Essex. It is the biggest single grouping of counties with which we have to deal; and the last. I think that if I were a visitor from abroad whose time is limited, and I wanted to see as much as possible of the almost endless variety of English cities, towns and villages, and of countryside generally, I should choose this area. If I were an American visitor and interested in the early history of the United States, I should not like to miss it, for it was this part of England which provided the New World with some of the best human stock from the Old. Many of the original settlers came from this area, and many great names in American history are those of its people.

A line drawn from Grimsby to St. Albans divides the area into two parts, of which the western is a continuation of the industrial Midlands. Here are Derby (pron. 'Darby'), a considerable manufacturing town with important railway works; Nottingham, a flourishing industrial city and headquarters of the lace and hosiery industries—situated almost in the geographical centre of England; Leicester, which also makes hosiery and boots and shoes; and ancient Northampton, which to-day has the making of footwear for its principal industry. Derby is a black industrial town, a great railway centre with far too much smoke for my liking. The others are bright, busy and cheerful places. And all these, and the minor industrial towns in the area, are set off by the beautiful countryside with which they are surrounded. Some of the best hunting country in England is in the East Midlands, in the part west of Lincolnshire and vaguely known as the Shires. Fox-hunting here has acquired a considerable folklore, and for many it is almost a way of life, because of the strange customs and conventions associated with a declining squirearchy. Famous packs, such as the Belvoir (pron. 'Beever'), the Cottesmore, the Quorn and the Pytchley (pron. 'Pyechley'), carry on the tradition, and in the hunting season (November to April) the visitor who is interested—and who takes the precaution of being introduced by a fox-hunting friend—can join in a hunt; or, with guidance, see one. The stranger is advised to move cautiously in all this, for English huntsmen and huntswomen are apt to be touchy about their conventions, though kindly and open-hearted to the visitor who shows interest in blood sports. In recent years they have been attacked as cruel. They survive. And, in the Shires, Man the Hunter can be seen in the delightful setting of the countryside and in traditional costume. It is a good sight for those whom the sport attracts.

The Peak District in Derbyshire—with Buxton spa as a Convenient Centre—is worth a visit. Whoever cannot go to Cumberland, Northumberland or Yorkshire will find compensation in the moorlands and hills of the Peak District, and in its deep valleys and rugged cuttings. From Buxton (which is 1,000 feet above sea-level) there are many interesting outings: to Chatsworth, home of the Duke of Devonshire, and Haddon Hall, a medieval house of great beauty, property of the Duke of Rutland. Izaak Walton, author of *The Compleat Angler*, made Dovedale famous, and the town of Ilkeston, mentioned in Domesday Book, is a perfect example of the busy, progressive type of Midlands town. It has the interesting combination of lace-making and mining as its principal industries. In the Midlands areas—that is, the West and East Midlands—there are dozens of such towns: towns with a population of less than, say, 50,000, and having their own chosen industries, which sometimes depend on what Nature can supply—coal, for example. In the Peak District is the quaint town of Chesterfield. It deserves mention for the 'leaning spire' of its ancient (*c.* 1350) and interesting parish church. Although this spire cannot compete with the leaning Tower of Pisa (the latter must be about 20 feet, whereas the Chesterfield spire is only 6 feet, out of the straight), it is a curious example of a distortion which is said to be caused by the warping action of the sun's rays on the south and west sides.

The word which best describes these East Midland counties

—especially Derby, Leicester and Northampton—is *versatile*. You can in most cases walk out of an industrial town straight into a very lovely countryside. There is almost every kind of industry, and almost every kind of countryside. When you move south into Buckinghamshire, industry is left behind, and here you are in rural England. The former county town, Buckingham, has been supplanted by Aylesbury, now famous for a succulent and much approved breed of ducks. No wonder those ducks are fat, for this is nearly all beautifully green grassland. The gentle Vale of Aylesbury is ideal for dairy-farming, and the farmers there concentrate on high-quality products. In Bedfordshire, just on the border of Buckinghamshire, is Whipsnade, three miles south of Dunstable, and in summer served by motor-coaches which run from near Baker Street Station in London. Whipsnade is notable for its very fine Zoological Park, 500 acres in area and situated in the Chilterns at a height of 700 feet above sea-level. Those people who love wild animals, but do not like to see them in cages, will be pleased to observe here lions, tigers, bears and many other animals enjoying the freedom of spacious enclosures and paddocks. You need a day to visit the Zoological Park; and it is well worth it. No animals in their native jungles could look finer or fitter than these. North of Whipsnade is the attractive country town of Bedford, where John Bunyan, in 1676, wrote *The Pilgrim's Progress* while in the town jail. Bunyan's birthplace, Elstow, is a suburb of Bedford. The River Ouse is good for boating, and altogether you could not wish for a pleasanter town. Admirers of John Bunyan will find much to interest them, especially in what is called the Bunyan Meeting, which was built in the middle of the 19th century on the site of a barn in which John used to preach. There are panels on the bronze doors which illustrate the Pilgrim's Progress and, in the vestibule, is the old door of the county jail. There is also a Bunyan Museum with many interesting relics, and in the public library a unique collection of documents. The county jail used to be at the corner of what is now High Street and Silver Street. He wrote *Grace Abounding* and other works here in 1666, and it was during a later sojourn in the town jail on the old bridge that he wrote the first part of *The Pilgrim's Progress*, a book which, it is claimed, has had immense influence, literary and spiritual, not only in England but wherever English is spoken. I often wonder what its influence is to-day. The noble language and the allegories are, I think, lost to the present generation of readers. I have to confess that it appeals to me only in small doses and, for preference, when I am sitting alone on a height overlooking a populous city in which the evil characters and bad goings-on now, as in the past, and as it ever will be in the future, can be assumed.

Beginning at St. Albans in Hertfordshire, the traveller can now usefully run northwards through the central part of the area under consideration, with the city of Lincoln as his ultimate goal. The county of Hertford is almost entirely agricultural, though in recent years industrialism in many forms has made headway, and often in towns where, before the Second World War, not a factory could be seen. During that war I found myself in the little town of Ware, from which I was able one day to go to the village of Hatfield and see Hatfield House, a magnificent Jacobean mansion built in 1610–1611 as the home of the Cecils, that astonishing family which, since the days when the great Lord Burghley (father of Robert Cecil, first Earl of Salisbury) was the power behind the throne of Elizabeth I. The exterior and gardens are in themselves worth a special visit but, if you are fortunate enough to be able to visit the interior, you may be favoured to see the wonderful collection of manuscripts, state papers, portraits and other valuable and interesting things closely associated with that great Queen. But, not entirely forgetting all about history and historical associations, it is interesting to scrutinize one of these small or fair-sized towns in the Hertford countryside. I would suggest Bishop's Stortford, which has about 10,000 inhabitants, a fine church, a boys' public school, and is notable as the birthplace of Cecil Rhodes.

The county of Hertfordshire—usually called Herts (the *e* is pronounced *a*)—is among the smallest in England. The general aspect of the countryside is very pleasant, with an undulating surface and in parts successions of hills, valleys and woodland scenery which is often very beautiful. No more English landscape could be found anywhere. The uplands are sparsely populated, but elsewhere the population has been steadily increasing, and to-day many towns in Herts are dormitories for a considerable number of people who go daily to London to work, returning in the evening. The county as a whole is one of rich arable lands, with many fine estates that are almost parks, some set off by woodlands, the seats of well-to-do people of the old and new squirearchy; all of which gives the county a comfortable and almost luxuriant appearance. It is an old county historically. Here the ancient Britons were displaced by West and East Saxons. In 675 the Witenagemot met at Hatfield; the county is mentioned as a shire in the Anglo-Saxon *Chronicle* (1011), and for a time a part of it was in the Danelaw. It suffered badly after the Conquest. William confiscated many estates, bestowing them on the Church. But the estates changed hands frequently, which accounts for the fact that Herts is lacking in great historic families, though fairly rich in families on the fringe of the landed gentry.

The prosperous market-town of Bishop's Stortford (about thirty miles from London) is on the River Stort, which forms the boundary with Essex. Before the Conquest the manor of the present town area belonged to Eddeva the Fair, Harold's wife, who sold it to the Bishop of London, from whom it was confiscated by the Conqueror. William gave it back later, but it is not until 1311 that we find the first mention of 'Bishop Stortford' as a borough. It is now in the parliamentary division of Hertfordshire, which has always been a 'safe' Conservative seat, though Labour votes have been increasing and have reached (1951 election) 13,396 against the Conservatives' 21,204. The town is in the centre of an area that is characteristic of the county, and it is a typical English market-town. There are maltings, a match factory and a factory which makes machinery for public contractors, but otherwise the town concentrates on marketing and providing consumers' goods for the inhabitants and the people who live in the immediate countryside. As there is so little industry and as the town is mainly a mart, the visitor gets a first impression of a rather easy-going, friendly and comfortable community that feels itself to be semi-rural and without need of the rush which one associates with cities.

It was precisely this easy-going atmosphere which I liked about Bishop's Stortford. With it goes a great variety of friendly pubs—Herts is a good county for beer—some of which confront the traveller unexpectedly, and inside are found to be just the sort of typical little country pubs one reads about. You can find a pub almost anywhere in the town. There are the major houses such as the 'George' and the 'Chequers', but I felt attracted by old names such as:

> The Feathers—The Falcon—The Anchor—The Swan—The Grapes—The Reindeer—The Boar's Head—The Half Moon—The Rising Sun—The Castle—The Royal Oak—The Bull—The Fox—The Bricklayers' Arms.

—most of them with their colourful, interesting signs. The names I have listed do not exhaust the possibilities of Bishop's Stortford, and merely represent what I recall easily. The little 'Bricklayers' Arms' on the road to Hadham had just received a fresh coat of paint the last time I was there. I thought it looked a very beautiful little pub from outside. Inside I was not disappointed: the beer was delicious, and Mrs. Morgan, the landlady, a great personality whom I am not likely to forget.

I should like to dwell on these pubs, some of which are very old, because of their importance as an institution of considerable import in the social fabric of this country. Hertfordshire, and, indeed, all of this eastern area, can provide examples of more than ordinary interest. At St. Albans there is the 'Fighting Cocks', which is said to be the oldest inhabited licensed house in England. Thomas Burke mentions A.D. 795 as the date of its foundation. The traveller by car who takes the Great North Road—the historic highway linking London with Edinburgh—will come upon many pub signs which will inevitably attract his attention and often make him stop for a closer scrutiny. A little conversation with landlords and knowledgeable local people will quickly show that the English public-house (as we usually call it now), with which one may include the terms 'inn' and 'tavern', embraces a vast social history that can be traced back to Saxon times. For over one thousand years the house which provides food and drink for the traveller and wayfarer, and *a centre or club for local people,* has been a part of English life. If I have not mentioned the subject until now, it is not because other areas of England are less rich in public-houses than this eastern part, but merely that it falls in more conveniently at this stage. What I say about the pubs here can be paralleled for most parts of England and, as it is, I can deal with it only in the most summary way. Take, for example, the 'Letchworth Hall' at Letchworth, formerly a manor-house and, some may say, too much of an hotel to be considered as a 'typical' pub. It is mentioned in Domesday Book. And the 'Sun' at Hitchin, which was used by the Parliamentarians during the Civil War (1642–1648), and, in 1745, was the place in which North Hertfordshire men enrolled for the Resistence Movement that was to face the advancing army of the Pretender. Some of these old buildings are architecturally and artistically extremely interesting, externally or internally, and sometimes in both senses. As we move northwards, a slight detour takes us to Buckden and Huntingdon, both in Huntingdonshire. The first town has the 'Lion' with a lounge beautifully adorned by some magnificent oak beams; the second town has the 'George', with its long frontage and a lovely row of fifteen windows. Stilton, where one of the world's great cheeses is made, has the 'Bell' dating back to the spacious days when men travelled on horseback, more often than not in companies in order to be able to cope with the activities of such gentry as Dick Turpin. Lincolnshire has some noteworthy houses: the 'George' at Stamford where, in 1746, William Duke of Cumberland put up after his victory over Bonnie Prince Charlie at Culloden; and the curiously named 'Ram Jam Inn', a haunt of Dick Turpin and his men. At Grantham there is another 'George', visited by Charles Dickens in 1838 and about which he wrote to his wife, ". . . the most comfortable inn I ever put up in". In Grantham there is also the ancient 'Angel and Royal' with seven hundred years of history behind it and originally a favourite house of the Knights Templars. Kings held their courts there; the present building dates from about the middle of the 14th century. These few dips will indicate the scope of the subject, but I think I have said sufficient to show the reader that the English pub is a very old, very strong institution and in every way worthy of his attention. I have never yet entered a pub, however humble, from which I did not emerge refreshed in mind and body, and I think that a good argument could be put up in favour of the pub as the most characteristic institution of the people of England: of the men, that is, for it is only in comparatively recent years that women are frequenting licensed premises—with the approval of the younger generation of men, of course, but often with the strong disapproval of old regulars. To these it is unbecoming to the spirit and atmosphere of their club that lively and frivolous girls—the more attractive they are, the worse it is! —often in slacks or even shorts, should lower the serious tone of the establishment with their disconcerting jazzing, crooning and giggling. This litle survival of Puritanism is quickly passing and in many places no longer exists. It will soon be gone. The pub will survive by adapting itself to the social environment: as it always has done in the past.

If we include Lincolnshire and certain parts of Nottinghamshire, the part of England known as East Anglia (Norfolk, Suffolk, Essex) is of considerable historic interest to Americans. This part of England gave the United States some of their earliest settlers and, as we know, they were mostly of Anglo-Saxon stock with an admixture of Scandinavian, and hence the characteristics to be expected: Saxon strength and stolidity, with more than a touch of the venturesome. Leader of the Pilgrim Fathers, William Brewster, was born in the Old Manor House at Scrooby in Nottinghamshire, and in the village church his pew can be seen. The Pilgrim Society of Plymouth (Mass.) have erected a tablet to his memory. This Brewster was a direct ancestor of some very important Americans: of President Zachary Taylor, of Longfellow, of General Ulysses S. Grant, and of John Howard Payne, immortalized by his song *Home, Sweet Home*. From another manor-house at Austerfield, a little village only three miles from Scrooby, William Bradford also sailed on the *Mayflower*. He was Governor of the Plymouth Colony. In the village church there is a tablet in his memory from the Society of Mayflower Descendants, and inscribed are these words: "The First American Citizen of the English Race who bore rule by the free choice of his brethern." His baptism is recorded in the parish register; the Norman font used at the ceremony is there for all to see. I could not help thinking how easily one can be led to misjudge the people of this part of England, and of all that eastern area, who did that great piece of pioneering. I should say that the people there to-day do not differ greatly from their upright ancestors and, until one knows them fairly well, their quiet, unostentatious demeanour, their matter-of-fact and one might say their almost humdrum way of life, gives a first impression of good and reliable but rather uninteresting people. Good and reliable they are, but uninteresting? Oh no! The history of the Germanic invasion of Lincolnshire is obscure, but it appears fairly certain that most of the invaders were Frisians—farmers and fishermen—and that later the Vikings established themselves firmly in many places whose Scandinavian names exist to this day. The nature of this part of the country—then forest and fen, to-day farmland and fen—conditioned life. After the Conquest, William built a fort or castle at Lincoln and portioned out the estates among Normans. Domesday Book shows that the Frisian-Norse population were leniently treated, and this busy area with its many mills, a good fishing industry, salt-works and many iron forges, was altogether flourishing. William was too astute a man to disturb so fine and lucrative a territory. Nevertheless, the industries declined in the centuries after the Conquest and, with disafforestation and drainage, agriculture took their place. To-day, Lincolnshire is largely a flat farming county, and its inhabitants are in the main descendants of those Frisians and Vikings, with all the reserves of strength to be expected from such a blending. One may be somewhat misled by their reserved manners, but all their apparently rather unexuberant façade is quickly thrown aside when something has to be done which demands initiative, energy and courage. That is how I have seen them. Yet I must say that it is always with great misgivings and doubts in my mind that I offer these estimates and judgments and interpretations of English character. All I can say in defence is that I have the same doubts as when I read the attempts of others to bring clarity into what by nature is neither white nor black but a nebulous grey. Generalizations about the character of a people are always of doubtful value, but the writer who attempts to deal with the nature and character of the English is dealing with something that is more incalculable than the English climate.

The traveller ought to visit the city of Lincoln, if only to see the cathedral, certainly one of the grandest Gothic churches in Europe and quite unusual because of the impressive triple towers which crown it to dominate that fenland country. The Chapter Library, incidentally, contains one of the four contemporary copies of Magna Carta. The racing enthusiast who comes here in March will enjoy the Lincolnshire Handicap, a fine prelude to the most formidable and spectacular steeplechase on this earth: the Aintree Grand National. No good American will pass by Boston, the historic town which has given its name to Boston, Massachusetts. The Rev. John Cotton, Patriarch of New England, was vicar of the mother-town for twenty-one years. He and other Puritans were tried at St. Mary's Guildhall, an interesting 15th-century building in which the old cells where the prisoners were held can be seen. From Boston, Governor Winthrop set out with his little expedition for the New World, in which they founded the namesake city. How deep is the love of country! Dotted along the eastern side of the United States are the names of English towns and villages which were established there by English people who mostly left the old country because of Governmental persecution. That persecution did not obliterate from their minds the fact that they came from this old country. It has been perpetuated in the names given by them to their new habitats.

I have always found Norfolk a county of great charm, and Norwich a fine old city with a flavour all its own. Throughout its long history, this has been an area of farmers. The excellent nature of the land attracted Angles from north Germany, and by the 7th century the territory of the 'North-folk' formed the northern part of East Anglia (it included the 'South-folk', hence the name Suffolk), which from A.D. 630 was also an important diocese. The area came successively under the dependancy of the great kingdoms of Mercia and Northumberland, but in 867 was united under Ecgberht. Then, from 867, it came under Viking rule and was for a time part of the Danelaw, but it appears that the population remained almost entirely Germanic, for the ancient Britains had been driven out in the first wave of the Germanic invasion. Norfolk was a part of Harold's earldom at the time of the Conquest. It offered no resistence to William, who built a castle at Norwich. There has been little change in the county boundaries since the establishment of the shire system before the Conquest: the lines recorded in Domesday Book are almost the same as those of to-day. Norfolk is the home county of the Howards, one of the oldest and most important of English families, and to-day represented by the Duke of Norfolk, first of the English dukes and hereditary earl marshal of England, with the earls of Suffolk, Carlisle and Effingham and Lord Howard of Glossop representing its younger lines in the peerage. The founder of this great family was a successful lawyer-politician, son of John Howard of Wiggenhall, who lived about 1260. William Howard prospered in the law, was knighted and twice married, in each case to the daughter of a knightly house. From then onwards the history of this extraordinary family is always colourful, often checkered and at times romantic. It is a Roman Catholic family of great influence: an Act of Parliament (1824) enabled the holder of the hereditary dukedom to act as earl marshal, and so it remains until this day. The present duke is the sixteenth: "Earl Marshal and Hereditary Marshal and Chief Butler of England." There is a whole folklore in the story of the Howards, all of which has not yet been written.

The Norfolk coast, from Hunstanton on The Wash to Great Yarmouth, is nearly all sand and many parts of it have suffered from inroads of the sea. This is an extremely bracing part of England, with Cromer as a very delightful and healthy seaside resort, and Sheringham as one of the best of places for invigorating bathing. From Hunstanton the interested visitor may go to Sandringham, the country home of Her Majesty the Queen, and then on to King's Lynn, a very quaint old port on the River Ouse, with its Tudor Guildhall of black flint and white stone and an interesting Grey Friar's Tower. And then there are the Norfolk Broads, shallow meres with low-lying banks massed with water-plants and luxuriant reeds often tropical in density. The Broads area is from Norwich to Great Yarmouth, with a slight extension into Suffolk. The Broads are irregular areas of water with an average depth of about 8 feet, the largest of them, Hickling Broad, being about three miles long and a mile across in the widest part. The whole, from Norwich to Great Yarmouth, is a favourite resort for those who like yachting, punting, fishing or living on a house-boat. At many places along the waterways—Wroxham Bridge, for example—it is possible for sporting men and women to hire almost any kind of small craft from luxurious house-boats to tiny canoes, and every summer they are hired in great numbers. I can recommend the Broads in dry, sunny weather, but I would warn those who dislike insects that at certain times—hot, dull or damp weather and after sundown—life on the Broads can be one unremitting scratch. For all that, the rewards are considerable: here one enjoys the presence of interesting waterfowl, and often in good numbers. I have seen a bittern near Stalham, the only occasion on which I got a good close-up view of this somewhat rare bird. Water-hens, herons, king-fishers, mallard, teal and snipe come to the Broads, and whoever cares to wander through the surrounding countryside will be delighted with the great variety of bird life. It was not without reason that George Borrow finally settled at Oulton Broad. The coast from Cromer to Great Yarmouth is usually regarded as uninteresting because, behind the fine sandy beach, there is little else than a long line of sand-dunes and cliffs covered with strong, tall grass which holds the sand and helps to prevent inroads by the sea. I find it a restful, healthy part for a quiet holiday. About half-way between the two towns is Happisburgh (pron. Hazzboro),* a mere hamlet beside which great chunks of sandy cliff have broken off, leaving some of the houses perilously perched on the edge. Mammoth tusks have been found in the sand off Happisburgh. This east coast, right down to the mouth of the Thames, suffered greatly from tidal floods in 1953. The damage was enormous, and called for an elaborate scheme to prevent a similar catastrophe in the future.

One can now either proceed southwards into Suffolk and Essex, or turn west into the Isle of Ely, then south to Cambridge, and conclude a tour of the area with Suffolk, Essex and a quick look at St. Albans. Continuity is better served by first going southwards. The bracing Suffolk coast is dotted with holiday resorts: Southwold and Aldeburgh, delightful little resorts; Felixstowe, Walton-on-the-Naze and Clacton-on-Sea, which are typical popular resorts; and in Essex Frinton-on-Sea, which (like Walton) is favoured by those for whom the more

* Also Hazeboro.

popular places are at times a little too popular; with Southend and Westcliff in the Thames estuary, and the port of Harwich including Dovercourt Bay. We see here something of a counterpart to the popular south coast of England. The difference is chiefly due to the difference in climate: the east coast is favoured by those who like the strong, invigorating air; the south by those who prefer the milder atmosphere, especially in the winter months. I mention Lowestoft (with Gorleston nearby) last because, like Great Yarmouth, it is both a busy fishing-port and a holiday resort. In the herring season there is extraordinary activity.

The Isle of Ely (Cambridgeshire), according to Bede, is so called from the quantity of eels in the waters about it: in Anglo-Saxon *ael*=eel, *-ig*=island. It was a borough in the time of William the Conqueror, when Hereward the Wake is said to have made his last gallant stand against the Normans. To-day the city of Ely is a pleasant market-town in the plains of this flat, agricultural county which, on the whole, does not differ greatly from Hertford, except that it is nearly all flatland. Ely Cathedral is architecturally interesting because of its graceful, lacelike character, and especially for its central octagon, often described by experts as the most beautiful design in all Gothic atmosphere. There is in the town a school with a remarkable historical record, one which begins much farther back than that of any of the great English public schools, for Edward the Confessor (1042–1066) learnt his letters at King's School, Ely! In this town there is a house in which Oliver Cromwell lived for some years. I often wonder why we should find interest in a house in which some great person lived; but it would hardly be natural not to do so.

The university town of Cambridge has been mentioned in Part I (pp. 108–9), and I need say little more about it here. Any comparison with Oxford would be invidious; the colleges and chapels of both are among England's greatest architectural treasures. Each has its own distinctive atmosphere. The town of Cambridge lies in flat country on the south border of the Fens, and at an elevation never more than about 50 feet above sea-level. To the south there are hills which rise gently to border the fenland, and the little river Cam runs through the town. The visitor will find enough of interest to occupy his time for as long as he wishes to remain, and more than that I need not say; except perhaps that whoever goes to Cambridge and misses King's College Chapel must be told that he has missed what many of us think is one of the loveliest buildings in the world—a 15th-century gem which I dare not pretend to describe, no more than the lovely 'Backs' of the University.

Finally, we come back to St. Albans in Herts, a town that is saturated in history and dating back to the time when it was the important Roman-British town of Verulamium. It is called after St. Alban, a Roman soldier who was the first Christian martyr in Britain. He was beheaded at Verulamium for harbouring the priest who had converted him. From then onwards until about 793 its importance declined, especially after the departure of the Roman legions. But in that year King Offa of the great kingdom of Mercia founded a Benedictine Abbey in honour of St. Alban, one which rose to great wealth, power and such eminence that its abbot became the premier abbot of England. In the Wars of the Roses, two important battles were fought here. The famous Sarah Jennings, Duchess of Marlborough (1660–1744), was born at St. Albans, and lived here at Holywell House until the vast Blenheim Palace was finished after the death of John Churchill, the great Duke of Marlborough and ancestor of Winston Spencer Churchill. St. Albans is a city, because of its cathedral, which, incidentally, is built on higher ground than any other in England. It began as a Norman building, has a massive Norman tower with a striking arcade and the longest medieval nave in existence: altogether a most impressive edifice and one of great charm.

With St. Albans this tour of the East Midlands and East Anglia comes to an end: at about twenty miles from London.

ENVOI

THE tour that has been suggested in pp. 253–318 is merely in the nature of a sampler that is not intended to be exhaustive but which should give the traveller a fair view of the country and its people. It would not be difficult to suggest a dozen or more other circuits—the charm of England being its astonishing variety—any one of which would be equally enjoyable or instructive. I hope that what I have said is enough to satisfy the stay-at-homes in England and those who do not live here that the little island holds much that is worth seeing. Whether the traveller decides to move from place to place to get general impressions, or prefers to settle for a time in some chosen town or locality to get a deeper breath of the atmosphere, I trust that what he has read will give him some ideas of what to expect, and at least an inkling of the impressive background that lies behind it. If at times I have stressed the historical background, this is because I cannot see that it is otherwise possible to understand or fully appreciate this old country at its true worth.

There is great beauty and great depth in England. And it can reasonably be claimed for the English of to-day that, after a thousand years of successful history—I choose the word 'successful' deliberately—they still hold their own, they are still as interesting as they ever have been, and they promise as much for the future as they ever did in the past.

THE END

APPENDICES

APPENDIX I

BIBLIOGRAPHY

In this list the numbers correspond to those in the text

PART I

[1] *British Prehistory*, by Stuart Piggott. London, 1949.
[2] *Ensayo de una reconstrucción de la etnologia prehistórica de la peninsula ibérica*, by Bosch Gimpera. Also other works by the same author.
[3] *The Archæology of Ireland*, by R. A. S. Macalister, London 1949.
[4] *Prehistoric England*, by Grahame Clark, London, 1948.
[5] *Stonehenge: To-day and Yesterday*, by Frank Stevens. The Official Guide to Stonehenge. H.M. Stationery Office, London, 1938.
[6] *The Rise of the Celts* and also *The Greatness and Decline of the Celts*, by Henri Hubert. London, 1934.
[7] *Roman Britain and the English Settlements*, by R. G. Collingwood and J. N. L. Meyers. In the *Oxford History of England*. Oxford, 1936.
[8] *History of England*, by George Macaulay Trevelyan. London, 1927.
[9] *Historical Geography of England and Wales*, by E. H. Carrier. London, 1935.
[10] *Along the Roman Roads*, by G. M. Boumphrey. London, 1935.
[11] *The Beginnings of English Society*, by Dorothy Whitelock. Pelican Book, 1952.
[12] *The Mabinogion*. New Translation by Thomas Jones and Gwyn Jones. Everyman Library, 1949.
[13] *Encyclopædia Britannica*, 13th edn.
[14] *Encyclopédie Nouveau Larousse Illustré*. Paris.
[15] *A Short History of the English People*, by John Richard Green.
[16] *Religion and the Rise of Capitalism*, by R. H. Tawney.
[17] *The Wealth of England: 1496 to 1760*, by G. N. Clark. Home University Library.
[18] Article on Jeremy Bentham in *Encyclopædia Britannica*, 11th edn.
[19] *The Population of Britain*, by Eva M. Hubback. Pelican Books, 1947.
[20] *Encyclopædia Britannica*, 11th edn., Vol. XI, p. 495.
[21] *The Ascent of Everest*, by John Hunt. London, 1953.

PART II

[1] *Times Literary Supplement:* 4/9/1953.
[2] *Query* (Book V): George Padmore in *Africa Speaks.*
[3] *The English, Are They Human?* by G. J. Renier. London, 1931.
[4] Sean O'Faolain.
[5] Defoe's *Tour Through England* and Cobbett's *Rural Rides.* Everyman Library.
[6] *England,* by L. Russell Muirhead. Blue Guides. An excellent all-round guide-book. London, 1950. (5th edn.)
[7] Bartholomew's ½ in. to 1 mile map, and their motoring map are excellent. Also excellent are the 'Geographia' series of maps. For close detail of particular areas, consult Ordnance Survey maps. (H.M. Stationery Office.) Excellent and easy to handle is *The Oxford Travel Atlas* of Britain (O.U.P., 1953).
[8] See *Don Roberto.* A Biography of R. B. Cunninghame Graham. By A. F. Tschiffely. London, 1937.
[9] Published by Phoenix House, London, 1953.

APPENDIX II

TRAVEL INFORMATION AND INFORMATION ABOUT PARTICULAR AREAS OR PLACES

The prospective visitor who lives in non-British territory should apply to the nearest British Consul for information about passports, visas, Customs and currency regulations, etc.

The most useful all-round source for general information about the whole of Great Britain and Northern Ireland is:

THE BRITISH TRAVEL AND HOLIDAYS ASSOCIATION,
64–65 St. James's Street,
London, S.W.1,
England.

The Association has offices in:

New York: 336 Madison Avenue. (British Travel Centre.)
Paris: 6 Place Vendôme, ler. (British Travel Centre.)
Australia: 252 George Street, Sydney. (British Travel Association.)
Canada: 372 Bay Street, Toronto, Ontario. (British Travel Association.)
331 Dominion Square Building, Montreal, P.Q. (British Travel Association.)
South Africa: Union House, Queen Victoria Street, Cape Town, South Africa.

The British Travel and Holidays Association in London can supply much interesting free literature about Britain. The visitor is advised to ask for the latest edition of HOTELS, with a list of London Restaurants. This list gives the essential information about each hotel: cost of rooms per night, weekly terms, facilities offered, and whether licensed for the sale of alcohol.

INDEX

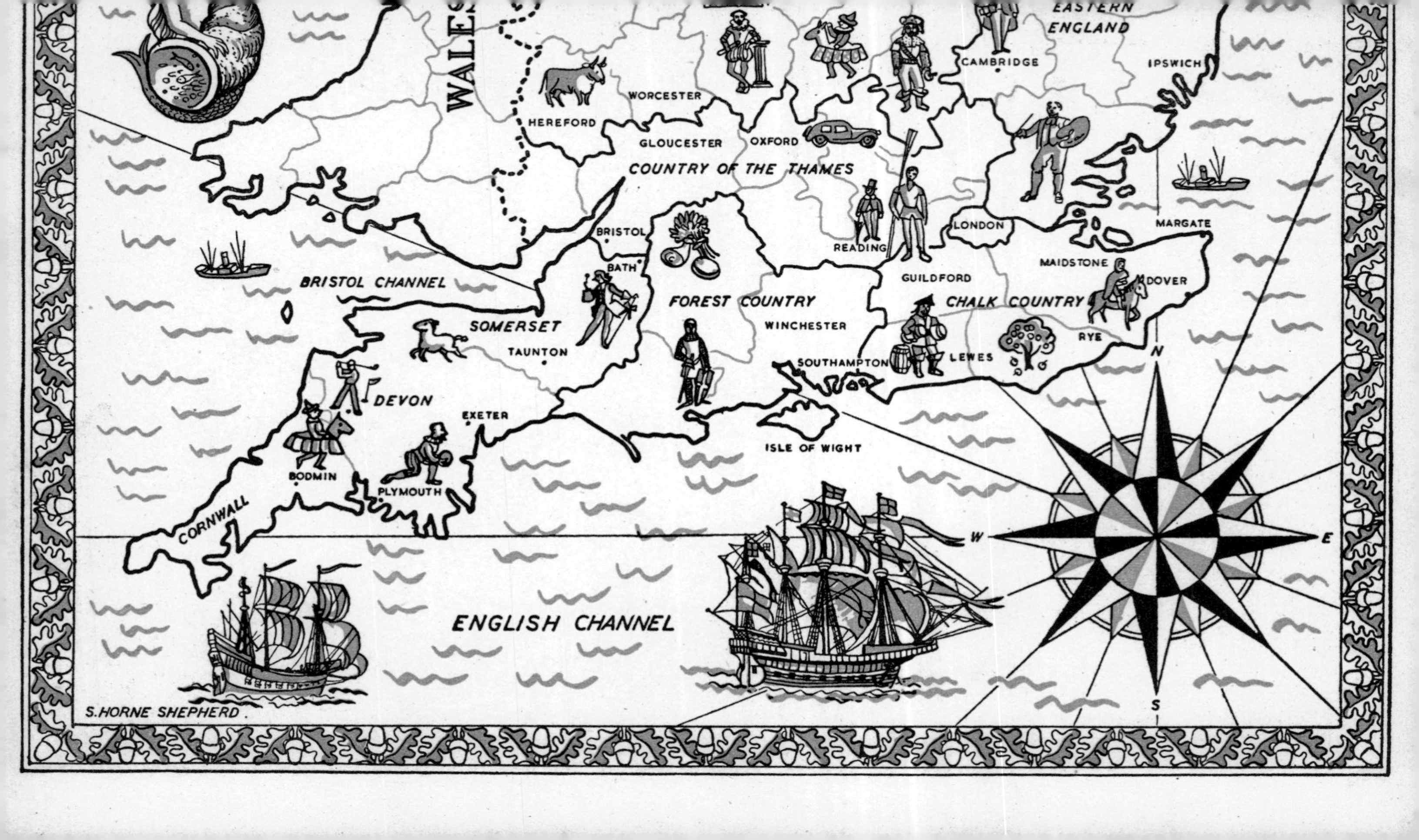

WALES
EASTERN
ENGLAND
CAMBRIDGE
IPSWICH
WORCESTER
HEREFORD
GLOUCESTER
OXFORD
COUNTRY OF THE THAMES
BRISTOL
LONDON
MARGATE
READING
BATH
MAIDSTONE
DOVER
BRISTOL CHANNEL
GUILDFORD
FOREST COUNTRY
CHALK COUNTRY
SOMERSET
WINCHESTER
TAUNTON
RYE
SOUTHAMPTON
LEWES
DEVON
EXETER
ISLE OF WIGHT
BODMIN
PLYMOUTH
CORNWALL
N
W
E
S
ENGLISH CHANNEL
S.HORNE SHEPHERD.